ROMMEL'S
LIEUTENANTS

ROMMEL'S
LIEUTENANTS

*The Men Who Served
the Desert Fox,
France, 1940*

Samuel W. Mitcham, Jr.

PRAEGER SECURITY INTERNATIONAL
Westport, Connecticut • London

Library of Congress Cataloging-in-Publication Data

Mitcham, Samuel W.
   Rommel's lieutenants : the men who served the Desert Fox, France,
1940 / Samuel W. Mitcham, Jr.
      p. cm.
   Includes bibliographical references and index.
   ISBN 0-275-99185-7 (alk. paper)
   1. Germany. Heer. Panzer-Division, 7—Biography. 2. Germany. Heer.
Panzer-Division, 7—Biography. 3. Germany. Heer—Officers—Biography.
4. Rommel, Erwin, 1891–1944—Friends and associates. 5. Germany. Heer.
Panzer-Division, 7—History. 6. World War, 1939–1945—Campaigns—
France. 7. World War, 1939–1945—Regimental histories—Germany. I.
Title.
   D757.56 Nr. 7 .M57 2007
   940.54'214092243—dc22   2006026012

British Library Cataloguing in Publication Data is available.

Library of Congress Catalog Card Number: 2006026012
ISBN13: 978-0-275-99185-2
ISBN10: 0-275-99185-7

First published in 2007

Praeger Security International, 88 Post Road West, Westport, CT 06881
An imprint of Greenwood Publishing Group, Inc.
www.praeger.com

Printed in the United States of America

The paper used in this book complies with the
Permanent Paper Standard issued by the National
Information Standards Organization (Z39.48–1984).

10   9   8   7   6   5   4   3   2   1

To Ben James
leader, mentor, and friend

CONTENTS

Contents

Photo essay follows page 84.

LIST OF FIGURES

List of Figures

PREFACE

Perhaps the most famous soldier to fight in World War II was Field Marshal Erwin Rommel, who achieved immortality as "the Desert Fox." He is also one of the most admired.

Rommel's first field command during the war was the 7th Panzer Division—also known as the Ghost Division—which he led in France in 1940. During this campaign, the 7th Panzer suffered more casualties than any other division in the German Army.[1] It lost 2,594 men, including 682 killed, 1,646 wounded, and 266 missing—20 percent of its entire force—as well as 39 tanks. During the process, it inflicted a disproportionate amount of casualties upon the enemy.[2] It took 97,486 prisoners; captured 458 tanks and armored vehicles, 277 field guns, 64 antitank guns, and 4,000 to 5,000 trucks; and destroyed dozens of others in each category. It captured or destroyed hundreds of tons of other military equipment, shot down 52 aircraft, destroyed 15 more on the ground, and captured 12 more. It also captured the commander of the French Atlantic Fleet and four of his admirals, a French corps commander, and 15 to 20 other generals, including the commander of the British 51st Highlander Division.[3] It barreled through the Ardennes, broke through the Meuse River line at Dinart, and raced through Belgium and northern France. It destroyed the French 1st Armored Division and the 4th North African Division, punched through the Maginot Line extension near Sivry, and checked the largest Allied counteroffensive of the campaign at Arras. It played a major role in encircling and destroying the mighty French 1st Army at Lille; then it redeployed rapidly to the south, stormed across the Somme and the Seine, and captured the major French ports of St. Valery and Cherbourg in heavy fighting, almost without assistance from the rest of the German Army. When France surrendered, the Ghost Division was within 200 miles of the Spanish border. No doubt about it—Rommel had proven himself a great military leader who was capable of greater things. His next command, in fact, would be the Afrika Korps, where the legend of the Desert Fox was born.

Rommel had a great deal of help in France—and much more than his published papers suggest. His staff officers and company, battalion, and regimental commanders were an extremely capable collection of military leaders, which included 12 future generals (two of them SS), and two colonels who briefly commanded panzer divisions but never reached general rank (see table at end of preface). They also included Colonel Erich von Unger, who would no doubt have become a general had he not been killed in action while commanding a motorized rifle brigade on the Eastern Front in 1941, as well as Karl Hanke, a Nazi gauleiter who later succeeded Heinrich Himmler as the last Reichsfuehrer-SS.

To my knowledge, no historian has ever recognized the talented cast of characters who supported the Desert Fox in 1940. No one has ever attempted to tell their stories. The purpose of this book is to remedy this deficiency.

I wish to thank my good friend, the late Theodor-Friedrich von Stauffenberg, who first called my attention to the relatively large number of future generals who served in the Ghost Division in 1940. He identified seven of them in the late 1980s, but it turns out that there were even more. (Friedrich was an expert on the German panzer officers and was the first cousin of the colonel who came so close to assassinating Hitler in 1944.) I also wish to thank my long-suffering wife, Donna, who has had to put up with a lot over the years in the interest of my research, and who turned out to be an extraordinarily competent proofreader. Professor Melinda Matthews, the head of the Interlibrary Loan Department at the University of Louisiana at Monroe, is also deserving of special praise for putting up with my insatiable requests for books and documents. (If Melinda can't locate it, it probably doesn't exist.)

I alone assume responsibility for any deficiencies or mistakes in this book.

Principal Commanders and Staff Officers, 7th Panzer Division, France, 1940

Division Commander: Major General Erwin Rommel
    Ia (Chief Operations Officer): Major i.G. Otto Heidkaemper[1]
    Ib (Chief Supply Officer): Captain i.G. Joachim von Metzsch[2]
    Adjutant: Captain Schraetler[3]
    Ic (Chief Intelligence Officer): Major i.G. Joachim Ziegler[4]
    Chief Medical Officer: Dr. Wilhelm Baumeister[1]
    Chief Orderly: Lieutenant of Reserves Karl Hanke[4]

25th Panzer Regiment: Colonel Karl Rothenburg[1]
    I Battalion: Major Franz von Lindenau[5]
    II Battalion: Major Casimir Kentel
    III Battalion: Major Rudolf Sieckenius[1]

7th Rifle (Schuetzen) Brigade: Colonel Friedrich Fuerst[1]
    6th Rifle Regiment: Colonel Erich von Unger[6]
        I Battalion: Major Paris
        II Battalion: Lieutenant Colonel Hans Junck
    7th Rifle Regiment: Colonel Georg von Bismarck[1]
        I Battalion: Major Hans Cramer[7]
        II Battalion: Major Bachmann

78th Panzer Artillery Regiment: Colonel Gottfried Froelich[1]
    I Battalion: Lieutenant Colonel Dr. Kessler
    II Battalion: Major Eduard Crasemann[1]
    II Battalion/45th Motorized Artillery[8]: Major Joachim von Kronhelm[9]

7th Motorcycle Battalion: Major Friedrich-Carl von Steinkeller[1]
37th Panzer Reconnaissance Battalion: Major Erdmann[10]
    Captain Hans von Luck[9]
42nd Antitank Battalion: Lieutenant Colonel Johann Mickl[1]
58th Panzer Engineer Battalion: Major Binkau
    Major von Mertens
83rd Motorized Signal Battalion: Major Mueller
59th Light Flak Battalion: Major Schrader

Notes:
[1]Reached the rank of general during World War II.
[2]Probationary member of the General Staff.
[3]Wounded in Belgium, May 1940; promoted to major (1940); killed in action, North Africa, late 1941.
[4]Reached general officer rank in the SS.
[5]Severely wounded in Russia, August 1941, and forced to leave the service.
[6]Killed in action in Russia, August 1941, while commanding the 7th Rifle Brigade.
[7]Promoted to lieutenant colonel on December 1, 1941, and to colonel on July 1, 1944, as commander of the 7th Panzer Grenadier Regiment. Not to be confused with General of Panzer Troops Hans Cramer, the last commander of the Afrika Korps.

(Notes continue on next page)

Preface

[8]The II Battalion, 45th Motorized Artillery Regiment, was a General Headquarters unit temporarily attached to the 7th Panzer Division. Later this attachment became permanent and the II/45th Motorized Artillery became III Battalion, 78th Panzer Artillery Regiment.
[9]Briefly served as acting commander of a panzer division but was never promoted to general officer rank.
[10]Killed in action, France, May 1940.

CHAPTER I

THE SOURCES OF ROMMEL'S OFFICERS

Rommel's officers came from three overlapping sources: the Imperial Army (the Kaiser's army), the *Reichsheer* or "Treaty Army" (as the German Army from 1919 to 1935 was called), and the *Heer*, which was Hitler's army. The term *Wehrmacht* is also sometimes used to refer to Hitler's army, but that term literally means "armed forces" and would thus include the navy and *Luftwaffe* (air force).

Rommel and his officers inherited a legacy that dates back to the days of Prussia and the rise of what became the House of Hohenzollern in the early 15th century. In 1701, Leopold, the Holy Roman Emperor, bestowed upon Frederick III, the Elector of Brandenburg, the ambiguous title of "King in Prussia." His son, Frederick Wilhelm I, retained the vague title under the Holy Roman Empire but simultaneously created the best-drilled army in Europe, although he avoided using it, despite a great many opportunities. His son, Frederick II (1712–86)—known to history as Frederick the Great—used it with great success and expanded his kingdom beyond its East Prussian and Brandenburger heartlands and into Silesia, which he took from the Hapsburgs. It was Frederick who established the reputation of the Prussian Army as the best in Europe, based on harsh discipline, unquestioning obedience, and the courage of its men, especially its officers. Prussia became, as Baron Friedrich von Leopold von Schroetter remarked, "not a country with an army, but an army with a country." Unfortunately for Prussia, however, Frederick's successors lacked his skills, strength of will, and intelligence. As a result, the army stagnated and was finally crushed and humiliated by Napoleon in the Jena campaign of 1806.

Following the Napoleonic Peace of Tilsit (1807), and the harsh Treaty of Paris (1808), the Prussian Army was built anew under the "reformers,"

Figure 1.1
General Regions of the Third Reich

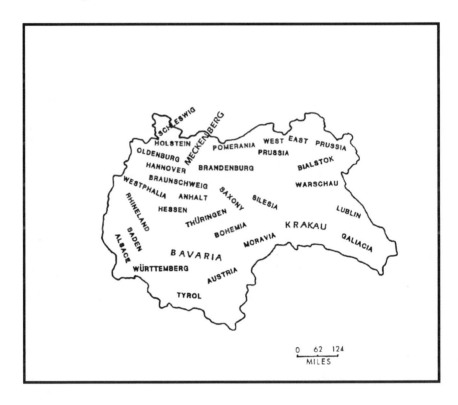

led by General Johann von Scharnhorst. Scharnhorst shifted the emphasis of Prussian military thought and doctrine from a volunteer army obsessed with iron discipline and rigid drill to a conscripted army, stressing technological expertise, operational planning, flexibility, and a highly trained and dedicated professional Officers' Corps. Discipline remained harsh. He and his young assistants, which included Count Wilhelm Anton Neidhardt von Gneisenau and Karl von Clausewitz, founded the *Landwehr* (the national militia), the Prussian General Staff, and the War Academy (*Kriegsakademie*), and laid the foundations for a tradition of military excellence that endured until 1945. Indeed, if there is one common characteristic that links the Imperial Army, the Reichsheer and the Heer, it is institutionalized military excellence.[1]

Scharnhorst himself died of wounds he suffered in the Battle of Luetzen in 1813, but the army he created helped smash Napoleon at Leipzig and Waterloo. Although the aristocratic military reactionaries were by no means a thing of the past after 1815 (thanks to their influence with the king), the Prussian Army continued its quiet, steady development under the supervision of the General Staff until it had, in effect, institutionalized the idea of professional military excellence at all levels of the army. General Staff training was especially vigorous. Entrance into the War Academy in Berlin (where the officers of the General Staff were trained) was by competitive examination, and well over 85 percent of all applicants were eliminated at the beginning. Of the 150 officers who succeeded in gaining admission each year, only about 50 completed the course, which was gradually expanded until it was three years long. The survivors were then assigned to the Great General Staff in Berlin for two years' more training in topographical mapping, map exercises, and war games. Following this assignment, they participated in the annual Staff Ride, under the personal supervision of the chief of the General Staff. Finally, the successful candidates were allowed to wear the distinctive red trouser stripes of permanent members of the General Staff. They could look forward to more rapid promotions and better duty assignments than their contemporaries. They usually spent most of their careers alternating between positions with the Great General Staff (*Grosser Generalstab*), housed in a red brick building in the northeast corner of the Tiergarten, near the center of the government sector of Berlin, and assignments with the field forces (*Truppengeneralstab*).[2] The king was, of course, still the official Supreme Commander of the Army, but by the 1860s his role was largely nominal: the chief of the General Staff was the real leader of the German Army.

From 1813 until 1871, the Prussian Army enjoyed a string of unbroken successes. After playing a major role in the defeat of Napoleon, it smashed the Revolution of 1848, overran Schleswig-Holstein in the Danish Wars of 1848 and 1864, crushed the forces of the Austro-Hungarian Empire in the Seven Weeks' War of 1866, and—to the surprise of the entire world—humiliated France in the Franco-Prussian War of 1870–71. As a result, Otto von Bismarck (the "Iron Chancellor") was able to unite Germany and make Wilhelm I the first *kaiser* (emperor) of the Second *Reich* (empire) at Versailles in 1871. The Prussian General Staff was generally considered the best trained professional military body in the world between then and 1914. It was copied and emulated by a great many countries during that era, including the three formerly independent German states, which retained the right to keep their own military establishments in peacetime: Bavaria, Wuerttemberg, and Saxony. (Even these were forced to recognize the hegemony of Berlin, however, and were subordinate to the Prussian General Staff in wartime.)

If the Prussian General Staff was considered a model for others to follow, German diplomacy after Wilhelm II ascended to the throne in 1890 was not. He sacked Bismarck and had maneuvered the Reich into

Figure 1.2
Major Cities of the Third Reich, 1937

a strategic corner by 1914, when it faced the prospect of a two-front war without a single strong ally, against all the other great powers of Europe and later the United States as well. General Count Alfred von Schlieffen, chief of the General Staff from 1891, recognized Germany's dangerous position as early as 1894 and devised a plan to deal with it. The famous Schlieffen Plan was based on the concept of a rapid mobilization and, making maximum use of railroads, called for concentrating the bulk of Germany's combat power on the right flank of the Western Front. Six of the Kaiser's eight armies would then overrun neutral Belgium and part of the Netherlands, debauch into France, and capture Paris before the British or Russians could decisively intervene.

The Schlieffen Plan probably would have worked had Schlieffen himself directed operations in 1914, but he died on January 4, 1913. Appropriately enough, his last words were "Strengthen the right wing." This advice his successor, General Helmuth Johann Ludwig von Moltke, known as "Moltke the younger," did not follow. When World War I broke out, he attacked through Belgium with 55 divisions, instead of with 71, as planned by Schlieffen. Moltke also dispensed with the 16-division follow-up force his predecessor had envisioned. Then, once the campaign had started, Moltke grew nervous about Russian advances into East Prussia, so he withdrew two corps from the main advance and sent them to the East. They arrived in Prussia after Generals Paul von Hindenburg and Erich Ludendorff won the Battle of Tannenberg, and the Czar's forces were in full retreat. Even so, the French government fled from Paris before French General Joseph J. C. Joffre halted the German offensive on the Marne. This defeat ruined Germany's prospects for a quick victory and doomed the Reich to a long war of attrition.

Moltke the younger was replaced as chief of the General Staff on September 14, 1914, by General Erich von Falkenhayn, the minister of war of Prussia. When Falkenhayn was unable to break the stalemate on the Western Front, Wilhelm replaced him with the Hindenburg-Ludendorff team in August 1916. Ludendorff, the First Quartermaster-General, received the title *Feldherr* (literally "warlord") and was called the "National Commander." Ludendorff achieved successes, most notably the defeat of Russia; however, he exhibited a flaw common to German General Staff officers before and since: untrained in geopolitics or international affairs, and uneducated in politics, he had too much faith in the invincibility of German arms and had too little grasp of what was practical or possible on the larger scale. As a result, his Great Offensive of 1918 failed. He also failed to appreciate the value of tanks until it was too late. He was replaced by General Wilhelm Groener in late October 1918. Less than three weeks later, Germany sued for peace.

During World War I, the corporate tactical and operational excellence of the Imperial Army was proven on the battlefield. French General Charles de Gaulle, for example, wrote:

[T]he superiority of good troops was abundantly clear. How else is one to explain the prolonged success of the German armies against so many opponents? For 1,700,000 deaths … the Germans, better trained than anyone else, killed 3,200,000 enemies; for 750,000 prisoners which they lost, they took 1,900,000.[3]

De Gaulle, of course, was no admirer of Germany or the Germans.

The military clauses of the Treaty of Versailles attempted to reduce the German armed forces to the status of an armed police and coast guard force by limiting the German Army to 100,000 men, including 4,000 officers.[4] So that it could never again wage offensive warfare, it was forbidden to have tanks, aircraft, poison gas, or field pieces larger than 105 mm. To ensure that no significant reserves were created, privates and noncommissioned officers (NCOs) had to enlist for 12 years,

Figure 1.3
Europe, 1920–38

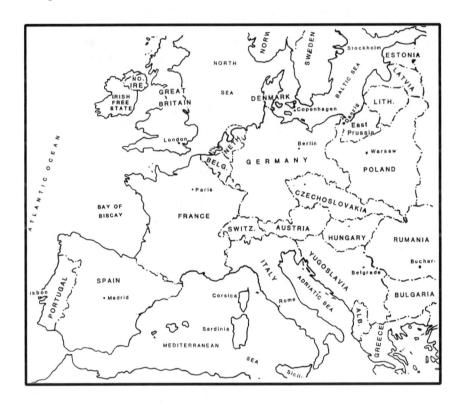

while officers were required to commit themselves to 25 years' service. The General Staff, the War Academy, and the cadet academies were banned; a yearly personnel turnover of more than 5 percent was prohibited; and even its ammunition supply was limited, to prevent stockpiling for a major war. It was subject to inspections by the International Control Commission.

The Law of the Creation of the Provisional Reichswehr passed the Reichstag on March 6, 1919, but it was only a stopgap measure, still leaving the army more than twice the size permitted by the treaty and without a permanent organizational structure. President Ebert assigned the task of submitting recommendations concerning the organization of the postwar army to a commission headed by Lieutenant General Hans von Seeckt. His recommendations were accepted with only minor modifications and became the basis of the new *Reichswehr* (Reich Defense Force). The nominal commander-in-chief of the Reichswehr was the president, but actual authority was normally exercised by the defense minister.

The Reichswehr consisted of the *Reichsheer* (army) and *Reichsmarine* (navy). The former played such a predominant role (it must be remembered that Germany was traditionally a land power) that many came to consider the Reichswehr and Reichsheer identical. The tiny navy amounted to little until after the rise of Adolf Hitler. Under the terms of the Treaty of Versailles, Germany was not allowed to have an air force.

Because the treaty forbade the army or navy to have a commander-in-chief, the Weimar Republic's defense ministry accepted Seeckt's recommendation and created the *Heeresleitung* (army command), initially headed by a 48-year-old Wuerttemberger officer named Walther Reinhardt. Under the Army Command came the Personnel Office, the *Waffenamt* (Armament and Equipment Office, or Ordnance Office), the *Truppenamt* (Troop Office), and the Army Administrative Service. The real power in the army was the Troop Office, which was headed by General Hans von Seeckt, a highly cultured Pomeranian nobleman. Known in the army as "the Sphinx with a Monocle," he was short, thin, neat, and dainty in his appearance. The son of a Prussian general, he was born in Schleswig on April 22, 1866, and was commissioned second lieutenant in the elite 1st (Emperor Alexander) Foot Guards Regiment at the age of 19. He completed the three-year course at the War Academy, became a member of the General Staff in 1897, and soon established a reputation as a brilliant staff officer. During World War I, Seeckt rose from the rank of lieutenant colonel to lieutenant general and proved that he was an extremely able general and staff officer. (See appendix 1 for a table of comparative ranks.) After the Armistice, he served as military advisor on the Treaty of Versailles and headed the reorganization commission, clandestinely rebuilt the General Staff (under the cover name *Truppenamt*), and established the organizational foundation that Hitler's generals would later expand into the most feared army of its century.

Seeckt's Troop Office was the chief planning agency for the army and consisted of five departments: T 1 (Operations), T 2 (Organization), T 3 (Statistics and Intelligence), T 4 (Training), and T 7 (Transportation). These were further subdivided into Office Groups (*Amtsgruppen*), Branches (*Abteilungen*), and Sections (*Gruppen*).[5] The lowest level of the General Staff was the *Referat* (desk). Each of these subdivisions dealt with various tasks, including a number forbidden by the Treaty of Versailles. Group L of the operations department, for example, handled Germany's clandestine air forces and kept up with developments in aviation and military aviation, while special section T 3V handled matters relating to the secret Red Army/Reichswehr agreements, and so forth. This organization was flexible and could easily be expanded to serve a much larger army.

The level of command below the Army Command was the *Gruppen-kommando* (Group Command). There were two of these field army level headquarters: Group 1 in Berlin controlled all units in north and eastern Germany, while Group 2 in Kassel controlled those in the south and west. Under these commands came the true functional heart of the German Army: the *Wehrkreise* (military districts). Each Wehrkreis was a corps-level territorial command that was responsible for recruitment, mobilization, supply, administration, logistical support, and all territorial and military-political (or military-civilian) matters within its area. Later, when the German Army took the field, the Wehrkreise also assumed responsibility for training as well. Initially there were seven military districts, all designated by Roman numerals. By 1939, there were 16 (see Figure 1.4). By 1940, there were 18 Wehrkreise, numbered I through XIII, XVII, XVIII and XX, as well as Wehrkreis Bohemia and Moravia (in what had been Czechoslovakia), and Wehrkreis *General Gouvernement* in what had once been Poland. In addition to directing the military activities in their territories, each Wehrkreis commander was also the commander of an infantry division, which bore the same number as the Wehrkreis, although the two commands were technically separate.

Figure 1.4
The Wehrkreise, 1939

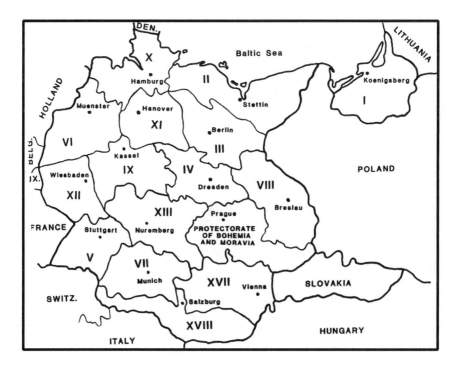

Each infantry division consisted of three infantry regiments, an artillery regiment, and reconnaissance, signal, engineer, and antitank battalions, as well as smaller medical, supply, administration, service, and veterinary units. Each division had approximately 12,000 men, although this figure increased to the 15,000–17,000 range after 1935. From then until the fall of 1941, it was not uncommon for a division to control 20,000 men, counting temporarily attached smaller units.

The most important officer on the divisional staff was the Ia, the chief of operations, who was, in effect, divisional chief of staff (although this term was used only at the corps level and higher). When the division went to the field, the staff usually divided into three separate operational groups: the *Fuehrungsabteilung*, the *Quartermeister*, and the *Adjutantur*. The *Fuehrungsabteilung* (or operational detachment) was the most important. Directed by the Ia, it formed with division's tactical nerve center and was known as the division's command post (CP). It also included the intelligence staff, which, under the Ic (chief intelligence officer), was subordinate to the Ia.

The supply headquarters (*Quartermeister*) was headed by the Ib (chief supply officer or divisional quartermaster). Physically separated from the CP, it included the IVa (chief administrative officer), IVb (chief medical officer), and V (motor transport officer), each of whom directed his own section. Most of these officers were not members of the General Staff; as a general rule, only I-type officers (the Ia, Ib, and so on) were War Academy graduates.

The personnel group (or *Adjutantur*) was the third staff grouping. Generally some distance to the rear, it was directed by the IIa (chief personnel officer or adjutant). He supervised the IIb (second personnel officer), the III (chief judge advocate), the chaplain (IVd), as well as various other units necessary to keep a staff headquarters and divisional rear area functioning normally, such as security detachments, construction engineer units, labor battalions, and replacement units.

The Reichsheer also had three cavalry divisions, which consisted of six small cavalry squadrons and one artillery battalion each—a total strength of 5,300 men. The commanders of the cavalry divisions were junior in rank to the Wehrkreise commanders, had no territorial responsibilities themselves, and were subordinate to the district commanders in times of emergency.

In 1920, before the 100,000-man army could be established, tens of thousands of officers and hundreds of thousands of other ranks had to be involuntarily discharged from the service. Some generals (most notably, General Reinhardt, the war minister of Prussia and the first chief of the Reichsheer) wanted to retain primarily frontline soldiers, but Seeckt wanted to keep as many General Staff officers as possible.

General von Seeckt—backed by Groener, who was now minister of defense—won the day, forced Reinhardt to retire, and personally replaced him as chief of the Army Command. Seeckt would be the undisputed dictator of the German armed forces for the next six critical years. He had a unique opportunity to build an army in accordance with his own ideas, and he took full advantage of it.

Hans von Seeckt considered the mass armies of 1914 obsolete. They were, he said, unmaneuverable, poorly trained, and far too expensive. The next war, he predicted, would be won by smaller, mobile armies with superior training and equipment. He attached the greatest value to training and emphasized the importance of mechanization, motorization, and air power. Overruling the recommendations of his own personnel staff, he insisted that at least 180 of the officers of the new Reichsheer be former Air Service officers.

To man the new 100,000-man army, and especially the 4,000-man Officers' Corps, General von Seeckt and his colleagues had the pick of the best of more than 34,000 German officers who had survived the Great War and wished to remain in the service. Their selections were based on high professional accomplishments and demonstrated efficiency; intelligence and high standards of educational achievement; "correctness" in both professional and private life; a strong sense of tradition; generally promonarchist political views; and a desire to isolate the army from the politics of the Weimar Republic. General Staff officers received preference in selection over non–War Academy graduates, and younger officers were preferred to older ones.

Seeckt and his staff drew their officers from three general categories: (1) General Staff officers, (2) Freikorps veterans, and (3) the junior officer ranks of the pre-1914 Imperial Army. Their selections were extremely important in the history of Nazi Germany and World War II, because the officers they selected led Hitler's army groups, armies, corps, and air fleets from 1939 until the very end. Some officers fell into all three categories, but most did not. The old Imperial Army had been devastated by the war. Of the 22,112 officers on active duty when the war began, 11,357—more than 50 percent—were killed in action before the armistice. As a general rule, the new army was disproportionately dominated by the aristocrats. In February 1927, for example, 25 of its 42 generals were noblemen, 45 of its 105 colonels were nobles, and 162 of the 724 officers assigned to the defense ministry were nobles. The cavalry was especially dominated by "the vons": 265 of its 596 officers were aristocrats. Only 0.74 percent of the general population was of noble birth.[6]

One type of officer not often retained was the *Einjaehrig-Freiwilliger.* Typically, these were 17 or 18 year olds who served at the front for a time and then underwent a hasty officers' basic course at an officers' training school. They were jeeringly called "90-day wonders" by enlisted men (but seldom to their faces, because they enjoyed some of the same rights as the most senior Prussian general—such as that of boxing an enlisted man's ears anytime they felt provoked. An "ear boxing" in the Prussian Army was designed to burst an ear drum.) Many of these volunteer officers entered the Freikorps after the war, joined the provincial police in the early 1920s, and ended up back in the army in the 1930s, typically as a major. A great many of them served as regimental officers during World War II, and quite a few became generals.

Seeckt would not tolerate prima donnas in his army. "The form changes, the spirit remains," he said when he set up the *Truppenamt*. "It is the spirit of silent, selfless devotion to duty in the service of the army. General Staff officers have no names."[7] For him, it was intolerable for officers to meddle in politics (although he periodically meddled in them himself). "Great achievements, small display; more reality than appearance" became a motto of the General Staff officer.[8]

After the initial selections, the decision on which officers to choose for the regimental and company-level appointments usually fell to the colonel involved. As one might expect, this man almost invariably selected candidates whom he believed to have outstanding leadership potential, largely because it was in his own best interests to do so. About 400 exceptionally talented NCOs and *Feldwebel-Leutnant* (sergeant-major-lieutenant or acting second lieutenant) received permanent commissions in this way.

Once an officer was selected for the Reichsheer, his rate of promotion was very slow, as is still typical in a small army. Erwin Rommel, for example, entered the Reichsheer as a captain in 1919, having been promoted the year before. He was not promoted again until 1932, when he had 14 years' time in grade. Kurt Student, a future colonel general and "father" of the German parachute branch, was a captain from 1917 until 1929. Bernhard Ramcke, a second lieutenant in 1918, was not promoted to first lieutenant until 1921 and did not become a captain until 1927. He spent 16 years as a company grade officer. Ramcke was a lieutenant general when he led the 2nd Parachute Division against the Americans in 1944. Most other junior officers were promoted with equal slowness. In fact, several future World War II generals served full 12-year enlistments without ever receiving their commissions. Examples of these include Major General Ludwig Heilmann, future commander of the 5th Parachute Division; General of Schutzstaffel (SS) Willi Bittrich, who distinguished himself as the commander of the II SS Panzer Corps in the Battle of Arnhem; and SS Major General Helmuth Becker, commander of the 3rd SS Panzer Division "Totenkopf."

The postwar intake of potential officers was very small; therefore, the standards they had to meet were high. Preference went to those under 21 years of age with a higher education. They served 15 months in their regiments as enlisted men and, if still considered suitable, took their *Fahnenjunker* examination. Before World War I, officer candidates coming straight out of schools or universities entered the ranks as *Fahnenjunkern* (officer-cadets). They ate in the officers' mess (but were not allowed to speak unless spoken to) and could sleep in private accommodations after six weeks' service. Then they went on to a war school (*Kriegschule*). These procedures were similar during the Reichswehr era, but the standards were much higher. If the Reichsheer candidate passed his *Fahnenjunker* exam, he was promoted to *Faehnrich* (senior officer-cadet or officer candidate) and sent to the corporals' course at the Infantry School at Dresden, regardless of his branch. Then he took the officers' examination. If the candidate passed, he was promoted to *Oberfaehnrich* (roughly equivalent to ensign or senior candidate) and joined the officers' mess of his regiment. After a certain period of time, he was accepted or rejected for the rank of second lieutenant by a vote of the officers of his regiment. This was usually just a formality; if the colonel wanted a Oberfaehnrich commissioned, it would be highly unusual for the officers to reject him. In any case, the entire process took between four and five years from the date of his enlistment.

Twice a year the recruitment of enlisted men took place. A successful volunteer had to be single, between 17 and 21 years of age, without a criminal record, and in excellent physical condition. The choice concerning who to accept was left to the company, battery, or troop commanders, who functioned as their own recruiting officers. They thus had a great deal of interest in only choosing the best men available. Most of the recruits had political views identical to those of the officer selecting him, which meant they were conservative, nationalistic, and often promonarchist, anti-Semitic, and anti-Republican. Men from rural areas were generally preferred to city dwellers, because they were usually in better physical condition, more easily adapted to life in the field, and tended to be more conservative. Their training and discipline were strict but generally fair and without the abuse and brutality of the Kaiser's day. The facts that the NCOs were more closely supervised and of a generally higher quality than those of the Imperial Army were the major reasons behind this change. Like their officers, enlisted men and NCOs could not marry without official permission. This was usually not granted until after a soldier's 27th birthday. The soldier's commanding officer investigated and usually interviewed the prospective wife. Once he was satisfied that she was morally unstained and came from a respectable family, he would forward the application with a recommendation for approval. Final approval had to come from the defense ministry, but an officer's recommendation was only very rarely reversed.

Under Seeckt's supervision, the army became a state within a state, but it was a highly professional body of dedicated men, all trained to assume command of the unit above their own. It was an army capable of extremely rapid expansion, should an emergency arise; that, indeed, was the cornerstone of its existence, what its members longed for. The German Army practiced mobile operations with dummy tanks and used balloons to simulate airplanes. Its sergeants were trained to be platoon leaders, its lieutenants were fully qualified as company commanders, and its captains were perfectly capable of commanding battalions. Its field maneuvers and training problems were the best in the world, and its men almost turned the staff study and war game into an art form, they became so good at them.[9]

"The officer instruction program of the Reichswehr was one of the most strenuous officer training systems ever devised," historian James Corum wrote later.[10] Typically, training for a new officer candidate (whose title was *Fahnenjunker*) began with 18 months in a line regiment, during which time he served as a recruit, private, and junior NCO. This was followed by two years at an officer training school. At the Infantry School at Dresden, the first year included 24 hours per week in academic classes and 13 hours of practical training. The academic instruction included an emphasis on tactics, as well as classes on weaponry, military engineering, geography, motor vehicles, and aerial warfare, among other subjects. Practical training included athletics, horse riding, infantry exercises, combat engineering, and a variety of live-fire exercises, including artillery, mortars, and machine guns. During the second year, about half of the instruction was on general army subjects, while half was branch specific (i.e., specific to the infantry, artillery, or cavalry). Common subjects included military history, army administration, weapons training, and close air support for ground forces.[11] These vigorous courses of instruction had a very high failure rate (unfortunately exact figures are lacking), but they also produced the best junior officers in the world by the late 1920s.

Even in this highly skilled collection of soldiers, the General Staff officers stood out. (Seeckt clandestinely reintroduced General Staff training almost as soon as the Allies outlawed it.) By 1920, for example, all officers who reached 10 years' service were required to take the Wehrkreis exam, which measured their professional ability. It lasted several days. An officer had to write three papers on applied tactics, one on theoretical tactics, one on military engineering, another on map reading, and another on weapons and/or equipment. There were general knowledge questions dealing with history, military history, civics, economic geography, mathematics, physics, and chemistry. The exam did not rehash the officer candidate exams, but went well beyond them. They included complicated problems in logistics, resupply, motorized warfare, artillery and mortar fire support plans, and so on. The test, which was changed every year, was a major event in an officer's career and was graded by General Staff officers in Berlin. If an officer failed the test, he was required to take it again the next year. A second failure could result in the loss of one's commission.[12]

Only those in the top 10 to 15 percent were considered for General Staff training. (Erwin Rommel was among those who did not score high enough for General Staff selection.) Of those selected, only about a third passed the rigorous course and became General Staff officers. Their training, of course, could not be conducted at the Kriegsakademie, which had been closed in March 1920 under the terms of the Treaty of Versailles. Under Seeckt and his successors, it was carried on in the Wehrkreise and by special courses held by the *Truppenamt*. Other than that, however, little had changed. The course was just as rigorous as it had ever been.

Hans von Seeckt was succeeded as chief of the General Staff by Wilhelm Heye (1920–22), Otto Hasse (1922–26), Wilhelm Wetzell (1926–27), Werner von Blomberg (1927–29), Kurt von Hammerstein (1929–30), and Wilhelm Adam (1930–33). His successors as chief of the Army Command were Colonel General Heye (1926–30) and General von Hammerstein (1930–34). After Seeckt retired, the higher levels of the army became increasingly dominated by Lieutenant General Kurt von Schleicher, who became defense minister on January 20, 1928.[13] Although Schleicher brought the army into politics to a greater degree than Seeckt would have ever allowed, he and his cronies did very little to change the basic structure established by Hans von Seeckt. It survived intact until 1935, and, in an expanded form, until early 1945—almost until the end of the Hitler regime.

The third source of Rommel's officers were those who entered the service in 1935 or after—that is, those who were commissioned during the Hitler era. For the most part, these men were the company commanders and junior staff officers of the 7th Panzer Division. They were the products of the officer training schools (*Kriegsschulen*). Rommel himself taught at the War School at Potsdam (1935–38) and was the commandant of the War School at Wiener-Neustadt (1938–39).[14]

The officer training schools taught officer candidates a much narrower range of lower-level tactical skills (battalion level and below) for the various arms, as opposed to the War Academy, which taught higher-level tactics and operational and strategic skills. The emphasis was on infantry training, which every would-be officer had to undergo. The case of Siegfried Knappe—one of Rommel's students—is typical.[15] He graduated from a Leipzig *Gymnasium* (high school) in March 1936 and then was confronted with a choice: enter a university or do his military service. Against the advice of his older sister, Ingeborg, Siegfried decided to get his service out of the way before continuing his education. Before he could join the army, however, he had to undergo six months' labor service in the RAD (Reich Labor Service).

Knappe reported to the Augustus Square in Leipzig on April 4, 1936, along with scores of other boys. They were placed on buses and driven to the village of Burglengenfeld, which was almost on the Czechoslovakian border. The labor service camp included a former villa that had been remodeled to house as many as 160 boys. Each room had four bunks, four lockers, and one table with four chairs.

Wake-up for the camp was 5:30 A.M. One boy from each room had to go to the mess hall to fetch breakfast, which consisted of a jug of coffee, a bag of hard rolls, and a small amount of jam and butter. The work day began at 6 A.M., with squad drill. Later that day they were issued an assortment of uniforms for parade, exercising, sports, and work. Lunch lasted an hour and consisted of soup, stew, bread and butter, and coffee or tea. This was followed by a one-hour indoctrination class on the subject of the "New Greater German Reich." Then there was more drill. After learning the very basics ("left face," "right face," and so forth), the boys were issued a spade, which was to be used strictly for exercising and for parades. These spades never touched dirt and had to be kept immaculately clean because there were countless spot inspections.

The first four weeks were taken up by military drill, in which the spade took the place of the rifle. The most important mission of the Labor Service was to free the army from having to do the most basic types of training, because every boy who went into the RAD would eventually be drafted into the military, and they would enter the service already partially trained. (A *Waffen-SS* [Armed SS] volunteer did not have to spend six months in the RAD. This significantly increased the appeal of the SS to young German men.)

The boys were not allowed out of the camp during the first four weeks, but the little base had a library and a recreation hall with ping-pong tables, card tables, and chess sets. There was little free time, however, as the daily schedules were filled with calisthenics, drill, and indoctrination classes. Even so, the first month passed quickly, as the young men acquired a familiarity with military life. Then came the first work day. The boys marched 40 minutes to a strip coal mine, where they removed layers of dirt from veins of coal, loaded the dirt into small tip-bed freight cars, and dug the coal. Lunch was 45 minutes long and consisted of a sandwich of cold cuts and butter, lemonade, and occasionally an apple. They marched back to the camp late in the afternoon, arriving at 5 P.M. Then they washed, ate dinner, and had an assembly, which featured either singing or a history lesson. They also did kitchen or guard duty periodically, just like men in the military.

The first days were very hot and humid, Knappe recalled, and the "work spades had worn blisters on my hands, and sweat poured from my body, making it extremely desirable to gnats, flies, and mosquitos." Then his Gruppenfuehrer appeared and inspected their parade spades, which had been stacked like rifles. "You call these clean?" he bellowed and kicked them into the mud. The young Leipziger recalled how his muscles ached, his hands hurt, and he now had someone else's grimy spade. "As I scrubbed and scraped ... Inge's face appeared before me, laughing in an 'I told you so' manner." That evening, they cleaned their spades until midnight.

The boys were free on weekends from 4 P.M. on Saturday until 10 P.M. on Sunday. Knappe and his friends took a train to nearby cities, where they visited historical and cultural sites, cathedrals and museums, had lunch in a restaurant, and perhaps went to a movie or a dance, looking for girls. These outings were financed by their parents; the Labor Service only paid them half a mark per day, which was barely enough to cover snacks and incidentals. In addition, they received a five-day furlough home in June.

Knappe was one of the 10 percent from his camp (and 1 of 10,000 young men from all over Germany) selected to represent the RAD and parade for the Fuehrer at Reich Party Day (*Reichsparteitag*) in Nuremberg on September 8. The indoctrinated young Germans were filled with pride to be selected. After the huge rally, which profoundly impressed young Herr Knappe, he was sent back to Burglengenfeld, was discharged from the RAD on September 24, and returned to Leipzig. Three weeks later, he took the train to Jena, 40 miles away, to begin his career as a soldier in the 24th Artillery Regiment. Lured into false expectations by the Goebbels' propaganda machine, Knappe expected to find a modern, mechanized artillery unit with self-propelled guns. To his dismay, he found himself in a horse artillery unit. "I wanted to turn around and go back home," he wrote later.

This, of course, he could not do. The next morning at 5 A.M. he was awakened by a whistle and got his first taste of stable duty. His first military experience was shoveling horse manure. This was to be his job every morning before breakfast. Then he met the German equivalent of a drill sergeant.

Basic training in the Wehrmacht in 1936 was somewhat similar to American basic training. As artillery soldiers, Knappe and his comrades underwent only six weeks of infantry basic training (as opposed to 12 months for infantry troops). They learned infantry tactics, how to handle and clean rifles, how to parade, how to read a tactical map, how to throw hand grenades, and how to operate machine guns. During this phase, the day usually ended at 10 P.M., when the recruits fell into bed, nearly exhausted. Then, around December 1, they began their three months' basic artillery training. Because he had a high school diploma, Knappe was selected for communications training as a radio-telephone operator for the battery's forward observers. Their big maneuvers took place in the summer, when they went to Jueterbog, a military facility near Berlin, where they could fire live ammunition. While there, Knappe and his regiment paraded for Hitler and Mussolini, but never saw them. "Nearly 300 horses and 100 cannon wheels raised so much dust that we not only could not see, we could barely breathe!"

On weekends, Knappe and his friends spent time in Jena, which readily accepted them. Then, in late February 1937, he and three other soldiers—all of them gymnasium graduates—were invited to become officer candidates. Knappe accepted and immediately began his training in "correct behavior" (i.e., how to behave in various social situations, how to act at mess, and so on). His military training was also intensified, with emphasis on tactics, and he began to learn the forward observer's and battery officers' jobs. They also continued their duties as enlisted men and helped the farmers with their harvests in the second half of July. The troops enjoyed the change of pace, and the farmers fed them extremely well.

In the late 1930s, there were four grades of officer candidates: *Fahnenjunker-Gefreiter* (equivalent to corporal), *Fahnenjunker-Unteroffizier* (equivalent to sergeant), *Fahnrich* (officer candidate), and *Oberfahnrich* (senior officer candidate or "almost an officer"). Candidates could be promoted to Fahnenjunker-Unteroffizier before beginning their intensive officer training at a Kriegschule. Successful candidates were promoted to Fahnrich about halfway through their training. Knappe was promoted to Fahnenjunker-Gefreiter on June 1, 1937, and to Fahnenjunker-Unteroffizier on September 1. After a 10-day furlough, he reported to the War School at Potsdam in mid-October to begin his officer's training.

The barracks at Potsdam were divided into suites, with four candidates per suite. All four men in each suite were from different branches of the service. Each suite was divided into a large study room with four desks and a bedroom with four beds, four lockers, and four washing facilities. There were approximately 1,000 students in the school at any one time, and there were four such schools in Germany. The Potsdam school was divided into two groups (500 students), and each group had 16 platoons of 32 men each.

One measure of the quality of the school and the quality of the training the young men received is the caliber of the officers responsible for their training. The school commandant at Potsdam was Colonel Wilhelm Wetzel, who went on to command the 255th Infantry Division, V Corps, and LXVI Corps in World War II. He ended the war as a general of infantry, commanding Wehrkreis X. Knappe's group commander was Lieutenant Colonel Erwin Rommel, the future "Desert Fox." His book, *Infantry in the Attack*, was then being used as a textbook in the course. Knappe's platoon leader was Major Erwin Kahnsnitz, who would rise to the rank of colonel. Kahnsnitz was commanding the elite Grossdeutschland Fuesilier Regiment when he was killed in action on the Eastern Front on July 20, 1943. He received a posthumous promotion to major general.[16] One of Knappe's unofficial instructors was also noteworthy. She was Lucie Rommel, the wife of the future field marshal, who assisted her husband on "evenings out," when the future officers were taught the social graces. Lucie, who had been a dance student in Danzig when she met her future husband in 1912, helped teach the young cadets proper social behavior and how to dance. By all accounts, the young men looked forward to and thoroughly enjoyed their "evenings out."

At Potsdam, all of the candidates were treated as infantry, and the mission of the school was to teach them all how to lead an infantry platoon, company, and battalion in combat. The training began immediately and continued without a break until Christmas. (They were, however, not subjected to the verbal abuse the NCOs heaped on them in basic training.) They studied topography, map reading, engineering, the construction and demolition of bridges, basic artillery, drill, parade, physical education, Luftwaffe coordination, and horseback riding. They spent six hours each day in the classroom and three in the field, and had a major exam every week. The most important subject was tactics, which counted more than all of the other subjects combined. In their tactical problems, there was no single "school solution." The candidates had to formulate, defend, and execute their own plans, and their success was based on how well they did it. They all had the chance to "play" battalion commander, as well as to serve as company commander and in various staff positions. They also spent a great deal of time studying military history (mostly the Prussian battles of the 17th and 18th centuries), and often took trips (now called "staff rides") to the actual battlefields. One trip to East Prussia lasted two weeks. They also studied the tactics of Alexander, Caesar, Napoleon (Rommel's favorite), and Frederick the Great, and the battles of ancient Greece and Rome. They learned how to handle barbed wire, antitank mines, dynamite (for demolitions), and various types of machine guns. They participated in sports, including swimming, highdiving, boxing, fencing, horseback riding, running, tennis, and others. Knappe started training in the modern pentathlon, which consisted of fencing, pistol shooting, horseback riding, 10-kilometer cross-country running, and 1,000-meter swimming. In addition, the school owned some small sailing boats, and everyone learned how to sail.

"Our lives were quite pleasant at Kriegsschule Potsdam," Fahnen-junker Knappe recalled. Their training was excellent, interesting, and challenging. Their mess hall was a like a cafeteria; the food was simple but good, and usually consisted of meat, potatoes, vegetables, and bread. The hall was used only for the noon meal. Each room was issued a two-pound loaf of *kommissbrot* (army bread) every other day, and they were issued butter, jam, and coffee every morning. Dinner was dispensed from the mess hall and eaten in the suite. It consisted of liverwurst or cheese, butter, and bread.

In addition to their military training, they received training in the social graces as well. They often had formal dances, to which the daughters of older officers and the local gentry were invited. The events were held in large ballrooms, with live orchestras, and dance classes were provided for those who needed them.

After a Christmas furlough, training resumed in the second week of January 1938. Knappe graduated 24th out of 4,000, and won an Inspector of the War Schools' Award. "I had really enjoyed the experience," he recalled. "The school had been hard work, and it was challenging, but it was also great fun."

Just before graduation, all of the candidates were asked whether they would like to join the Luftwaffe. Not enough candidates volunteered, so several were drafted into the air force. Knappe graduated on July 2, 1938, and returned to his unit as an Oberfahnrich, to complete his speciality training. Because no officer-candidate could be assigned to a base where he had served as an enlisted man, Knappe was assigned to the I Battalion of the 24th Artillery Regiment (I/24th Artillery), which supported the 18th Infantry Regiment at Plauen. Those who had not performed well enough to earn a commission were returned to their regiments as sergeants. Knappe, however, received his commission on September 1. He ended the war as a major of the General Staff and as operations officer of the LVI Panzer Corps in the Battle of Berlin.

Although Knappe was an exceptional young man, the training that he had received to this point in his career was typical. Like his superiors up through the rank of corps commander, he had received the best military training available anywhere in the world. Also, like most of his peers, he had faith in his country and in the peaceful goals and ideals of his Fuehrer. He had no idea that he would be required to use what he had learned in the very near future.

CHAPTER II

KARL ROTHENBURG: HERO OF TWO WARS

Rommel's most important subordinate during the French campaign was Karl Rothenburg, another war hero and fellow holder of the *Pour le Merite*.

Rothenburg was born in Fuerstenwalde, near the river Spree in Brandenburg, on June 8, 1894, and entered the Imperial Army as a private in the 5th Foot Guards Regiment on April 1, 1914. Four months later, World War I broke out. Rothenburg first saw action near Namur, Belgium, but was soon on his way to Silesia with his regiment. The 5th Foot Guards fought against the Czar's armies in Poland, Galacia, and in the Carpathians. After serving on the Eastern Front, Rothenburg was involved in the trench warfare that characterized the Western Front. He distinguished himself in combat, both as an enlisted man and as an officer. On November 8, 1915, he was awarded a direct battlefield commission as a second lieutenant of reserves. Later he was awarded the *Pour le Merite*, also known as the "Blue Max," which was the equivalent of the Congressional Medal of Honor when awarded to someone of such junior rank. By the time the Armistice was declared, however, Karl Rothenburg had obviously had enough of war and the army. He was discharged at this own request on December 18, 1918.[1] Because he left the service so quickly, he did not receive the customary honorary promotion to the next highest grade (i.e., first lieutenant).

Rothenburg spent the next 14 years in the police. On July 26, 1935, however, he rejoined the army as a major. He foresaw that the future lay in mobile warfare and, as the holder of the "Blue Max," he was in a much better position to influence his own assignments than the average major. In 1936, he was named commander of the II Battalion of the

6th Panzer Regiment, despite the fact that he had no experience in tanks and was a grade junior to his appointment.

The 6th Panzer was part of the Berliner 3rd Panzer Division, which was known as "the Bear Division" from its emblem and mascot. During the 1937–39 period, the regiment furnished cadres and volunteers for the 88th Panzer Battalion, which was part of the Condor Legion in Spain. Thus, it had more highly experienced combat veterans than any other panzer unit in the German Army when Hitler invaded Poland in 1939. Before that, the 6th Panzer took part in the *Anschluss* (the occupation of Austria, 1938) and the occupation of the Sudetenland (1938). Meanwhile, Rothenburg was promoted to lieutenant colonel on April 1, 1938.

Karl Rothenburg was promoted to the command of the 6th Panzer Regiment on March 1, 1939, and led it in the Polish campaign. As part of Heinz Guderian's XIX Motorized Corps, it attacked from Pomerania to Thorn in northern Poland and cut the Polish Corridor, uniting East Prussia with the rest of the Reich. It then redeployed to the east and attacked to the southeast, and ended the campaign with the capture of the Polish fortress of Brest-Litovsk. Figure 2.1 shows the German invasion of Poland, 1939.

During the conquest of Poland, the German light divisions (numbered 1st through 4th) proved too cumbersome in combat. Hitler and *Oberkommando des Heeres* (OKH, the army high command) therefore decided to convert them into panzer divisions. Each division, which already had a tank battalion, was given two more panzer battalions and a panzer regiment headquarters. Rothenburg was named commander of the newly formed 25th Panzer Regiment of Lieutenant General Georg Stumme's 7th Panzer Division, which was nicknamed "the Ghost Division." A poorly equipped unit by German standards, it had no Panzer Mark IIIs (PzKw IIIs)—the best tank in the German Army until 1942. As of April 12, 1940, the regiment had 72 poor Panzer Mark IIs (armed with a 20mm main battle gun), 37 nearly useless Panzer Mark Is (which did not even have a main battle gun), and 23 Panzer Mark IVs, whose short-barreled 75mm main battle gun seriously limited their effectiveness. Its main tank was the Panzer 38 (t), a Czech tank which had been incorporated into the German Army after the occupation of the Sudetenland and Czechoslovakia in 1938 and 1939. It was not a bad tank by 1940 standards, but it was too light to match up effectively with many of the Allied tanks. Also, the fact that its operators' manuals and maintenance manuals were written in Czech—which few (if any) of Rothenburg's men could read—created further headaches, especially for the maintenance units.

After the reorganization was completed, the division redeployed to the Rhine sector, just behind the Western Front. This was the "Phony War"

Figure 2.1
The German Invasion of Poland, 1939

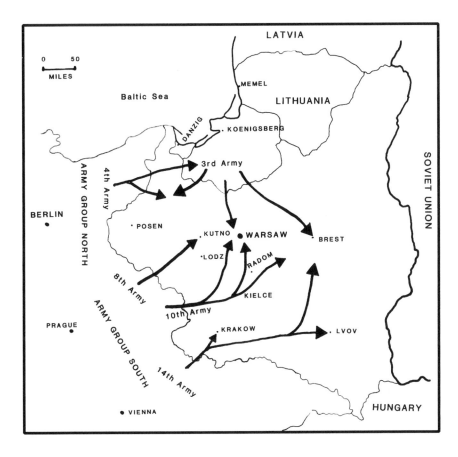

period and the division was allowed to train unmolested. On February 10, 1940, Stumme was promoted and given command of the newly formed XXXX Corps.[2] A relatively junior *Generalmajor* named Erwin Rommel arrived at the divisional headquarters at Bad Godesburg to succeed him. He initially made a very unfavorable impression by greeting his senior commanders with the Hitler salute. (Although he was forced to commit suicide in 1944 for his part in the anti-Hitler conspiracy, Rommel had commanded Hitler's bodyguard battalion in 1939 and was definitely a Nazi sympathizer in 1940.) He also offended the officers when he made a sneering reference to the fact that most of the 7th Panzer's enlisted men were Thuringians, supposedly an area not noted for producing good soldiers. Then he ordered a general inspection for the next day—a Sunday—which was very unusual and not at all popular.

A few days later, General Rommel returned to Berlin for a last interview with Hitler. While he was gone, his disgruntled officers met to discuss their new commander. The fact that Rommel was an infantry officer without armored experience did nothing to increase his popularity. Of the 10 senior officers, only Rothenburg and Lieutenant Colonel Rudolf Sieckenius, the commander of the III/25th Panzer Regiment, urged patient cooperation. When he returned, Rommel had a gift. He presented each of the 10 senior officers with a copy of his book on tactics, *Infantry in the Attack*.[3] This further aggravated some of the already unhappy officers.

Rommel realized that there was dissension in the senior ranks and his solution to the problem was to exhibit his inflexible determination. On February 29, he abruptly fired a battalion commander and had him packed and out of the divisional area in an hour and a half. His remark that this would cause the other dissidents "to pull up their socks" was quite correct. The division quickly embraced Rommel's vigorous training program.

Rommel, in fact, had little to be dissatisfied about in the 7th Panzer Division, as the ensuing battles would prove. Despite its maintenance problems, Rothenburg's 25th Panzer Regiment performed brilliantly in the French campaign. It broke through the Allies' Meuse River defenses, smashed through Belgium and France, and overran the French 1st Armored Division, destroying more than 100 French tanks and some 30 armored cars in the process. It helped check the British counterattack at Arras, overran the French 31st Motorized Division, and helped destroy the 1st French Army at Lille. It then turned south, captured Cherbourg, and pushed almost to the Spanish border by the time the French surrendered. The 7th Panzer Division amassed a tremendous record of accomplishment in the Western Campaign and Rommel, as the division commander, naturally received the lion's share of the glory. Rothenburg's part, however, did not go unnoticed, either by Rommel or Berlin. (Early in the campaign, Rothenburg's personal tank rescued the future Desert Fox by picking him up on the battlefield after his own tank had been knocked out. Rommel, in fact, relied more heavily on his panzer regiment's commander than on any other subordinate in the French campaign.) Rothenburg was decorated with the Knight's Cross on June 3, 1940, and was promoted to full colonel on August 1, 1940.

Rothenburg's attitude in battle was entirely fatalistic: he simply did not fear death. Perhaps because Rommel had a similarly fearless view of the world, he often rode with Rothenburg in the colonel's command tank. They were, in fact, kindred spirits. Like Rommel and many other German panzer commanders, Rothenburg habitually placed himself at the forefront of each advance. This fearless attitude cost Rommel his life when he joined the anti-Hitler conspiracy, and it would cost Rothenburg his life in the next campaign.

The 25th Panzer Regiment was engaged in occupation duties in the Bordeaux region until February 1941, when it was sent to East Prussia. It crossed into Russia on June 22, 1941, and was immediately involved in what became the Battle of the Minsk Pocket. In the early stages of this huge battle of encirclement, Colonel Karl Rothenburg was critically wounded near Grodeck-Ostrochichy (south of Minsk) on June 27 and died two days later.[4] He was thus one of the first of Rommel's old "Ghost Division" to suffer the fate awaiting many of them. By April 1944, the division, which in 1940 boasted a strength of more than 15,000 men and 218 panzers, was down to a total fighting strength of 1,872 men, 9 guns, 11 antitank guns, and 9 tanks—one of which was a captured Russian T-34. By early 1945, it did not have a single tank left.

A hero of two wars, Karl Rothenburg was buried with full honors. He was posthumously promoted to major general, effective June 1, 1941. For the rest of the war, the 25th Panzer was semi-officially referred to as "the Rothenburg regiment."

CHAPTER III

RUDOLF SIECKENIUS: THE SCAPEGOAT

The best battalion commander in the 25th Panzer Regiment (and probably in the entire 7th Panzer Division) was Rudolf Sieckenius.

Rudolf was born in Ludwigstal, Silesia, on May 16, 1896, the son of Alexander Sieckenius, a successful businessman. Both men planned for Rudolf to follow in his father's footsteps. In school, he studied accounting and industrial mathematics, as well as French, because the family business required trips to the south of France and Lorraine.[1]

The outbreak of World War I in August 1914 totally disrupted the family's plans. Rudolf was no less affected by the patriotic fervor that swept Germany than the typical 18 year old, and he joined the 5th Foot Artillery Regiment of the Silesian 9th Infantry Division on the 22nd of that month. He fought on the Western Front as part of the Crown Prince's 5th Army, taking part in the invasion of Lorraine. In September, the division (along with the 10th Infantry Division from Posen) established itself in the Côtes de Meuse (the Calonne trench), where it remained for two years. Sieckenius, meanwhile, transferred to the cavalry and applied for officers' training. More infantry officers were needed than cavalry officers, however, so Sieckenius again changed branches. He underwent a brief training course and, on December 27, 1916, graduated as a "90-day wonder," as the enlisted men somewhat derisively called the new second lieutenants (but never to their faces, for the reason explained in chapter I). Commissioned in the 154th Infantry Regiment (also of the 9th Infantry Division), Sieckenius served as platoon leader in the trenches and became a battalion adjutant in November 1917. He fought in the Côtes de Meuse again (from February through the end of April 1917), in the California Plateau sector (May to September 1917), and at Chemis des Dames (September to December 1917). Sieckenius's unit was pulled out of the line at the end of 1917 and partially rebuilt. It did not return to combat until March 1918, when it suffered heavy losses at the Battle of Picardy. Withdrawn again, it fought in the Battle of Aisne, where it lost another 3,000 men.

Sieckenius and his comrades fought in the Second Battle of the Marne in the summer of 1918 and in the Champagne district that fall. A first-class division from 1914 through 1917, its performance deteriorated in 1918 and, on November 4 alone, 1,800 of its men were captured. Rudolf Sieckenius was not among them, however; he was still fighting at the end of the war. Following the collapse of the Second Reich in November 1918, he was discharged from the army on October 20, 1919.

When Sieckenius returned to Silesia in 1919, the new Germany—which was called the Weimar Republic—was characterized by civil unrest, rebellion, political confusion, occasional anarchy, and economic turmoil. Like many former officers, Rudolf decided to join the police. He applied for a post with the Silesian *Landespolizie* (State or Provincial Police) and entered the service on April 29, 1920. Two months later, he was a police lieutenant.

Rudolf Sieckenius did well in the Weimar civil service. He became a qualified instructor in calisthenics and physical fitness (and retained his thin waist throughout his life), attended the excellent Equestrian Training School at Bamberg, and was named commander of the elite Escort Company of the Silesian Mounted Guards Police Battalion. He was promoted to first lieutenant in 1923 and to captain of police in 1928.

Hitler came to power in 1933 with the avowed intention of expanding the army, a program he secretly began in 1934. When Sieckenius read a memorandum from the Reich's Defense Ministry soliciting former soldiers in the civil police to resume their military careers, he jumped at the chance. On May 27, 1934, he was gazetted *Rittmeister* (captain of cavalry) in the I Squadron of the 11th Cavalry Regiment, which was based in Breslau. (See appendix 1 for a table of comparative ranks.) Initially, he was OIC (officer-in-charge) of the regimental stables. On April 1, 1935, however, he was transferred to Stuttgart as chief staff officer of the 7th Heavy Cavalry Regiment. Shortly thereafter, he was placed in charge of the motorized elements of the regiment—the 1st, 2nd, and 3rd Motor (Truck) Detachments. He was thus in a position to become familiar with motorized warfare.

In October 1935, General of Mobile Troops Oswald Lutz and Colonel Heinz Guderian created the first three panzer divisions.[2] Sieckenius quickly transferred to the new panzer branch and was named commander of the 6th Panzer Company, 2nd Panzer Regiment (6/2nd Panzer Regiment), which was part of the 1st Panzer Division at Weimar. He was promoted to major on March 1, 1936.

Despite his rank, Sieckenius continued to command his company until October 6, 1936, when he was appointed *Ordnance* (Orderly) Officer to Lieutenant General Baron Maximilian von Weichs, the divisional commander.[3] In October of the following year, Weichs was promoted to the command of Wehrkreis XIII at Nuremberg, and Sieckenius was transferred to the command of the I Battalion of the newly formed 15th Panzer Regiment at Oppeln. Here he found that he could not get along with Lieutenant Colonel Johannes Streich, the mediocre commander of the 15th Regiment, who was a difficult superior.[4] Their relationship deteriorated to the point that, in January 1939, Striech shouted at both of his battalion commanders (Sieckenius and Paul Goerbig) in public— and they shouted back. The division commander remedied this impossible situation by arranging for both Sieckenius and Goerbig to receive lateral transfers. Goerbig was given command of the 67th Panzer Battalion of the 3rd Light Division, while Sieckenius received command of the 66th Panzer Battalion of the 2nd Light.[5]

Sieckenius's new division was commanded by Georg Stumme, a competent but pleasure-loving general. The atmosphere, Friedrich von Stauffenberg wrote later, was "very congenial" and the 2nd was "a crack, well-officered division."[6] Sieckenius soon developed a close personal friendship with Major Walter von Neumann-Silkow, the commander of the 37th Reconnaissance Battalion.[7]

The 2nd Light went into battle in southern Poland in September 1939 and acquitted itself well. Every officer in a position to know, however, recognized that the light divisions had proved to be unbalanced and difficult to command in Poland. No one was sorry when OKH announced in mid-October that they were to be converted into panzer divisions. The 2nd Light became the 7th Panzer, and Sieckenius's battalion became the III Battalion of Rothenburg's 25th Panzer Regiment. Sieckenius, meanwhile, was promoted to lieutenant colonel on October 1, 1939.

Sieckenius did well in France and, at one point in the pursuit, his battalion was the only one that could keep up with the hard-charging Rommel. The III remained in the Bordeaux region of France until February 1941, when Rommel was transferred to North Africa and was replaced by the more congenial Major General Baron Hans von Funck, who would command the 7th Panzer Division for the next three years.[8]

Funck's first task was to move his division back to its home base of Gera in Germany. The 25th Panzer Regiment was then supplied with a shipment of new tanks. Sieckenius and his men were busy running them in; meanwhile, Hitler decided to double the number of his panzer divisions by cutting the tank strength of each in half. Experienced panzer officers were in great demand and, on April 30, Rudolf Sieckenius said farewell to his officers, men, and friends, and traveled to Bucharest.

There, he joined the newly formed 16th Panzer Division, which was in the process of loading aboard trains for a move back to Niesse, Silesia.

When he arrived in Bucharest, Sieckenius found that he was there to replace Colonel Hero Breusing, the commander of his own old regiment, the 2nd Panzer. The circumstances were not the best. Although every major panzer leader except Walter Nehring thought Hitler's plans to create 20 panzer divisions from the original 10 was a bad idea, only Hero Breusing said so publicly. A highly respected expert in mobile warfare, Breusing had served in the Motor Transport Branch under both Lutz and Guderian since as early as 1930. He taught armored tactics to the General Staff aspirants at the War Academy, and he contributed numerous articles on that subject to various military journals. He had led the 2nd Panzer Regiment with considerable distinction in Poland and France. When Hitler cut the strength of the tank divisions in half, Breusing wrote a number of critical articles on the subject. They were published without comment in several military journals, where they attracted the attention of the High Command of the Armed Forces (OKW) staff. Someone took one or more of the articles to Hitler, who had Breusing summarily relieved of his command.[9] Rudolf Sieckenius therefore inherited a very unhappy regiment, and his officers greeted him with guarded hostility and suspicion.

Fortunately for the uncomfortable Sieckenius, his new division commander was the very experienced and competent Hans Valentin Hube.[10] This major general had lost an arm at Verdun in 1916 and, as far as I am able to determine, was the only handicapped officer selected for the Reichsheer. Hube understood the situation and let it be known that he expected his officers to give the new regimental commander their full support and cooperation, and to try to make him feel at home. Sieckenius's transition was further aided by the rush of events. The division almost immediately moved to its jump-off positions on the west bank of the Bug River. On June 22, 1941, Operation Barbarossa, the German invasion of the Soviet Union, began. The 16th Panzer followed the 11th Panzer Division across the river at Sokol-Krystinopol and was immediately involved in the fierce frontier fighting.

The Russian border area was fortified and strongly defended, but the division fought its way through in a matter of days. Then, from June 27 to July 1, the Red Army counterattacked in almost overwhelming strength, using hundreds of tanks that were mostly superior to the German panzers. The division, however, held its positions and beat back every attack. When the Soviets finally retreated, they left 243 burned-out tanks on the battlefield. Most of them had been destroyed by the 2nd Panzer Regiment. For his part in the victory, Hube personally presented Sieckenius with the coveted Knight's Cross on July 15.

Sieckenius continued to lead the 2nd Panzer Regiment in the huge battle of encirclement at Uman and the subsequent Russian breakout attempts in and around Monasterischtse and in the dense Oratov Forest (July 25 to August 2). There was no time for rest, however. Sieckenius set off immediately down the meandering Bug and his I Battalion (under Reserve Major Count Hyazinth Strachwitz) seized Pervomaisk by *coup de main*.[11] The next day, Sieckenius personally led a surprise attack and captured the bridge at Vosnesenk.

The furious pursuit continued until August 6, when the division was checked outside the Black Sea naval base of Nikolaev. The base was screened and the battle turned over to the infantry, which captured it on August 20, while Hube's division moved north to Kirovograd. Meanwhile, near Novo-Danzig, Soviet forces surprised and captured the 6th Company of the 79th Rifle Regiment. After it surrendered, every man was mercilessly massacred.

News of this atrocity was received with shock and rage by the men of the 16th Panzer Division. Sieckenius and his men had been aware of Hitler's "Commissar Order," which had been issued before the invasion began, under which captured Soviet political officers were to be summarily executed as war criminals. Field Marshal Gerd von Rundstedt, the commander of Army Group South, had not made much of an effort to disseminate the order and Colonel General Ewald von Kleist, the commander of the 1st Panzer Group, had ignored it altogether.[12] His units, including the 16th Panzer Division, had behaved remarkably well—until now. After Novo-Danzig, however, everything was different, and the war became increasingly brutal.

Meanwhile, the recon battalion of the 16th Panzer (Major von Witzleben) seized a bridgehead over the wide Dnieper River near Kremenchug on September 11. The next day, the entire division was across the river and barreling through the rear areas of the Soviet armies defending Kiev and the Ukraine. On September 16, near Lubny on the Sula River, the 16th Panzer Engineer Battalion linked up with Walter Model's 3rd Panzer Division of Guderian's 2nd Panzer Group, surrounding more than 700,000 Soviet soldiers. By the time the battle ended on September 26, five Red armies had been destroyed and 667,000 men surrendered, along with 3,718 guns and 584 armored vehicles. Hube's division was not there for the finish, however. Figure 3.1 shows the major battles of encirclement on the Eastern Front in 1941. Led by von Witzleben, Strachwitz, and Sieckenius, it was off and running to the southeast, where it played the major role in smashing the Soviet 18th Army around Melitopol. The division found the body of the Russian army commander, General Smirnoff, on October 6. Hube ordered him buried with full military honors.

Figure 3.1
Major Battles of Encirclement, Eastern Front, 1941

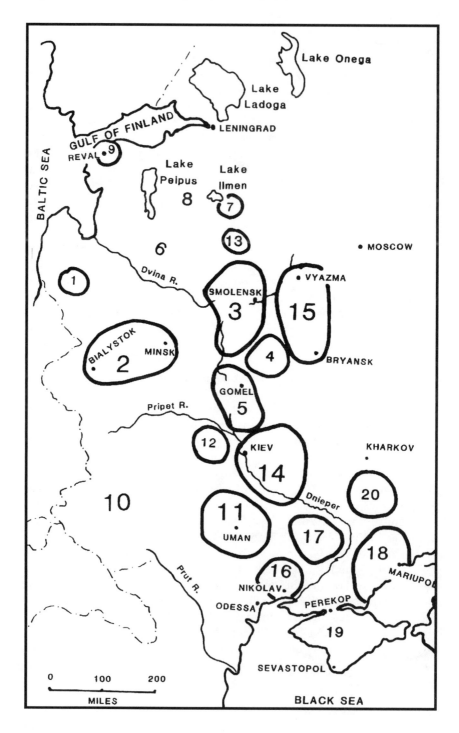

For his services to date, Rudolf Sieckenius was promoted to colonel on October 1, 1941, with seniority to date from February 1.

The target for the next advance was Rostov, and it was harder. It began on October 12, and was hampered by supply problems and maintenance difficulties. The rainy season set in on October 27 and the division, which had clearly outrun its supply lines, halted. The offensive was not resumed until November 17–18, when the first severe frost hardened the soil. Rostov was captured by the III Panzer Corps on November 20, while the 16th Panzer covered its northern flank.

Stalin's winter offensive on the southern sector began on November 22—earlier than elsewhere. Hube's division alone faced 10 Russian divisions. On November 28, in near blizzard conditions, the 1st Panzer Army finally retreated and Rostov was abandoned. Sieckenius and his two battered battalions fell back to the Mius, where the Reds were finally halted. While his regiment huddled in their bunkers near the front, Sieckenius spent much of his time that winter in Stalino, supervising the arrival of new tanks and begging for more.

The summer campaign of 1942 began in June. Hube moved up to the command of the XIV Panzer Corps in September, and Lieutenant General Gunther Angern took over the division, which was then on the Volga and fighting in the northern suburbs of Stalingrad.[13] It was committed to street fighting by the 6th Army commander, Colonel General Friedrich Paulus, who did not seem to understand that armored divisions should not be sent into combat in built-up areas.[14] By mid-November, the division had been reduced to a strength of 4,000 men—about one-quarter of its strength in May 1941.

Finally, on November 20, the 94th Infantry Division completed the relief of the 16th Panzer in the line at Stalingrad, and the depleted division headed west for the Donetz, where it was to undergo a complete refit. Angern instructed Sieckenius to command the vanguard while he personally directed the rearguard. As fate would have it, however, Stalin's counteroffensive began on November 19. The northern pincher overwhelmed the 3rd Rumanian Army in one day and cut right across the line of march of the 16th Panzer Division on the evening of November 20. The fighting was fierce, but Sieckenius was cut off from the rest of the division on November 21. Sieckenius had the 2nd Panzer Regiment, the I/64th Rifle Regiment, the 16th Panzer Reconnaissance Battalion, most of the 16th Engineer Battalion, and the 16th Tank Destroyer Battalion, which was led by Major Curt von Burgsdorff, a 56-year-old reservist who had volunteered for frontline duty after his only son was killed near Moscow in early 1942.[15] Angern was left inside the pocket with the 79th Panzer Grenadier Regiment, most of the 64th Panzer Grenadier (led by Lieutenant Colonel Dr. Woermann), and the entire 16th Panzer Artillery Regiment (led by Colonel Ernst Strehlke), as well as assorted divisional troops and the staff of the 16th Panzer Brigade under Major General Hans Adolf von Arenstorff.[16] Figure 3.2 shows the Stalingrad encirclement.

Sieckenius divided his command into two (later three) combat groups and did yeoman's service, bolstering and often restoring the thin German line as it was pushed westward, back across the frozen

Figure 3.2
The Stalingrad Encirclement, 1942

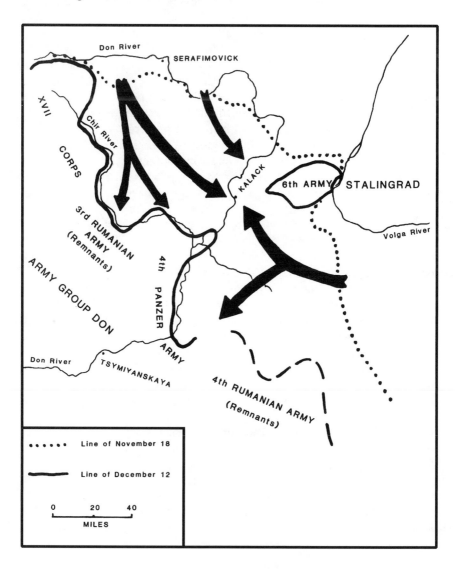

Line of November 18

Line of December 12

0   20   40
MILES

Donetz. Sieckenius was severely wounded in mid-January 1943 and was shipped home to recover. Strachwitz assumed command but was himself seriously wounded two days later, so command devolved on Major Bernhard Sauvant, the former commander of the II/2nd Panzer Regiment, who was the senior surviving officer outside the pocket.[17]

Soon Sauvant would be the senior surviving officer of the division, period. In Stalingrad, the rest of the 16th Panzer Division was crushed. Rather than surrender to the Russians, General Angern committed suicide on February 2, and the ranking surviving officer, Lieutenant Colonel Dr. Woermann, surrendered the remnants of the division that same day.

The forces still with Sauvant were sent back to Stalino and put on trains for France, where the division was to rebuild. Meanwhile, on February 5, 1943, Colonel Sieckenius visited the commander of Wehrkreis II in Stettin and reported for duty. He now wore the Wounded Badge in Silver, which was awarded only after a soldier received his third wound.[18] He was allowed to recover for 10 more days and was then ordered to report to Panzer Troop Command VI Headquarters at Warendorf for reassignment. After two weeks of light duty, he flew to Mayenne, France, where he replaced Colonel Burkhart Mueller-Hildebrand as commander of the reception staff of the rebuilding 16th Panzer Division.[19] He assumed formal command of the division near Laval on March 5. It initially consisted of 3,400 men who returned from service in Russia and 600 Russian volunteers, who were called "Hiwis." These were soon joined by thousands of new inductees, and dozens of new tanks, self-propelled guns, artillery, and new Mercedes half-tracks, which were called "bucket cars."

On May 23, General of Panzer Troops Hans Hube—en route to Italy as the commander of the rebuilt XIV Panzer Corps—visited the division to take its salute on the anniversary of the Battle of Mont Morion, which the original 16th Panzer had won in 1940. That evening, Sieckenius and his officers entertained their former commander at dinner at Mayenne, and, as a body, entreated Hube to request their unit be assigned to his corps. It did not take too much pleading.

Hube was one of the very few army generals Hitler respected and trusted throughout the war, so he readily agreed to assign the new division to the XIV Panzer Corps. On May 25, the 16th Panzer began its trip to northern Italy. The infantry went by way of Munich and the Brenner Pass; the heavy equipment traveled via Avignon and Nice. They rendezvoused near Siena in Tuscany in early June. Meanwhile, Rudolf Sieckenius was promoted to major general, effective June 1, 1943.

Hube defended Sicily with the 15th and 29th Panzer Grenadier Divisions and the Luftwaffe's Hermann Goering Panzer and 1st Parachute Divisions. Meanwhile, on July 25, the 23-year reign of Benito Mussolini ended when he was deposed by the king and was arrested as he left the palace. The new government under Field Marshal Pietro Badoglio hotly proclaimed its loyalty to the Third Reich, but Adolf Hitler knew the Italians were lying. They were just waiting for the right moment to defect.

Sieckenius, meanwhile, moved his division south and deployed every available unit along the Gulf of Salerno, but positioned them about three miles from the beaches, in case the Allies tried to land paratroopers in Hube's rear. He also kept a wary eye on his Italian counterparts, General Gonzaga's 222nd Coastal Defense Division. In the meantime, Hube successfully evacuated Sicily. Montgomery's 8th Army crossed the Straits of Messina on September 3 and invaded the Reggio da Calabria, the toe of the Italian boot.

Hitler was right about the Italians. They surreptitiously signed surrender terms with the Allies at Cassibile, Sicily, but the news was not made public until Wednesday, September 8, when General Mark Clark's Anglo-American invasion force, the U.S. 5th Army, was already on its way to Italy.

As soon as he heard the news, Sieckenius dispatched his intelligence officer, Major von Alvensleben (who spoke fluent Italian), along with an armed motorized detachment, to General Gonzaga's headquarters to arrest and disarm the Italian coastal defense division. On the way, Alvensleben found that half of Gonzaga's men had abandoned their posts and headed for home. Once at HQ, the remaining senior officers surrendered immediately and made no trouble; Gonzaga, however, refused to capitulate. One word led to another, and Alvensleben slapped his holstered Luger as a threatening gesture. Gonzaga at once pulled his service revolver, waved it at the major, and shouted for help, which was not forthcoming. One of Alvensleben's soldiers, believing that the major's life was in danger, opened up with his Schmiesser automatic. Gonzaga was killed instantly. Sieckenius saw to it that his body was sent home with appropriate honors.

The 222nd Coastal Defense Division ceased to exist on September 8, and it was not too soon. On September 9, the Anglo-American invasion force landed at Salerno and on its neighboring beaches. Sieckenius pounded the sector with artillery and multiple rocket launchers, while his own units were blasted by the big guns of the Royal Navy and later the U.S. Navy. The 16th Panzer Division began launching counterattacks on September 10.

The Battle of Salerno was hard fought on both sides, and the 16th Panzer gave the Americans some very bad moments. At one point, Sieckenius penetrated almost to the invasion beaches, and Lieutenant General Mark Clark, the commander of the U.S. 5th Army, was contemplating a retreat to his ships. The 16th Panzer was halted in front of the last American defensive line.

Reinforced by battle groups from three other divisions, Sieckenius attempted to launch a massive tank attack on September 16 and 17, but both efforts were aborted when Allied naval guns and airplanes blasted the units in their assembly areas. The Germans began to retreat on September 18. OKW considered that, at the very least, they had won a major prestige victory. Casualties had been very high: almost 7,000 Allies were killed, wounded, or missing. The Germans lost 840 killed, 2,002 wounded, and 630 missing. At least 90 percent of these were from Sieckenius's division.

Meanwhile, Sieckenius conducted a perfectly orchestrated withdrawal to the Avellino-Olfante line. He personally commanded the rearguard and inflicted heavy damage on the U.S. VI Corps around Teora on September 24–25. Figure 3.3 shows the German retreat to the Gustav Line.

With the German right flank secured, Sieckenius was called to stabilize the left, where Montgomery's British 8th Army had secured a bridgehead over the Biferno River at Termolin, near the Adriatic coast. The division made a long 95-mile road march along the difficult mountain roads of the Apennines during the night of October 4–5. As a result, it was badly strung out and went into battle against the British piecemeal. In a tough battle against two British armored brigades, Sieckenius lost most of his remaining armor, mainly to British air strikes. Now a burned out unit at *kampfgruppe* (regimental) strength, the 16th Panzer covered the retreat of the LXXVI Panzer Corps to the north. It was, however, unable to prevent Montgomery's commandos from seizing a small bridgehead across the Trigno, south of the town of Vesta. The bridgehead was quickly sealed off by the 16th Panzer, and the entire Allied advance was halted by the onset of the rainy season, which turned the entire country into mud.

Meanwhile, Field Marshal Albert Kesselring, the OB South[20] and commander-in-chief of Army Group C, had promised Hitler he would hold the Volturno-Biferno line until at least October 16. He had failed, and now Berlin was demanding scapegoats. For no good reason, Rudolf Sieckenius and the 16th Panzer Division were selected. Sieckenius was relieved of his command on October 31, 1943, and his career was ruined.

How Hitler, OKW, and OKH could have found any legitimate cause for dissatisfaction with the performance of the 16th Panzer is impossible to understand. It fought the Battle of Salerno almost single-handedly and, despite the tremendous odds against it, narrowly failed to throw the Americans back into the sea. It then checked the U.S. VI Corps at Teora and, after a difficult forced march, stabilized the German left flank against greatly superior British forces. In the process, it lost more than half of its men and most of its tanks and artillery.

Figure 3.3
The German Retreat to the Gustav Line, 1943–44

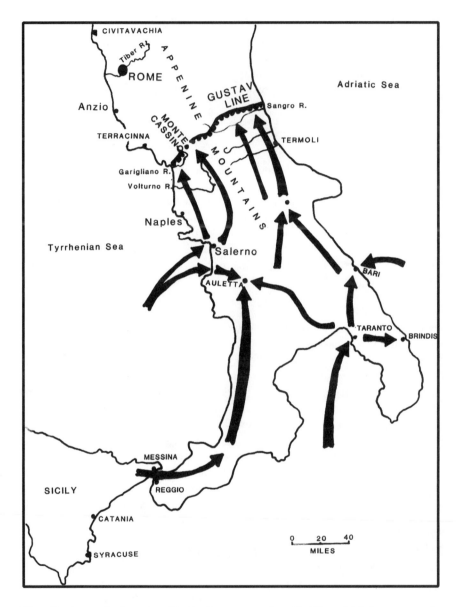

Despite its truly heroic efforts, however, the divisional history records that not one member of the 16th Panzer Division was awarded the Knight's Cross or the German Cross in Gold in September or October 1943.[21]

General Sieckenius was placed in Fuehrer Reserve in Kassel, Wehrkreis IX, and his rank was permanently frozen. He was forced to take a course in National Socialist Leadership Procedure, as well as the short Division Commanders' Course, which was given only to officers who had been earmarked to command a division but had not yet done so (unless it was briefly and on a temporary basis only). This was an insult, because he had already commanded a division in combat and had done so with considerable skill. Thoroughly bewildered and frustrated, he was unemployed until February 21, 1944, when he was ordered to report to the Army Personnel Office in Berlin. He was attached to the 1st Bureau as a reserve division commander. A month later, he was sent to Army Group North in Russia for use as a backup division commander, to be used if a regular divisional commander went on leave, was wounded, or was killed.

Sieckenius hung around headquarters until May 2, when Lieutenant General Konrad Heinrichs, the commander of the 290th Infantry Division, went back to Germany on leave. Sieckenius defended a sector near Lake Ladoga until May 23, when General Heinrichs returned.[22]

Meanwhile, on May 21, Lieutenant General Werner Richter, the commander of the 263rd Infantry Division, was mortally wounded while defending a sector on the Duna River.[23] Although unacquainted with static (completely unmotorized) units, Sieckenius took command at once and directed the division in a skillful retreat to the Dvina during the massive Soviet offensive of June–July 1944.

Sieckenius led the 263rd Infantry until August 14, when Major General Adolf Hemmann arrived to replace him.[24] Next, he was sent to Breslau, to supervise the dissolution of the 221st Security Division, which had been smashed by Stalin's massive offensive of June–July 1944. (The permanent commander, Major General Hubert Lendle, had committed the sin of escaping death or capture, so he had been summarily dismissed.)[25] General Sieckenius completed this unpleasant task by August 31.

Meanwhile, the 391st Field Training Division was reforming in Breslau as a security division. It had been smashed in the Minsk-Bobruisk encirclements, and its previous commander, Lieutenant General Baron Albert Digeon von Monteton, had been transferred to Army Group North as the commandant of Lerpaja (Libau), and Rudolf Sieckenius was selected to replace him.[26]

Sieckenius's new command included the 312th Field Training and 566th Security Regiments. The men were mainly overage volunteers or draftees, rear-area personnel (including bakers, typists, clerks, postal people, maintenance personnel, and so on), and returning wounded. The 312th consisted of rear-area veterans of the defunct 206th Infantry Division, which had been destroyed at Bobruisk. Its commander had a serious health problem and would have been sent home, except for his determination to continue soldiering. The commander of the 566th was a 62-year-old reserve officer who had commanded the supply depot at Pinsk until it was captured by the Red Army. With one or two exceptions, all of the officers were from the noncombatant branches. Sieckenius had no artillery, no heavy weapons companies, and no signal, engineer, or reconnaissance units. Worse yet, he did not have any horses to speak of—much less motorized vehicles.

Sieckenius made the best of a bad situation and instituted a rigorous training regimen, including a physical fitness program. Unlike the typical security or field training division in 1944–45, the 391st was not raided for trained men and replacements for regular combat units because of the need for a permanent defensive force at Breslau and on the southern reaches of the Oder River.

Meanwhile, in December 1944, Sieckenius was eligible for promotion to lieutenant general. He was summarily passed over.

In late January 1945, the Soviets launched another massive offensive. Sieckenius had done such a marvelous job that the 391st Security Division was now actually considered a potentially battle-worthy unit. The 9th Army, which was responsible for defending the lower Oder, allocated Sieckenius a fleet of ancient trucks, as well as replacement and training companies of signal troops and engineers, heavy machine guns, and two batteries of self-propelled artillery. With these reinforcements he hurried to the Oder, where he joined the V SS Panzer Corps, which was holding the river from Guben to Eberswalde, on the right flank of the 9th Army.[27]

The V SS Panzer Corps was not a panzer corps and did not have a single tank unit. It was commanded by SS Lieutenant General Friedrich-Wilhelm Krueger, who was soon replaced by SS Lieutenant General Friedrich Jeckeln, a mass murderer who had commanded an *Einsatzgruppen* (an SS murder unit) in 1941.

The last Soviet offensive began on April 16 (see Figure 3.4). Its objective was Berlin. Despite overwhelming odds, the German line held until April 19; then it broke, and the 9th Army was cut in two. The LVI Panzer and the two security divisions of the V SS Corps were pushed back to the north, on Zepernick and Ladeburg, while the rest of the army was in danger of being encircled behind the Spree River, between Erkner and Zossen. Sieckenius and Major General Emmo von Roden, the commander of the 286th Security Division,[28] lost contact with the Headquarters, V SS Corps, and more or less by default placed themselves under the command of General of Artillery Helmuth Weidling, the commander of the LVI Panzer Corps. Weidling found himself named Battle Commandant of Berlin on April 25, the day the city was surrounded.[29]

Figure 3.4
The Battle of Berlin, 1945

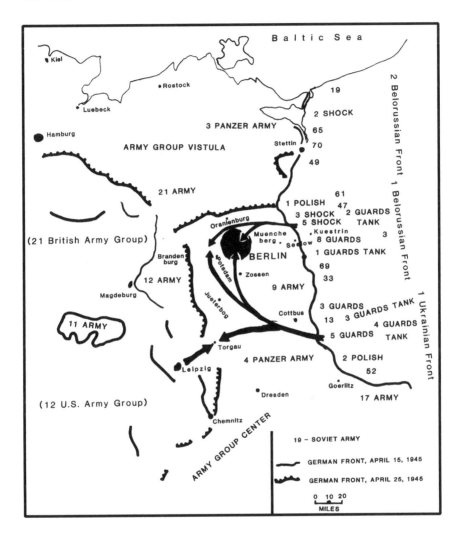

The remnants of the 391st Security Division were incorporated into the defensive perimeter of the capital. Initially, Sieckenius's forces held positions along the Landwehr Canal, supporting SS Major General Joachim Ziegler's SS Nordland Division. Weidling, however, considered Ziegler a worn-out force, so he replaced him with SS Major General Gustav Krukenberg, whose 33rd SS Grenadier Division "Charlemagne" had virtually ceased to exist.[30] He placed Sieckenius in charge of the entire sector.

During the next three days, Sieckenius tried to hold his positions while the German defensive lines were pressed ever backward, toward the center of the city. Tempelhof airport was overrun on April 27 and, on the morning of April 28, Sieckenius found himself surrounded in Goerlitzer Station. His main forces had already been destroyed and the Russians had pushed beyond him, toward the Fuehrer Bunker.

With their ammunition almost gone, Sieckenius and a handful of survivors held out until late afternoon, although they knew that their position was doomed. General Sieckenius then ordered the survivors to save themselves, if they could; meanwhile, he and a handful of stalwart volunteers would launch a final suicide attack against the enemy to provide cover for their escaping comrades. The general himself charged forward firing a Schmieser machine pistol. A few moments later, Rudolf Sieckenius and his entire band were cut down by Soviet machine guns.

CHAPTER **IV**

KARL AUGUST HANKE: NAZI POLITICIAN

Not all of Rommel's officers were professionals, like Karl Rothenburg and Rudolf Sieckenius. Some were reserve officers, and a few were opportunistic Nazi officials who were more interested in furthering their own political careers than anything else. Perhaps the most interesting of these was Karl August Hanke, who eventually succeeded the infamous Heinrich Himmler as chief of the German police and was the fourth (and last) Reichsfuehrer-SS.[1] Less than five years before that, he served the Desert Fox as a lieutenant of reserves.

Hanke was born in Lauban, near Liegnitz in Lower Silesia, on August 24, 1903, the son of a locomotive engineer. His older brother was killed in action in World War I, but Karl Hanke was too young to see action before the armistice. Karl did, however, serve as a temporary volunteer (*Zeitfreiwilliger*) in the 19th Infantry Regiment at Frankfurt/Oder in the early 1920s. Hanke, meanwhile, obtained an education as a milling engineer by attending the German Milling School at Dippoldiswalde. He then obtained a year's practical experience as a railway workshop apprentice before returning to milling. From 1921 to around 1926, he worked mainly in the milling industry, serving as a business manager for mills in Silesia, Bavaria, and Tyrol. He then attended the *Berufspaedagogischen Institut* in Berlin and in 1928 received a degree, qualifying him to teach milling at vocational schools. Later that year, he went to work as a master miller in Berlin-Steglitz and became a vocational instructor at a technical school in Berlin. He joined the Nazi Party (NSDAP) on November 1, 1928.

Hanke started his National Socialist career at the relatively low level of *Amtswalter*—a low-ranking speaker and a factory cell organizer. He joined the Brownshirt (Stormtrooper or SA) Reserve in 1929, became a deputy street cell leader that same year, and was promoted to street cell leader (*Strassenzellenleiter*) in 1930. Later that year, he became a section leader (*Sektionsfuehrer*) in Berlin. He was fired from his teaching job in April 1931 because of his Nazi activities, and he went to work for the party full time. By late 1931, Hanke was *Kreisleiter* (ward leader) of the West End District in Berlin, working directly under the Gauleiter, Dr. Paul Joseph Goebbels. By 1932, he was also chief Gau organizational director and personal adjutant and *Referent* (advisor) to Goebbels in the latter capacity as propaganda director of the Nazi Party (*Reichspropagandandaleiter der NSDAP*). He had risen rapidly, but he wanted much more.

Even as a young man, Karl Hanke combined a certain charm and directness with German competence and German arrogance. Adolf Hitler took an early liking to the outspoken and handsome young Nazi, and Hanke became a NSDAP delegate to the Prussian *Landtag* (provincial legislature) in April 1932 as a result. By the end of the year, he was elected to the *Reichstag* (the German National Parliament) on the Nazi slate, representing Potsdam. (He would hold this seat until the end of the war.) In November of the same year, he became an office leader in the party propaganda department, and in March of the following year (less than two months after Hitler took power) became secretary and personal assistant to Dr. Goebbels in the Ministry of Popular Enlightenment and Propaganda. Goebbels—another arrogant Nazi—convinced himself that the competent Hanke was loyal to him personally and wanted nothing more than to serve him. Hanke, Goebbels thought, would be content to remain in his shadow. For this reason, among others, Goebbels promoted the young Silesian to state secretary to the minister of propaganda and public enlightenment on November 26, 1937, making him the number two man in the entire ministry. Goebbels, however, was laboring under a delusion. He was too busy with his duties and his whores to realize that Hanke wanted not only his job, but his wife as well.

Karl Hanke, meanwhile, skillfully solidified his position within the party and with Hitler. He joined the SS in early 1934, did a temporary duty assignment as a special duties officer on the staff of the Reichsfuehrer-SS (1935–36), and became second vice president of the *Reichskulturkammer* (Reich Chamber of Culture) in 1937. He also made it a point to introduce Hitler to Alfred Speer, an architect who refurbished Hanke's Berlin-Grunewald villa (and headquarters) in 1932. Speer owed much of his initial success in the Third Reich to his connection with Hanke, and the two friends helped each other at every opportunity from then on. By 1938, Hanke was very well connected in the Reich, was second in command at the propaganda ministry, and held the rank of *Oberfuehrer* (roughly equivalent of brigadier general) in the

SS.[2] He was, however, still bidding his time. He was sure that the incautious Goebbels would slip up on a grand scale. Then he—Karl Hanke—would have both the minister's post and Magda Goebbels as well.

Meanwhile, oblivious to Hanke's plotting, Joseph Goebbels fell in love.

His sexual exploits were a national joke, and he was known as the *Giftzwerg* (the foul-mouthed toad), the limping devil, and "the goat of Babelsberg" (the German counterpart of Hollywood) because of the number of starlets he had taken to bed. When his charms were insufficient to unclothe a woman to whom he was attracted (and they frequently were not), he would promise the woman important parts in certain movies in exchange for sex. If she still refused to yield, he would threaten to end her acting career if she did not at once satisfy his primeval urges. This usually got him what he wanted. He was a direct contradiction to a part of the official Nazi world view: that people should lead wholesome family lives. "We used to polemicize against Jewish bosses who sexually coerced their employees," Heinrich Himmler sneered. "Today it is Dr. Goebbels."[3]

The *Giftzwerg* also had his wife completely fooled. In 1938, she dumbfounded her best friend by saying, "Joseph and I are now just as close to one another as ever before. It makes me so happy that he is resisting temptation and being true to me."[4] Her world came falling down around her one day when Goebbels returned home to their mansion, Schwanenwerder, for tea with Lida Baarova, a shapely, dark-haired, slender, and beautiful 28-year-old Czech actress, who had a definite exotic appeal. Goebbels brought his wife flowers, and the three chatted harmlessly for about a half an hour. Then, Goebbels turned to his wife and said, "I have something very serious to discuss with you. Frau Baarova and I love one another."

"Yes, indeed," the beautiful actress confirmed. "We love each other."[5]

Magda Goebbels put down her tea cup, speechless. She was so stunned that she could not grasp what was happening. Goebbels went on to say that Lida would be sort of a second wife for him. "You naturally are the mother of my children and the wife who belongs to me. But after so many years you must of course understand that I need a lady friend, I mean a steady and serious friend." Frau Goebbels, still stunned, could not speak. Goebbels took her silence for consent. "I knew I could rely on you, dearest Magda," he said, "you are and remain my good old wife." Then the propaganda minister got up and returned to Berlin with his beautiful mistress. Soon he was taking her everywhere with him, as Himmler's agents did not fail to notice. Goebbels made a mistake, however, when he took her with him on an outing aboard his yacht, the *Baldur*, and tactlessly carried his wife and some of her friends along. Lida was wearing a bathing suit that left little to the imagination when she went into the small ship's cabin, to change for tea. Apparently she was not aware that Frau Goebbels was already there. They were only alone in the little room for a few minutes, and what was said was never revealed, but it was undoubtedly very interesting. When Lida returned to the deck, she made it clear that she was mortally offended. From this point on, her behavior toward the minister's wife was rude and arrogant. When Magda was present, both Goebbels and his "second wife" acted as if she did not exist. They even held hands, both in public and in front of Frau Magda, who was by now desperately unhappy. The fact that Hermann Goering had bugged Lida's telephone and was spreading the details of the unsavory affair to Berlin society with malicious glee did nothing to improve Magda's mood.

Frau Goebbels was not without her friends, however. A sophisticated and attractive society woman, she had quickly charmed Hanke when they first met in the early 1930s. He was soon secretly in love with her.

Hanke was a true believer in the Fuehrer and the principles of National Socialism, and, through his hard work and dedication to the cause, as well as an unshakable faith in his own ability, had risen to the rank of state secretary. He had also come to regard the amoral Goebbels as a traitor to the cause, because his immoral behavior was a threat to Nazism and a potential embarrassment to the Fuehrer. When Magda needed a friend and an adviser, he immediately made himself available and counseled her to divorce her faithless husband. Because he knew about a great many of Goebbels' affairs (no doubt informed by his friend, Heinrich Himmler), he supplied the names of actresses who had slept with the propaganda minister and even helped collect sworn depositions from them, stating that the "goat of Babelsberg" had forced his attentions on them by threatening their careers. Finally, Hanke arranged for Magda to meet with Adolf Hitler, the supreme judicial authority in the land. If he vetoed the divorce, there would be no divorce, no matter if every judge and lawyer in the Reich ruled in her favor. He had already arbitrarily refused to allow divorces in six cases involving high-ranking party or government officials, because they would embarrass the party.

Hitler received the ash-blonde wife of the propaganda minister on October 21, 1938. They were old friends, and it is almost certain that they had once been lovers. In fact, Magda told Frau Otto Meissner that Hitler had sired her son Helmut during a vacation on the Baltic coast in 1934. I have no doubt that Magda actually made this remark to Frau Meissner, but it is extremely unlikely that Hitler was, in fact, the father of this child, both because the Fuehrer had only one testicle (according to Soviet autopsies) and because one only has to look at a photograph of the unfortunate child to *know* who his father was. This, of course, does not mean that Hitler and Magda did not have an affair; all the evidence suggests that they did. Hitler commented to Gauleiter Otto Wagener and others that he was attracted to Magda Goebbels; he had spent a great deal of time in the Goebbels' home before his involvement with Eva Braun; and he was the godfather of the Goebbels' children. Adolf Hitler, however, was not a man to take any woman particularly seriously, and he also liked Lida Baarova. When they first met (at a tea in the chancellery) in 1935, when she was 25, he commented that she reminded him of Geli Raubal, someone tragic who was gone from his life. Later, to her horror, Lida found out that he was referring to his niece and lover who had committed suicide after a fight with him in 1931. Geli was 23 years old at the time of her death.[6]

In contrast to his normal behavior, Hitler listened attentively, while Magda spoke for an hour. Hitler was very much angered by what he heard and the documents Frau Goebbels showed him. He knew, of course, about Goebbels' promiscuity and about Lida Baarova from the routine Gestapo reports, but he was inclined to look upon Goebbels' love for Baarova as just another affair that would burn itself out. He was, however, angry about the way Goebbels used his official position to force himself on women and was furious when he learned that that Goebbels had kept a foreign diplomat waiting, in spite of a scheduled appointment, while he enjoyed himself with a woman in an adjacent room.

Frau Goebbels was disappointed and hurt that Hitler showed more concern about the possible political consequences of Goebbels' behavior than about her suffering. The next day, Hitler called Goebbels in. Neither man ever spoke about this meeting, so what was said is not known. It is known that Goebbels emerged with his career undamaged. Hitler accepted whatever he said and had confined himself to telling the minister to reconcile with his wife. It seems likely that *Kristallnacht*, the pogrom against the Jews, was discussed, but this is not certain.

Karl Hanke was not satisfied with this result and demanded to see the Fuehrer. Hitler quickly agreed to meet with him; he had a high opinion of this hard-working and idealistic young man and considered him an exemplary National Socialist.

Unlike Magda, Hanke also knew which buttons to push. "Joseph Goebbels has betrayed our ideals," he bluntly told the Fuehrer. "The whole world is laughing at us.... In the past in a thousand speeches Goebbels has asserted that any actress who wishes to make a career for herself in Germany must first go to bed with the Jewish film producer. Today Goebbels himself is the greatest film Jew."[7]

When it came to politics, Adolf Hitler never really took women seriously; Karl Hanke was another matter. Before the young state secretary was through, he had Adolf Hitler hopping mad, literally jumping up and down, banging his fists on the table and screaming that Goebbels had lied to him. From that moment, Joseph Goebbels was in deep disgrace. He was not allowed to have meals with the Fuehrer, either at the Berghof or in Berlin. He was informed that he was not invited to Hitler's evening parties, and Goebbels' repeated requests for a personal discussion with the Leader were all coldly rejected. It was even rumored that his political career was in jeopardy, but this was not true. Hitler had told Hanke that he was not going to dismiss Goebbels, because "I shall be needing him again soon."[8] This cryptic remark was probably an allusion to Crystal Night.

On October 23, Hitler called Magda in and told her that there was no question of a divorce: she and the propaganda minister were too well known to the public. When Magda said nothing, he asked her to outwardly remain with Goebbels for one year. If she still wanted a divorce at the end of that time, he would grant it, on her own terms. In the meantime, she would continue to live in Schwanenwerder, and Goebbels could go there only to see their children, and then only with her permission. He also promised that, if she still wanted the divorce after waiting the year, as he requested, she would be allowed to keep Schwanenwerder, the children, and a substantial amount of money. She agreed to these terms. Goebbels was informed of them later; he was not invited to the meeting, but Karl Hanke was.

So the sins of the "foul-mouth toad" came home to roost. Julius Schaub, Hitler's adjutant, appeared at Lida Baarova's house that same evening and told her that she had 24 hours to leave Germany. She telephoned her lover but was told that he was not available. She then threw a hysterical fit, which ended in a heart attack. Dr. Theodor Morell, Hitler's personal physician, was called in and injected her with sedatives. She was then packed off to do a film in Italy. Her affair with Goebbels was ended.[9] She only saw him once more, at the 1942 Venice Film Festival. He ignored her.

Paul Joseph Goebbels now began his political comeback. He moved into a palace behind the Wilhelmstrasse and, as Hitler instructed, dropped all of his lovers and began living the life of a monk. Himmler's Gestapo agents continued to shadow him but never caught him in a compromising situation, so it must be assumed that his clandestine affairs were temporarily at an end. Magda, on the other hand, was soon seen in Berlin with Hanke, who openly proclaimed his love for her. They had an affair, and he asked her to marry him after her divorce from Goebbels. She seriously considered his proposal, but, in the end, decided that he was not glamorous enough to suit her; besides, the Goat of Babelberg was a man of higher rank.

Goebbels knew all about this, of course. Privately he called Hanke a traitor, but he did not feel secure enough to dismiss his estranged deputy until 1941. Meanwhile, he had to work his way back into the Fuehrer's favor, step by step. The first step would be an attack on Hitler's most hated enemies, the Jews. Hitler had already instructed Goebbels to meet with Reinhard Heydrich, a man as amoral as Goebbels himself, to work out the details. The result would be Crystal Night: a night of terror and unprovoked violence against Germany's Jews. Now only a pretext was needed to set events in motion.

Nazi Germany was not the only government in Europe that was anti-Semitic: Warsaw had no use for Jews either. After the Anschluss, the Polish government was fearful that Hitler would repatriate thousands of Polish Jews from Vienna, so it passed a Law of Expatriation, depriving these unfortunates of their Polish citizenship. Now, after the signing of the Munich Accords, Warsaw ruled that, as of October 31, no expatriated Poles would be allowed back into the country without a special entry visa. As a result, in the last days of October, the Nazis took this window of opportunity to dump thousands of Jews of Polish extraction back into their mother country. Approximately 10,000 Jews were rounded up and thrown into boxcars. Soon dozens of unscheduled trains, loaded with Jews and guarded by the Gestapo, and unimpeded by sleepy border guards, crossed the Polish frontier. Some of the trains, however, were stopped. Poland would not accept their human cargo, and Germany would not take them back. The boxcars were emptied and the Jews were dumped into extremely primitive refugee camps in a sort of no-man's land between the borders, pitiful and innocent pawns in a game of international politics. Some of the luckier ones were "housed" in stables, pigsties, or border railroad stations. Others had to sleep in the fields between the Polish border guards and German Storm Troopers—armed with fixed bayonets—who made sure they did not try to reenter Germany. Quite a few of these Jews died of typhus and some went insane before Warsaw finally yielded to international outrage and took them in some weeks later.

Among these abandoned victims was a Polish-Russian couple named Grynspan, who had been deported to a Polish camp at Zbonszyn. They were the parents of Herschel Grynspan, who was born in Hanover in 1921. Young Grynspan had fled the anti-Semitism of Nazi Germany in the early 1930s, intending to go to Palestine. He only got as far as Paris, where he became an unemployed and underfed drifter. He had already been served with a deportation order from the French police on November 3, 1938, when he received a postcard from his sister, informing him of the plight of his parents. Full of hatred and thirsting for revenge, he walked into the German legation in Paris on November 7, intent upon killing the ambassador, Count Johannes von Welczeck. When he saw Ernst vom Rath, the third secretary of the embassy, however, Grynspan apparently mistook him for Count von Welczeck, so he pulled his pistol and shot him instead, mortally wounding the innocent young diplomat.[10]

Hitler now had his excuse for Crystal Night. It is one of history's minor ironies that Ernst vom Rath was an anti-Nazi. At the time he was shot, he was under investigation by the Gestapo for his opposition to the Fuehrer. Hitler nevertheless immediately promoted vom Rath to the rank of embassy counselor and sent one of his own surgeons, Dr. Karl Brandt, to Paris, to try to save Rath's life. Simultaneously, Goebbels' propaganda ministry beat the anti-Semitic drum, working the German public into a white heat. Meanwhile, orders were sent out to Brownshirt and Hitler Youth headquarters throughout Germany. "Spontaneous" anti-Jewish riots were to erupt throughout the Reich the following night. Orders were also sent out by telegraph to all Gestapo and Security Service headquarters. They read, in part:

Only such measures may be employed as will not endanger German lives or property—for example, synagogues may be burned only when there is no risk that fire will spread to neighboring structures. Jewish stores and dwellings may be destroyed, but not plundered.... The police must not interfere with the demonstrations that will occur.... Only as many Jews—particularly wealthy ones—should be arrested as can be accommodated in available jails.[11]

These Jews were to be sent to the concentration camps as quickly as possible.

During the afternoon of November 9, while Hitler and his cronies were engaged in the annual ceremonies commemorating the Beer Hall Putsch, word came from Paris that Ernst vom Rath had died. Spontaneous anti-Jewish demonstrations took place in Kurhessen and Magdeburg-Anhalt. After speaking with Hitler, Goebbels spread the word to party officials that, if the riots spread throughout Germany, they were not to be discouraged. "The party leaders took this to mean that they were to organize demonstrations while making it appear that they had nothing to do with them," Toland wrote later.[12]

November 9–10 was a night of horror throughout Germany, as riots broke out all over the country. One German, coming home late in the evening, recalled:

I saw several thugs beating a man until he collapsed. They dragged him onto the streetcar tracks and left him there. A policeman who happened to come by helped me carry him to the Elizabeth Hospital. He was an old man with white hair—a lawyer, I think. On the way back I saw a woman with two small children, with coats over their nightclothes. They were in a state of utter terror.

"Why are they beating us?" the woman screamed. "We haven't done anything!"

The policeman who helped carry the old man to the hospital was also terrified that he would be turned in and punished for helping a Jew. "Berlin's main streets looked as though they had been under bombardment," one witness recalled. "In the radio shops all the sets and installations were in fragments, in the wine shops broken bottles were knee high—everywhere, everywhere an indescribable chaos."

In Duesseldorf, a mob of hysterical Nazis armed with hammers broke into Rabbi Eschelbacher's synagogue shouting, "Revenge for Paris! Down with the Jews!" They burst into the rabbi's living quarters, where they beat him with their fists, smashed his furniture, mirrors, and windows, and threw his books and typewriter into the street. Eschelbacher felt sure he would be beaten to death; instead, the Storm Troopers demanded a sermon. The rabbi began by deploring the murder of vom Rath and saying that it was more a misfortune for the Jews than for the Germans, and that the Jewish people were in no way responsible for the death of the young diplomat. This did not suit the Brownshirts, who threw Eschelbacher against the side of a house. A Kreisleiter then arrested the bleeding rabbi, and he was carted off to Dachau. By this time his synagogue was on fire.[13]

Even the Jewish hospital in Duesseldorf was stormed by the Brownshirts. All except the patients who had recently been operated on were forced out into the streets at 4 A.M. The Jewish nurses were ordered to leave, so Catholic nuns took their places. Even the 50 or so children from the Jewish orphanage were rounded up. Finally, at 7 A.M., the women and children were released and the men removed to Dachau. In the capital of the Reich, electricity and heat were cut off in all Jewish buildings. The SA behaved with particular savagery in Nuremberg, where they were directed by Gauleiter Julius Streicher, Nazi Germany's most notorious Jew-baiter. At least nine Jews were murdered—most of them beaten to death or tossed off balconies, although at least one throat was cut. Another Jew died of a heart attack while being beaten. Ten Jews (five of them women) committed suicide. In Fuerth, all of the Jews in the town, including pregnant women, small children, and sick people, were rounded up and, half-dressed, were taken to a theater, where some were made to watch as other Jews were hauled onto the stage and fiercely beaten. Eventually, the women and children were released and the men sent to Dachau.[14]

Synagogues burned all over Germany—in Freiburg, Heidelburg, Karlsruhe, Berlin, and all of the major cities. Jews were rounded up in market squares and forced to urinate toward the burning synagogues while the Brownshirts kicked them in the buttocks. The pogrom was particularly vicious in the Rhineland, where Ernst vom Rath was lying in state, but there was violence and broken glass everywhere. All over Germany thousands of Brownshirts, SS men, and Motor Corps men were smashing windows, sacking synagogues, beating Jews, or helping the attackers. Count Fritz-Dietlof von der Schulenburg, the vice president the Berlin police, is reported to have sat down on the sidewalk and cried; as he saw it, his duty was to help victims, not criminals.[15] Law and order broke down throughout the Reich. Even Hitler Youths were ordered to plunder synagogues and desecrate Jewish graves and cemeteries. All over Germany the streets were covered with broken glass, where tables, chairs, and goods were thrown through the windows of Jewish shops (hence the name *Kristallnacht*, "the night of the broken glass").

The experience of Alfons Heck, a 12-year-old Hitler Youth living in Wittrich (in the Mosel Valley of the Rhineland), was somewhat typical. "I watched open-mouthed as small troops of SA and SS men jumped off trucks on the market place, fanned out in several directions, and began to smash the windows of every Jewish business in town." One major target was the shoe store, next to the city hall.

Shouting SA men threw hundreds of pairs of shoes into the street. They were picked up in minutes by some of the nicest people in our town. When the singing gang reached the synagogue, they broke into a run and literally stormed the entrance. Seconds later, the intricate lead crystal window above the door crashed into the street, and pieces of furniture came flying through doors and windows. A shouting SA man climbed to the roof and waved the Torah. "Wipe your asses with it, Jews," he screamed.

Some people turned away from the scene in disgust, others simply watched, and still others joined the vandals. "The brutality of it was stunning," Heck recalled, "but I also experienced an unmistakable feeling of excitement. 'Let's go in and smash some stuff,' urged my buddy Helmut." He picked up a rock and threw it through a window. Heck was on the point of deciding whether or not to join the attackers, when both he and Helmut felt a heavy hand on the back of their necks. Heck's Uncle Franz grabbed both boys, kicked them briskly in the seats of their pants, whirled them around, swore at them, and ordered them to go home at once. They dared not disobey. For two young Nazis, Crystal Night was over.[16]

Unfortunately for Germany and the world, there were not enough Uncle Franzes to go around in 1938.

Crystal Night was, indeed, the night Germany lost its innocence. It was a giant step down the path that led to the extermination camps. The damage figures, according to Heydrich's official report, were as follows: 814 shops destroyed, 171 houses set on fire or destroyed, 191 synagogues set on fire, another 76 completely destroyed, 20,000 Jews arrested, 36 deaths reported, 36 seriously injured, 7,500 Jewish shops looted, and several Jewish women raped. Author Werner Maser, however, estimated that 30,000 to 40,000 Jews were arrested on Crystal Night and sent to concentration camps,[17] and Heydrich himself admitted that his figures "must have been exceeded considerably."[18]

Goering handled the financial problems associated with Crystal Night by making the Jews pay for everything, including the destruction of their own property. Insurance monies owed to Jews were confiscated by the state; in addition, the Jews were fined a collective punishment of 1,000,000,000 Reichsmarks. Goebbels, meanwhile, insisted that Jews be excluded from every aspect of civil life: schools, movie theaters, plays, resorts, public beaches, parks, and even forests. Jews should be forced to sit in segregated railroad coaches, but only after all Aryans were seated.

Despite Hanke's best efforts, Goebbels had survived the Baarova affair because Hitler had needed him to help launch his pogrom against the Jews. Shortly thereafter, Goebbels decided to try to take another step in his political comeback when he began to write a book about the Fuehrer. Hitler, however, squelched the idea as soon as he heard about it because he didn't want someone of Goebbels' questionable character writing about him. Hitler then made sure that his words were conveyed to the propaganda minister. This indicated to Dr. Goebbels that he still had a long way to go before he regained his former favor at the Fuehrer's court. This message made Goebbels very angry. Not Joseph, but Magda. She let it be known that she thought Hitler was being very ungrateful to the man who had subdued "Red Berlin" during the early 1930s. She was soon denouncing Hitler's inner circle as "slimy rabble" and was also indignant when she learned that Hitler no longer allowed Goebbels to stay in the main house when he visited the Berghof on official business; now he had to stay in the adjutants' house.

Throughout their separation, which really did last almost 12 months, Goebbels had waged an active campaign to win Magda back from Hanke. In 1939, while she took a trip to Bad Gastein to take a cure, Goebbels went to the Salzburg Festival. The distance between the two places is not far, so he drove over and invited her to attend the performance with him. She accepted, and Goebbels exerted all his charm on her. The evening ended in his hotel room. Later that night, she telephoned Hanke and broke off their relationship by bluntly telling him that she was reconciled with her husband. Hanke could hardly speak for the tears, but Magda made no attempt to console him. She simply hung up the telephone. As part of the reconciliation, Goebbels had to agree to certain conditions. Among other things, Lida Baarova was never to be allowed to return to Germany, and the propaganda minister had to agree to be civil to his mother. He also had to agree to permanently ban certain women (all his former lovers) from their home. Magda had a list. On it were the names of at least 30 women.[19]

Because he spearheaded Crystal Night, Goebbels' stock with the Fuehrer improved significantly. His propaganda efforts leading up to the outbreak of the war also improved his standing at Hitler's headquarters. He had defeated Hanke's efforts to replace him (both as a minister and with Magda) and he gradually worked his way out of the Fuehrer's doghouse.[20] Hanke, meanwhile, in addition to his propaganda ministry duties, joined the army reserves in 1937, as a member of the Panzer Lehr Regiment, and was commissioned second lieutenant the following year. In the summer of 1939, he attended the panzer school and was called to active duty in July 1939, even though—with his contacts—he could easily have avoided military service. He served with the 3rd Panzer Division in Poland, where he was wounded. He was promoted to first lieutenant of reserves in early 1940 and commanded a company in the 33rd Panzer Regiment of the 9th Panzer Division from December 1939 to February 1940. He was then assigned to the 7th Panzer Division as an *Ordonnanzoffizier* (orderly) to Major General Rommel.

Hanke got along very well with Rommel in the beginning. The future Desert Fox had an almost American sense of public relations and was delighted to have the secretary of state of the propaganda ministry in his division. Certainly, the two assisted in advancing each others' careers. Just before the invasion of France began, for example, Rommel gave Hanke command of the heavy tank company of the 25th Panzer Regiment, which was equipped with his most modern Panzer Mark IV tanks.

Karl Hanke proved to be a very competent combat leader. Early in the campaign, Rommel got himself into a tight spot near Sivry on the Belgian frontier, and Hanke and his Panzer Mark IVs charged forward and extricated him, possibly saving his life. At one point during the fast-moving campaign, a French heavy tank column counterattacked, destroyed several panzers, and broke into the rear of the 7th Panzer Division. Hanke, with a single tank, reacted quickly and drove it off, almost single-handedly, before it could do any serious damage. A delighted Rommel promptly recommended Hanke for the Knight's Cross.

For Hanke, the worst moment of the Western Campaign occurred on June 11, when he was ordered to lead an assault on the French coastal city of St. Valery. He protested that he was not trained for this type of mission, but Rommel insisted that the attack go forward anyway.

(At this moment, Rommel was up front with the spearhead and had only limited forces available. He had been in full pursuit mode for days, and the rest of the 7th Panzer Division was strung out behind him for miles.) Hanke did as he was ordered and was soon in serious trouble. He had to be rescued by his regimental commander, Colonel Rothenburg.

Karl Hanke continued to distinguish himself throughout the Western Campaign of 1940. Shortly after beating back the French tank column, he captured a French convoy of 40 trucks. On another occasion, he machine-gunned a French bicycle unit and helped Rommel out of another tough situation. In addition, Hanke personally presented Rommel with the Knight's Cross, shortly after Hitler granted it to him. Rommel was the first divisional commander in the French campaign to receive this award.

Hanke never received his own Knight's Cross because his arrogance exceeded his bravery, and he again overplayed his hand—and this time for no good purpose whatsoever. He commented to other officers that, as a state secretary, he outranked a "mere" major general and could have Rommel replaced, if he so desired. His remarks were soon relayed to Rommel, who sacked Hanke immediately. He also sent his adjutant to Fuehrer Headquarters to intercept and quash the recommendation that Hanke be decorated with the Knight's Cross (although the Nazi official did receive the Iron Cross, 1st and 2nd Classes). Rommel's act caused considerable resentment among Hanke's troops, who felt he deserved the award, but Rommel's action was upheld. And Hanke discovered that he did not outrank the Desert Fox.

Hanke also soon discovered that he did not outrank Reichsminister Goebbels either. That winter, the former Goat of Babelberg decided that his political comeback had progressed far enough that he could dispose of Hanke. Taking advantage of Hanke's fall from grace with Rommel and his own growing stature with Hitler, Goebbels relieved the young lieutenant of reserves of his post as state secretary of the propaganda ministry on January 28, 1941. Hitler and Himmler, however, still held him in high esteem. As a sign of their respect, Hanke was promoted to SS-Brigadefuehrer (on January 30, 1941) and to SS-Gruppenfuehrer (SS lieutenant general) on April 20, 1941—Hitler's birthday.

Hanke was not unemployed for long. Martin Bormann, Hitler's secretary and a leading official in the Nazi Party, had long plotted against Joseph Wagner, the Gauleiter of Silesia. (Bormann hated Christians and Wagner was a devout Catholic.) In February 1941, he finally persuaded Hitler to sack Wagner and divide the Gau in two. Upper Silesia (*Oberschleisien*) was given to Fritz Bracht (with headquarters in Kattowitz) and the more important Lower Silesia (*Niederschlesien*) was given to Hanke, who was simultaneously named *Oberpraesident* of the province.

This move also got the young Nazi out of Berlin, which was a major plus in Goebbels' eyes.

Hanke's capital was the major industrial city of Breslau. He ruled here as the Gauleiter and Oberpraesident from 1941 to 1945. He also continued to add to his power and prestige. He became chief of the Agricultural Office and Waterways Directorate for the province, as well as director for a major bank in Berlin. In 1942, he became General Plenipotentiary for Labor Allocation in Lower Silesia, and was thus head of the slave labor program for the district. From the fall of 1943 through June 21, 1944, he was also temporary head of the Central Office of the Reich Ministry of Armaments and War Production under his old friend, Albert Speer. He was also named director of *Volkssturm* (Home Defense Forces) for Lower Silesia by Martin Bormann on September 25, 1944.

Back in Breslau, Hanke had a long affair with Baroness Freda von Fircks, the daughter of a wealthy landowner and University of Berlin lecturer. They were finally married on November 25, 1944, after she bore him his only child (a daughter) in December 1943.[21] In the meantime, Hanke was promoted to reserve captain in the army (January 30, 1942).

Karl Hanke worked vigorously within his district to ensure a German victory in the war and to obey the Fuehrer's wishes. This included playing a role in the persecution of the Jews and their transportation to the death camps. He was not a complete monster, however, and apparently did not know about the Holocaust until the summer of 1944, when he made the mistake of accepting an invitation to Auschwitz. He returned a very shaken and disturbed man. He told his friend Speer that he could not tell him what he had seen, but strongly advised him never to visit the place under any circumstances.

By the end of 1944, the Soviets were on Germany's doorsteps. On January 12, 1945, Stalin launched a major offensive against a depleted Army Group Center, which had 400,000 men, 4,100 guns, and 1,150 tanks and assault guns. It was outnumbered 9 to 1 in men, approximately 9.5 to 1 in artillery, and 10 to 1 in tanks and assault guns. By January 17, Army Group Center was smashed, and even the Soviet marching infantry units were gaining 18 miles a day.

Gauleiter Hanke threw himself into the defense of Breslau with his typical fanatical energy. On January 19, he organized the evacuation of the districts east of the Oder River, and the next day ordered the evacuation of most of the women and children of Breslau, while simultaneously doing everything he could to put the city in a defensible state. He had waited too long, however; the partial evacuation had to be conducted in subfreezing temperatures and most of it in a snowstorm. Many of the evacuees (old men, women, and children below the age of 15) froze to death, suffered severe frostbite, or died of exposure and malnutrition.

Meanwhile, the Red Army poured over the borders of the Reich, and Breslau was encircled by the 3rd Guards Tank Army on February 16. Thirty-five thousand soldiers and 116,000 civilians were trapped inside the city.

Hanke called on the soldiers, the population, and the Volkssturm to resist with fanatical determination. They responded with a courage born of desperation, because nobody wanted to fall into the hands of the Red Army, which was then robbing, raping, and murdering German civilians in occupied areas with unrestrained zeal. In Lower Silesia, no weakness was tolerated. When the deputy Buergermeister of Breslau, Ministerialrat Dr. Wolfgang Spielhagen, tried to flee, Hanke had him shot for "cowardice in the face of the enemy," despite the fact that they were formerly personal friends. He then ordered that the body be thrown into the Oder.[22] On April 21, he also conscripted the young women of Breslau into the defense. When some of them rebelled against this order, Hanke had them arrested. The fighting continued for weeks.

Hitler was inspired and excited by Hanke's spirited defense and called him "a devil of a fellow."[23] Even Goebbels was won over. After Hanke delivered a speech over the radio on March 3, Goebbels wrote in his diary that his address "was movingly impressive.... If all our Gauleiters ... acted like Hanke, we should be in better shape than we are. Hanke is the outstanding personality among our eastern Gauleiters. One can see that he was brought up in Berlin."[24] Later, Goebbels recorded, "one can see that Hanke is absolutely on top of his job. He is representative of today's most energetic National Socialist leader."[25]

The Russian heavy artillery pounded Breslau day after day for weeks, but the defenders checked every major attack. Gradually, however, the Red Army pushed them back, one block at a time. Hanke's ruthless measures to strengthen the defense of the Silesian capital excited the admiration of all of the Nazi big-wigs, although his failure to cooperate with the army's commandant of the city did little to improve the situation.

Hitler awarded Hanke the German Cross in Gold for his courage on April 8. Breslau held out until May 7—a week longer than Berlin itself. When the battle ended, between 80 and 90 percent of the city had been destroyed and about 17,000 civilians had been killed—22 percent of the total population. Probably half of the soldiers were also killed or wounded. In addition, the Red Army suffered 60,000 casualties during the siege—an astronomical number in a battle for a city so far behind the front lines. After the surrender, enraged Red Army soldiers entered Breslau and went on a rampage of looting, raping, and murdering that lasted for days. Naturally, the city's fire department had already ceased to exist. The fires raged out of control for more than a week. At the university library, 500,000 books burned on May 11.

Later, Breslau was incorporated into the Polish state and was renamed Wroclaw. The surviving Germans were "encouraged" to emigrate and most of them did.

Meanwhile, on April 29, 1945—the day before he committed suicide—Adolf Hitler named Karl Hanke *Reichsfuehrer-SS* and chief of the German Police, replacing Heinrich Himmler, who had been stripped of his posts when Hitler learned that he had been conducting secret, unauthorized negotiations with the Allies behind the Fuehrer's back. At 3:30 P.M. the next day, with the Russians within 300 yards of the Fuehrer Bunker, Adolf Hitler committed suicide. Hanke did not learn of his appointment (or of Hitler's death) until May 5. That night, he flew out of the doomed fortress. Sources differ as to whether he escaped via a Fieseler "Storch" reconnaissance airplane or aboard one of the few helicopter prototypes with which Germany was experimenting at the time. In any case, he managed to reach German lines, only to learn that Berlin had fallen. He flew on to Hirschberg, where he met with Field Marshal Ferdinand Schoerner. Then—for reasons this author has never been able to fathom—he flew to Prague. He found the city in the throes of an anti-Nazi uprising. The chief of the SS tried to return to the airport, only to find the way blocked by Czech partisans. He then joined an ad hoc band of isolated *Waffen-SS* (Armed SS) men from the 18th SS Volunteer Panzer Grenadier Division "Horst Wessel." They fought their way up the Karlsbad Road but were captured in the vicinity of Neudorf bei Komotau (now Nova ves) near Pilsen in the Sudetenland on May 6. At that time, Hanke was in a plain SS uniform, without any insignia of rank.

Remarkably, prisoner Hanke was not recognized by his captors or betrayed by his comrades for more than a month. He was held in temporary POW camps and was eventually transferred to a camp at Neudorf/ Komotau, where he was guarded by Czech partisans. Knowing that it was only a matter of time before his identity was discovered, Hanke decided to make a dash for freedom on June 8. He did not make it. The last Reichsfuehrer-SS was shot and killed by Czech guards while attempting to escape early on the morning of June 8, 1945. He was 40 years old.

CHAPTER V

JOACHIM VON METZSCH: THE SUPPLY OFFICER

Rommel's chief supply and logistical officer in the French campaign was Joachim von Metzsch. Born on April 28, 1907, he entered the service in 1925 as a member of the 12th Cavalry Regiment. Later he earned his commission and transferred to the 9th Reconnaissance Battalion. In 1936, he was selected to attend the War Academy (*Kriegsakademie*) at Berlin for General Staff training. He was there from October 6, 1936, until October 1938, when he graduated and was assigned to troop duty on probationary status. He was sent to the operations staff of the 2nd Light (later 7th Panzer) Division, where he was named Ib (chief supply officer or quartermaster) on November 10, 1938. He reported directly to General Stumme and later to Rommel. (In Rommel's absence, he reported to the Ia, Major Heidkaemper.)

After performing well in the invasion of Poland, young Metzsch was admitted to the General Staff (full status) on November 1, 1939.[1] He did very well as quartermaster of the 7th Panzer. During the drive through Belgium and France, its neighboring division, the SS Motorized Infantry Division "Totenkopf" (later the 3rd SS Panzer Division "Totenkopf") suffered from an appalling lack of qualified staff officers. (It only had one, and he collapsed from overwork, stress, and exhaustion.) The ensuing logistical failure slowed the advance of the "Death's Head" division and thus threatened to expose the flank of the 7th Panzer. Rommel ordered Heidkaemper and von Metzsch to assist his less-than-competent neighbor, General of SS Theodor Eicke. The main responsibility fell, of course, to von Metzsch. He accomplished his task without any fuss, and soon the SS combat units were receiving a smooth and uninterrupted flow of supplies, which enabled them to maintain the pace of their advance.

Metzsch's success as quartermaster of the 7th Panzer was noticed by several senior officers, including General of Cavalry Erich Hoepner, the commander of the XVI Motorized (later Panzer) Corps. On July 29, 1940, he secured Metzsch's transfer to his own staff.[2] (Rommel was very suspicious toward and often harsh with General Staff officers at this time; luring them away from him consequently was not particularly difficult.)

Young von Metzsch served as quartermaster of the XVI Panzer during its redeployment from France to Germany in the summer of 1940, and in its subsequent transfer to East Prussia in September. On February 15, 1941, it was redesignated 4th Panzer Group and was later upgraded to 4th Panzer Army on January 1, 1942. Metzsch, meanwhile, was promoted to major and left the largely thankless post of quartermaster for the more appreciated operations staff. As an assistant operations officer, he played a role in planning the 4th Panzer's invasion of the Soviet Union, the quick conquest of Lithuania, the massive tank battle at Dubysa, the capture of Duenaburg, the battle of the Duena bridgehead, the drive to Lake Ilmen, the Battle of Staraja-Russia, the battle of the Luga Bridgehead, and the subsequent drive on Leningrad. He also took part in the defensive battles of Yelnya and Smolensk, as well as the drive on Moscow and Stalin's subsequent winter offensive. After Hitler sacked Hoepner for ordering an unauthorized retreat, Metzsch worked for Colonel-Generals Richard Ruoff and Hermann Hoth.[3] He continued to excel in the defensive battles and retreats of 1942−43. On New Year's Day, 1943, he was promoted to lieutenant colonel.

An older and much more experienced Joachim von Metzsch finally left Russia on December 15, 1943, after two-and-a-half years on the Eastern Front. He took a leave until January 10, 1944, when he took up his new post: Ia (chief of operations) of the 90th Panzer Grenadier Division in Italy. Because divisions do not normally have chiefs of staff, Metzsch was 1st General Staff Officer and de facto chief of staff of the division. His commander was the eccentric Lieutenant General Ernst-Guenther Baade, a veteran of the Afrika Korps.[4]

As chief of operations of the 90th Panzer Grenadier, Metzsch took part in the battles of Cassino, the retreat to Rome and Florence, the battles of the Gothic Line, and the indecisive defensive battles in the Appennines. He further improved his growing reputation as a highly competent officer.

General Baade was seriously wounded on December 9, 1944, and was replaced by Lieutenant General Count Gerhard von Schwerin (December 9−26) and Major General Baron Heinrich von Behr (December 27, 1944, to the end of the war). Metzsch himself left the division on January 20, 1945, and, after a brief leave, assumed command of the

1060th Grenadier Regiment of the 362nd Infantry Division, also on the Italian Front. This represented another step up for Metzsch, who no doubt would have become a general had the war lasted longer. It did not, however. The Allies launched their final offensive on April 14, 1945, and in overwhelming strength. Metzsch fought at Ferrara and in the retreat to the Po. Remnants of the 362nd Division were still resisting near Padus when the German forces in Italy surrendered on April 29, 1945.

CHAPTER VI

DR. WILHELM BAUMEISTER: THE MEDICAL OFFICER

The 7th Panzer Division suffered more casualties than any other German division in the French campaign; therefore, its chief medical officer, Dr. Wilhelm Baumeister, was a very important person.

He was born in Disteln on December 7, 1887. He earned his medical degree, distinguished himself in his profession in the civilian world, did not serve in the Reichswehr, and did not enter the Wehrmacht until 1936, when he was 49 years old. Because of his reputation and experience, he was immediately commissioned as an *Oberfeldarzt* (lieutenant colonel of medical services). He was named chief divisional medical officer of the 2nd Light Division and simultaneously commander of the 47th Medical Unit in 1938. This was followed by a promotion to *Oberstarzt* (colonel of the medical service corps) on March 1, 1939.[1]

Dr. Baumeister was a fine medical officer and hospital administrator. He served the 2nd Light/7th Panzer well in Poland, Belgium, and France. This led to a promotion and, on February 15, 1941, he became chief medical officer of the VIII Corps, which was then on the coast of the English Channel. In May, however, the VIII deployed to Poland and served as part of Army Group Center during the invasion of Russia. It was sent back to France in the fall of 1941 to rest and refit and was for a time stationed in Paris. In March 1942, however, it was sent back to the Soviet Union, fought at Kharkov and on the Don, and ended up in Stalingrad. Fortunately for Dr. Baumeister, he was promoted to *Generalarzt* (major general in the medical service corps) on October 1, 1942, making him a rank too high for the position he occupied. He was soon named chief medical officer of Wehrkreis XVII (XVII Military District) in Austria and was allowed to fly out of the Stalingrad pocket. He assumed his new post in Vienna on December 16, 1942. His former corps was destroyed on January 31, 1943.

Dr. Baumeister did not remain in Vienna long. A new VIII Corps Headquarters began to form on January 22, 1943 (even before Stalingrad fell), and Baumeister was placed in charge of organizing its medical units. This appointment was also short-lived. On March 23, 1943, Baumeister was named chief medical officer of the newly reformed 6th Army.

Major General Dr. Baumeister directed 6th Army's medical efforts in the battles between the Donetz and the Mius, as well as in the retreat across southern Russia, across the Dnieper, in the successful defense and evacuation of the Nikopol bridgehead, in the retreat through the southern Ukraine, in the retreat across the Dniester, in the disastrous Rumanian campaign, in the battles in Hungary, and in the final battles in Austria, Moravia, and the eastern Alps. He surrendered to the Western Allies at the end of the war.

CHAPTER VII

HANS VON LUCK: THE CHARMING ARISTOCRAT

Hans-Ulrich von Luck und Witten was a charming, highly cultured, sophisticated, aristocratic gentleman of the Old World, who had a wonderful talent for making friends. These factors, along with his professionalism and tremendous competence, made him a great success in life, both on and off the battlefield.

He was born in Flensburg on July 15, 1911, the son of Otto von Luck, a naval officer. His roots, however, were in the Prussian Army. He could trace his ancestry back to 1223, when they fought against the Tartars in Silesia.[1] Shortly before graduating from the Monastery School in Flensburg in 1929 (where he received a classical education), young Hans decided to follow in the extended family tradition. He applied for acceptance into the Reichsheer as a *Fahnenjunker* (officer-cadet) in the cavalry. There were only 140 vacancies and more than 1,000 applicants, but Luck was successful. Initially he was assigned to a mounted regiment in Silesia but was soon involuntarily transferred to the 1st Motorized Battalion in Koenigsburg, East Prussia. Cadet von Luck was greatly disappointed, but the move turned out to be very good for his career. Each of Germany's seven Wehrkreis had a motorized battalion, and they soon formed the nucleus of the *Panzerwaffe* (armored branch).

In 1931–32, Hans attended the Officers' Training Course in Dresden. Here he met and became a staunch admirer of Major Erwin Rommel, one of the instructors at the school, and one he was destined to meet again.

Luck graduated, was commissioned in 1932, and was assigned to the 2nd Motorized Battalion at Kolberg, a resort town and commercial center on the Baltic Sea coast of Pomerania. He enjoyed his new station and his work, and, like most Germans, failed to appreciate the threat Adolf Hitler posed, both to Germany and Western Civilization. Luck and his colleagues were initially quite pleased with him, because he expanded the Wehrmacht, renounced the Treaty of Versailles, built the autobahns, and put more than 6 million unemployed people back to work. Only gradually would they read the danger signs and, when they did, it would be too late for people like Luck to do anything about it.

Second Lieutenant von Luck was transferred to the 8th Panzer Reconnaissance Regiment at Potsdam—a garrison town on the outskirts of Berlin—in 1936, as a platoon leader in the motorcycle company. As a young bachelor officer, he thoroughly enjoyed the delights of the capital. In 1938, he was posted again, this time to the 7th Panzer Reconnaissance Regiment of the 2nd Light Division at Bad Kissingen, a health resort near Wuerzberg in northern Bavaria. Here he was chilled by the Nazis' behavior during *Kristallnacht,* in which the Stormtroopers went on a rampage and smashed thousands of windows in Jewish homes and synagogues. Luck described the entire incident as "gruesome" and "shameful."[2]

In autumn, 1939, the 7th Panzer Recon was sent to Gleiwitz on the Polish frontier (in what had been Czechoslovakia) for "maneuvers." Fall maneuvers was a tradition in the German Army dating back centuries, and Luck (who was now a company commander) suspected nothing until August 31, when his regiment was issued live ammunition and received orders to invade Poland the next day. Luck did not share the enthusiasm the typical Prussian officer felt for the invasion, which he considered senseless. This campaign was relatively easy, however, and Luck—a personable and highly cultured young aristocrat with piercing blue eyes—made friends easily, even among an enemy population in wartime. He visited a famous Polish animal painter, who gave him a watercolor. Another new friend gave him an Irish setter puppy. By early October, Luck was back in Bad Kissingen, none of the worse for the wear.

That winter, the 2nd Light was converted in the 7th Panzer Division. The reconnaissance regiment was reduced to a single battalion (the 37th), which was commanded by Major Erdmann, a veteran of World War I. Luck (the leader of the 3rd Company) and the other company commanders had full confidence in him. Young Luck also had every confidence in the new division commander, Erwin Rommel. In addition, the battalion was reequipped with a three-axle reconnaissance vehicle, which mounted a 38mm gun, a significant improvement over the scout vehicle of 1939.

Along with most of the rest of the German Army, the 7th Panzer Division attacked the French and Belgian armies on May 10, 1940. Luck (who was now a captain) was in the forefront of the battle and proved again that he was an excellent reconnaissance officer. At one point, he discovered the division was facing a battalion of the Grenadier Guards, which was commanded by an old friend of his. Only shortly before the war, they had relaxed together in the Marborough Club in London. "How senseless it all was," Luck thought.[3]

South of Lille on the morning of May 28, von Luck and Major Erdmann conferred with Rommel near the general's command post. Afterward, Erdmann remained behind while Luck and his driver went to breakfast. They had hardly started their meal, however, when a runner summoned them back into Rommel's presence. There they found the general dusting himself off. At his feet lay the body of Major Erdmann. Moments after Luck had departed, Allied heavy artillery had opened up on the command post and had killed the battalion commander. Rommel, who seemed greatly affected by the death of this veteran leader, turned to Hans von Luck and promoted him to the command of the 37th Panzer Recon on the spot, despite the fact that he was the youngest company commander in the battalion. Rommel was not worried by this fact, but it did concern Luck, who pointed out his junior status.

"You are in charge," he snapped. "If the company commanders obstruct your orders, I will replace them."

Luck wrote later: "This again was typical of Rommel's unorthodox measures. With him, performance counted for more than rank or seniority."[4]

Luck led the 37th throughout the French campaign and was involved in the capture of Fecamp, Cherbourg, St. Nazaire, and La Rochelle. After the French signed the armistice, Luck accepted the surrender of Bordeaux. Here he became friends with the madam of a brothel. He then got Rommel's permission to move his battalion to Arcachon, an Atlantic resort on the Cap Ferret peninsula, where he and his men enjoyed the fresh oysters from the nearby oyster beds, the excellent local white wine, and swimming in the sea. In July, however, the division was transferred to assembly areas west of Paris, where they trained for the invasion of the United Kingdom. During this stop, Captain von Luck billeted in the villa of a Swiss national, who gave him access to his well-stocked wine cellar for the token price of 1 franc per bottle. As the invasion of England became less and less likely, Luck and his men spent more and more time in Paris. Finally, however, they were transferred to a sector north of Bordeaux, and the plans for the invasion were quietly shelved.

Back in Bordeaux, Luck renewed his friendship with the madam, who voluntarily promised to always provide him with free champagne. He also made friends with at least two people whom he quite correctly suspected were members of the resistance. His personal wine collection, meanwhile, grew to almost 1,000 bottles, including several with hand-written labels which would never appear on the market.

Meanwhile, new replacements arrived from Germany. Among them was Major Riederer von Paar, a World War I veteran who superseded Luck as battalion commander. Luck returned to his company. In early February 1941, Rommel departed for Africa and was replaced by Major General Baron Hans von Funck, an officer who never fully had von Luck's confidence. (Unlike the dashing Rommel, who led from the front, Funck was more traditional and directed the division from his headquarters in the rear.) Funck nevertheless appointed Luck his adjutant, even though the young captain wanted to remain with his unit.

Luck served General von Funck during the first phases of the Russian campaign, including the battles of Minsk and Vitebsk. In the final stages of clearing the Vitebsk pocket, however, Major von Paar was killed in action. Funck immediately ordered Luck to replace him as battalion commander, much to the delight of the young adjutant. He left for the front that same evening.

Captain von Luck led the 37th Panzer Reconnaissance Battalion in the final stages of the clearing of the Vitebsk Pocket, the Smolensk encirclement, the battles of the Dnieper crossings, the Battle of Vyasma, and the drive on Moscow (see Figure 7.1). In North Africa, meanwhile, Erwin Rommel selected Luck to command the 3rd Panzer Reconnaissance Battalion. Funck objected, however, and began a battle of influence between the two generals in which Hans von Luck was the prize. Initially, Funck managed to block the captain's transfer, and Luck narrowly escaped death in the winter campaign of 1941–42. In mid-January 1942, Rommel threatened Funck with consequences if he persisted. Realizing that Rommel had considerably more political influence with the Nazi regime than he, Funck relented, and the young battalion commander and his driver were soon on their way to Berlin. Once there, however, von Luck was informed that he would have to go on leave, whether he wanted to or not. After a few weeks in Flemsburg (where he visited his mother) and in Paris (where he again sampled the delights of the City of Light), Luck finally arrived in Libya in early April. He had, in the meantime, been promoted to major.

The 3rd Panzer Reconnaissance Battalion was Rommel's favorite battalion. It had initially been commanded by Lieutenant Colonel Irmfried von Wechmar, and then by Captain Wolfgang-Dieter Everth, who returned to his company when Luck arrived.[5] Luck's immediate superior was General von Bismarck, whom Luck knew well from the French campaign.

Luck's first battle with the 3rd Reconnaissance was almost his last. During the night of May 26–27, Luck and his men outflanked the

Figure 7.1
The Eastern Front

Gazala Line to the south. The next day, however, they were counterattacked by a British armored unit, which was equipped with American Grant tanks. Luck immediately set up a defensive front and was deploying his 50mm antitank guns when a British shell knocked out one of his armored cars. A piece of shrapnel caught him in the upper right thigh and hurled him to the ground. Fortunately for Luck, the shell fragment missed both his genitalia and a major artery by a narrow margin. A scout car picked up the nearly unconscious commander and carried him to an aid station, a few hundred yards to the rear. The doctor injected him with morphine and ordered that Luck be sent to a hospital in the communications zone. This proved to be impossible, however, because the Afrika Korps had been surrounded east of the Gazala Line—in an area soon to be known as "the Cauldron"—and the 3rd Panzer Recon was isolated in the desert east of that, even further behind British lines.

For the next five days, Major von Luck commanded his battalion from his jeep, until Rommel was able to break the encirclement to the west and clear a route through the minefields to the east. The 3rd Reconnaissance managed to rejoin the main army via this lane on June 1. By now, however, Luck's wound had become infected, so he turned his command over to Captain Everth and was evacuated to Derna. After an operation, he and General Gustav von Vaerst (the commander of the 15th Panzer Division, who had also been wounded) were evacuated back to Italy by hospital ship.[6] By the end of July, Luck had largely recovered. It was September, however, before the medical staff deemed that the impatient young major was again fit for combat.

Like many young men of his generation, Hans von Luck was quite dissatisfied while he was on wounded leave. He managed to spend part of it in the barracks at Kissingen, where he met several recovering veterans he knew from the 7th Panzer Division or the 37th Panzer Reconnaissance Battalion. He also spent time visiting friends in Berlin, which was now being bombed on a regular basis. Luck was glad when he returned to North Africa and the front.

By now, Rommel had overrun Libya, captured Tobruk, invaded Egypt, and had been checked in the First Battle of El Alamein. He and his men now awaited Montgomery's inevitable counteroffensive. The 3rd Panzer Reconnaissance, however, had the best duty in the entire panzer army. It occupied the Siwa Oasis on Rommel's extreme southern flank, 200 miles deep in the desert. Originally called Ammonion, the oasis had been the site of Cleopatra's bath and palace from 51 to 30 B.C. Now it was inhabited by 5,000 friendly Bedouins. The palace was gone by 1942, but the bath was still intact. It was a well, about 30 feet in diameter, with a constant temperature of 18°C, and was so clear that the men could see the bottom, 20 feet below. Luck and his troops found it immensely refreshing.

While Luck and his men covered Rommel's deep right flank, Montgomery launched his major offensive on October 23. Rommel checked attack after attack but, by November 2, the exhausted Panzer Army Afrika was in remnants and on the verge of collapse. That day, the supply units and bakery platoon of the 3rd Reconnaissance evacuated the Siwa Oasis. The combat units fell back the next day.

On the far desert flank of Rommel's army, Luck's task was to identify and report or defeat any attempt to outflank it from the south. He skirmished with the Royal Dragoons and the 11th Hussars for the next four months. Within the first few days, the three battalions had established a gentlemen's agreement, whereby all hostilities ended at 5 P.M., and they exchanged information on prisoners via radio.

Following the loss of Libya, Luck fought in Tunisia and earned the Medaglia d'Argento, an Italian decoration roughly equivalent to the Knight's Cross. He would have been captured when Tunisia fell, but Rommel's successor, Colonel General Juergen von Armin, also learned of Luck's charm and potential skills as an emissary. After consulting with the Desert Fox and Lieutenant General Alfred Gause, his chief of staff, von Armin sent the major on a mission to Fuehrer Headquarters, to personally convince the dictator of the need to evacuate Tunisia immediately, in order to save at least a portion of Army Group Afrika. Armin hoped that the personable major might even charm Adolf Hitler, but Colonel General Alfred Jodl, the chief of operations of OKW, refused to allow Luck to see the Fuehrer. Instead, Luck was briefly assigned to the staff of OB South in Italy, and then was placed in Fuehrer Reserve. His former orderly officer, a motion picture director in civilian life, loaned Luck his penthouse in Berlin; if Hans von Luck was in the professional doghouse, at least it was a luxurious doghouse.

Major General Rudolf Schmundt, the pro-Hitler chief of the Army Personnel Office, decided to keep Luck in reserve for an entire year. Horrified at the thought of such inactivity and wanting another command, Luck visited Schmundt and talked himself into a six-month assignment as an instructor at the Panzer Reconnaissance Commanders' School in Paris, which would last from August 1943 to March 1944, followed by a new combat command.[7] Meanwhile, he enjoyed a two-month furlough in his friend's penthouse. One night during this leave, Luck went to a party thrown by a Prussian princess, whom he had met through Franz von Papen, the son of the former chancellor. At the party he met Dagmar, the daughter of the owner of Europe's largest tree nursery. She was 21, attractive and sophisticated, well-educated, and fluent in French and English. The fact that she was 11 years his junior and officially classified as one-eighth Jewish did not deter Luck in the slightest.[8] They were soon lovers, and she joined him in Paris after he reported to the panzer reconnaissance school.

In August 1943, two weeks after Hans von Luck left Berlin, the penthouse he was using was destroyed by an incendiary bomb.

Luck's tour of duty at the Reconnaissance Commanders' School ended at the end of April and he happily reported to Fritz Bayerlein, the commander of the newly formed and exceptionally well-equipped Panzer Lehr Division. Bayerlein (an old friend from Africa) had earmarked him to be the new commander of the elite (130th) Panzer Lehr Regiment, but when Luck arrived, Bayerlein had some bad news for him. Major General Edgar Feuchtinger, the politically well-connected commander of the newly reconstituted 21st Panzer Division (15,000 men), had learned of Luck's availability and had used his influence at Fuehrer Headquarters to have Luck transferred to his unit.[9] When he reported to the 21st Panzer, Feuchtlinger named him commander of the 125th Panzer Grenadier Regiment,[10] which was stationed northwest of Caen in Normandy. The mission of the division was to counterattack against the Allied D-Day invasion—if it came in Normandy—and to throw the Anglo-Americans back into the sea. Figure 7.2 shows northwest Europe in 1944.

Figure 7.2
Northwest Europe, 1944

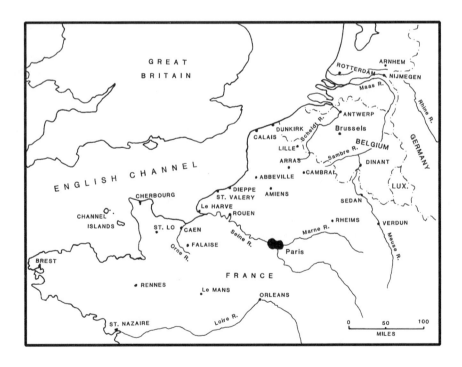

Luck's regiment had only two battalions (I, equipped with SPW armored half-tracks, and II, which rode in trucks), and was reinforced with two batteries of assault guns. The 125th was in action from the very beginning of the D-Day invasion, although its counterattack was badly mishandled by General Feuchtinger.[11] By June 9, Luck's command (which was now designated Kampfgruppe Luck) included his own regiment, the 21st Panzer Reconnaissance Battalion, a company of the battered 22nd Panzer Regiment, three batteries of the 200th Assault Gun Battalion, and a company of the 220th Antitank Battalion, which was equipped with 88mm guns. His task was to contain the British airborne bridgehead east of the Orne. The battle group clung to its positions in the Norman hedgerows and cornfields and was in action every day, as the British forces (the British 6th Airborne and 51st Highland Infantry Divisions and an assortment of attached units) doggedly tried to expand their positions to the south and southeast, because the Normandy bridgehead had inadequate depth. June and July were very hot and the mosquitoes and lack of relief made the conditions even more miserable.

By the middle of July, Luck's battle group had received considerable reinforcements and consisted of his own depleted 125th Regiment, all five companies of the 200th Assault Gun Battalion, the 503rd Heavy Panzer Battalion (equipped with superior Tiger tanks), a battalion of the 16th Luftwaffe Field Division, three sections of 88mm antitank guns, and a detachment of rocket launchers. Kampfgruppe Luck was backed by the 155th Panzer Artillery Regiment and strong elements of SS General "Sepp" Dietrich's II SS Panzer Corps.[12] Unknown to the Germans, however, Montgomery was secretly reinforcing the bridgehead at night and on a massive scale. By July 17, he had the 7th, 11th, and Guards Armored Divisions positioned east of the Orne, along with five armored brigades.

Meanwhile, on July 14, at the urging of Dietrich and Feuchtinger—who assured him that no major British offensives were expected for 10 days—Luck went on a three-day furlough to Paris, where he spent his birthday with Dagmar, who was now his fiancé. (Dietrich knew of her Jewish blood but had nevertheless asked Fuehrer Headquarters to give them permission to marry. When the request was denied, Dietrich promised Luck to make a personal appeal to Hitler the next time he was at Berchtesgaden. Unfortunately, he had not been able to do so, because of the invasion.)

When Luck returned to his command post shortly after 9 A.M. on July 18, he found his staff tense and nervous. They reported that the Allies had carpet-bombed the kampfgruppe's front lines, followed by a creeping artillery barrage from hundreds of guns. The aerial and artillery bombardment had lasted about four hours; now the staff was unable to contact any of the frontline units. Later, Luck learned that 2,500 Anglo-American bombers, 1,000 field guns, and massive amounts of heavy naval artillery had been employed in the attack.

Luck immediately suspended (and later relieved) his second-in-command, who had become paralyzed during the crisis and had done nothing. He then set out on the main road to Caen. When he arrived at what was left of the village of Cagny, he found that his I Battalion had been smashed and that 25 to 30 British tanks had already crossed the main Caen Road and were heading south, with dozens of others behind them, driving from north to south. Luck also found a Luftwaffe battery of 88mm guns, all of which were aimed at the sky. He quickly ordered the young captain in charge to open up on the Allied flank to halt the British advance. To his amazement, the captain calmly replied that he had orders to shoot down enemy airplanes; fighting tanks was the army's job.

Luck immediately drew his pistol, aimed it at him, and declared, "Either you are a dead man or you can earn yourself a medal!"

Realizing that Luck was serious, the air force captain opted for the medal.[13] Moments later, his men were blasting the British tanks, which were defenseless against the heavy flak guns. Fortunately for the Germans, the confused British did not react quickly and launch an infantry attack against the battery, which was extremely vulnerable.

Gradually the truth of the situation became clear. The Allies had blasted a huge gap in the German front line east of Caen and were pouring through it with their armor. Luck found that the Tiger battalion and a nearby Panzer Mark IV battalion had been knocked out, but Major Becker had two intact batteries of assault guns ready for action. Luck committed them to the right of Cagny, to prevent the British from flanking the village to the north. He also reinforced the Luftwaffe battery with a platoon from his staff company, fighting as infantry. Soon, at least 40 British tanks were burning in the cornfields, most of them knocked out by the 88mm guns. With the remnants of his own regiment and the panzer reconnaissance battalion, he formed a thin line on the eastern edge of the British armored corridor.

Luck's line held on July 18 and all day on July 19. With only 400 infantrymen, his position was definitely vulnerable, but the British did not launch any major attacks against his front. Finally, at about 5 P.M., the vanguards of the depleted 12th SS Panzer Division arrived to relieve Kampfgruppe Luck. By this time, the main British offensive (dubbed Operation Goodwood) had been halted. It had gained less than five miles. Several weeks later, Luck was awarded the Knight's Cross for his part in this defensive victory.

Luck's battle group was relieved during the night of July 19–20, an operation made more difficult by a terrible rainstorm. In the German rear, he and his staff rebuilt the I Battalion, which had been almost wiped out by the British and American bombers. Luckily for him, the division had just received a well-trained battalion of replacements from Germany, complete with brand new SPW-armored personnel carriers. The task of rebuilding the I Battalion was completed in no time.

That was fortunate for Major von Luck. After less than a week's rest, the entire 21st Panzer Division was shifted to the sector south of Villers Bocage, to block the important Highway 175, which ran from Bayeux to Falaise.

The Allies rained blow after blow against the German line throughout the summer of 1944. Finally, on July 25, the Americans broke through on the German left flank. On August 17, two Canadian divisions and the 1st Polish Armored Division broke through the 21st Panzer Division, trapping Kampfgruppe Rauch (100th Panzer Regiment, 192nd Panzer Grenadier Regiment, and the 21st Reconnaissance Battalion, all under Colonel Joseph Rauch) in the Falaise Pocket.[14] Kampfgruppe Luck was lucky: it had been on the division's right flank and thus escaped encirclement. Rauch managed to break out but lost many of his men and all eight of the division's remaining tanks in the process. On August 21, Feuchtinger handed command of the operational units of the division over to Luck and took Rauch's shattered units back across the Seine, where they were to be rebuilt. Luck had the unenviable task of trying to delay Montgomery's advance and then escaping across the river with his battle group. This he did on August 29 in an amphibious Volkswagen car. It was a harrowing adventure because of Allied fighter-bomber attacks and because no one knew if the VW would actually float. Most of his men escaped using pontoon ferries and by constructing miniferries, made from doors of local houses and empty fuel cans. Luck then had to march in a wide circle to the north and west, trying to avoid being trapped by Patton's rampaging army in the process. This he managed to do by a narrow margin, arriving at his assigned positions west of Strasbourg on September 9. By now his average company was down to a strength of 50 men. Figure 7.3 shows the situation on the Western Front as of September 5, 1944.

Shortly after Luck arrived in the Strasbourg area, Colonel Rauch fell sick and returned to Germany.[15] Luck (now a lieutenant colonel) was given command of his battle group, which he led in Hitler's ill-fated attempts to turn Patton's right flank in September 1944. He then led his kampfgruppe in the retreat to the West Wall, fighting in the western Vosges, and in the battles around Saarbruecken, Saarlautern (Saalouis), Dillingen, and Merzig.

On Christmas Eve, 1944, a Nazi official arrived at Headquarters, 21st Panzer Division, to investigate Edgar Feuchtinger's behavior on D-Day and the night before. He was shocked to find that, while his division

Figure 7.3
Western Front, September 5, 1944

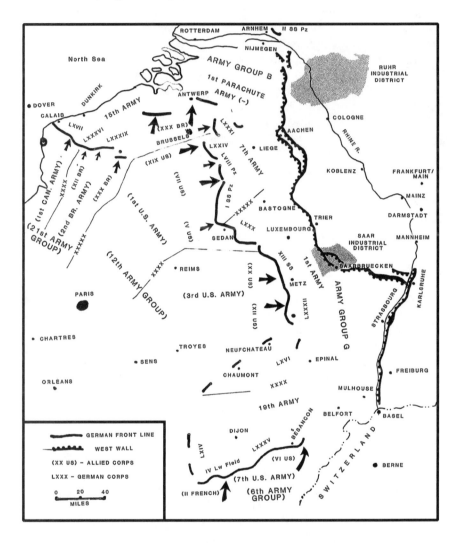

was fighting the Americans, the general had gone home for the holidays and was away without leave (AWOL). The investigator saw to it that Feuchtinger was relieved of his command, arrested, and court-martialed. He was replaced by Major General Werner Marcks—a strong Nazi. It would be several days, however, before Marcks could arrive. For six days, Hans von Luck was acting commander of the 21st Panzer Division. When Marcks finally turned up, Luck returned to the command of his regiment. In this capacity, he served in Operation Northwind (Himmler's badly managed offensive aimed at recapturing Strasbourg) and in the battles for the twin villages of Hatten-Rittershoffen, which involved some of the fiercest fighting of the war. The bitter house-to-house fighting in the snow and brutal cold lasted almost two weeks until January 21, 1945, when the Americans finally withdrew. By this point, the 21st Panzer Division had lost 16,000 men since June 6, 1944—more than 100 percent of its strength on D-Day.

Hatten-Rittershoffen was Hans von Luck's last battle on the Western Front. In February, the 21st Panzer was transferred to the Eastern Front. From February 7 to 9, Luck's 125th Panzer Grenadier Regiment spearheaded an attack that temporarily relieved Kuestrin, an ancient fortress about 50 miles east of Berlin, which had been surrounded by the Russians. Here, to his great surprise, he was visited by Dagmar, whose father had just died in a concentration camp. He managed to place her on a transport back to Berlin before the day ended.

After it left Kuestrin, the 21st Panzer Division was assigned to defend the Neisse-Oder line from February 20 until the last Soviet offensive began on April 16. This was the last natural barrier east of Berlin and the Germans struggled fiercely to hold it, but they were outnumbered 6 to 1 in men, 10 to 1 in artillery, 20 to 1 in tanks and 30 to 1 in airplanes. They had no chance. By nightfall on April 19, most of the 9th Army—including Luck's command—were virtually surrounded in the Halbe Pocket, about 60 miles southeast of Berlin. General Theodor Busse, the commander of the 9th Army, ordered Luck to spearhead a breakout to the west, across the Dresden-Berlin highway. He did not make it. Vastly outnumbered and pulverized by Stalin tanks, the battle group broke up. A few of the men managed to make it back across the Elbe and surrendered to the Americans. Colonel Hans von Luck, however, was not among them. With a handful of men, he surrendered to the Soviets near Baruth on the morning of April 27, 1945—three days before Hitler committed suicide in Berlin.

As a prisoner of war, Luck was sent across the Caucasus Mountains to Georgia and the Elbrus Mountains—a trip which took 35 days. During the next two years, about half of the prisoners died because of the cold and disease. The guards were brutal and often examined the prisoners for gold crowns. When they found one, they would break them off with a pair of pliers. This happened to Luck several times. Meanwhile, he was forced to work in coal pits and as a road construction worker. He was eventually allowed to write one 25-word postcard (including the address) home per month. In 1948, he was allowed to write one letter home every three months.

Luck quickly adjusted to prison life and eventually organized a construction crew, which he rented out to minor Soviet officials for money and extra rations. He also succeeded in impressing the camp prison officials, who promoted him to chief engineer, despite his lack of training in that area. Finally, in late 1949, he even managed to impress a Soviet colonel who headed a committee responsible for discharging prisoners. Although this man hated the "vons," he made an exception and decided to let Luck go. The former colonel was transported back to Germany and discharged at Hamburg on January 5, 1950. He was 39 years old and almost penniless.

Hans von Luck immediately returned to his home town, Flensburg, which was still largely bombed out. From there he telephoned Dagmar, who had become a well-known and highly successful radio and then television journalist in northern Germany and Berlin. They spent two days together. She, however, had become a self-sufficient career woman for the past five years, while Luck—trapped behind prison bars—had stagnated. They had little left in common. He realized that they had grown apart and ended the relationship with his typical tact. He only saw her once more. A few years later, she appeared out of nowhere and announced that a man had proposed to her. She asked Luck to approve the match! If he did not like the man, she added, she would not marry him.

Luck laughed, but consented to the interview and decided that the man in question was a decent sort who could make her happy, so Dagmar did marry him. Tragically, she was killed in an automobile accident two years later.

Meanwhile, Hans von Luck started life anew in a Germany he hardly recognized. Initially, he got a job as a night receptionist at a hotel in Hamburg. Finally, however, he received an offer to work for a businessman who intended to set up a firm in Angola, West Africa. Luck demurred and pointed out his lack of business experience. "The mechanics can be learned," his would-be employer responded. "Good management and reliability are innate."[16] He convinced Luck to accept the offer, and the former colonel's business career began. Then, in 1955, he answered a mysterious summons to Bonn, where he met with an anonymous officer. West Germany, the man declared, was about to organize the *Bundeswehr* (West German Armed Forces). Would Luck be interested in joining such a force? Luck asked to be guaranteed an appointment as a military attaché or a place in the new panzer force. When the officer refused to offer any guarantees, Luck thanked him and turned down the appointment.

Like F. W. von Mellenthin and Hasso von Manteuffel, among others, Hans von Luck was a successful business executive and achieved prosperity as a coffee merchant. He met a lady named Regina, who married him. Eventually she gave him three sons. Then, in the 1960s, he was astonished to receive an invitation from the British Staff College at

Camberley. They wanted him to speak about his experiences in Normandy. He was reticent because he realized that he had served an evil regime, but eventually accepted. He found the young British officers did not hate him but rather were anxious to learn from him. Both Luck and the officers enjoyed his speech, and he was invited back regularly. He also spoke on a number of television shows and to other service academies, as well as at the University of Innsbruck and the University of New Orleans, where the coeds expected to meet a high-ranking Nazi officer. Instead, they were charmed by an Old World aristocrat.

Luck's last years were enjoyable ones, and he never missed an opportunity to visit a friend from his World War II days—even if they were French. He passed away at Hamburg on August 1, 1997, at the age of 86. His wife and sons survive him.[17]

CHAPTER VIII

JOACHIM ZIEGLER: THE SS GENERAL

Hanke was not the only one of Rommel's commanders from the Ghost Division to achieve a high rank in the SS. Joachim Ziegler did as well.

He was born in Hanau on October 18, 1904, the son of August-Heinrich Ziegler, a lieutenant in the Prussian-Thueringen 6th Ulan Regiment. August-Heinrich rose to the rank of major and was adjutant of the 4th Higher Cavalry Command on September 3, 1914, the day he was reported missing in action in the Battle of Courtemont. He was never seen again. His son nevertheless followed in his footsteps and joined the 16th Cavalry Regiment as a Fahnenjunker on April 5, 1923. By 1929, he was a first lieutenant and a member of the 15th Cavalry Regiment at Paderborn.[1]

Young Ziegler's career took a decisive turn during the week of March 19–24, 1934, when he took his Wehrkreis exams. He scored at the top of the officers tested, earning him a slot in the next General Staff training course. For reasons not made clear by the records, his training was abbreviated, and he became a probationary member of the General Staff. He returned to Paderborn on October 1, 1934, as the adjutant of his regiment. He was promoted to captain 15 days later.

From September 30, 1936, until October 12, 1937, Captain Ziegler was attached to the Luftwaffe and served with Colonel Ritter Wilhelm von Thoma's tank units in the Spanish Civil War,[2] where he received a high Nationalist decoration. His personal extract does not say what he did during the following year, which is strange; apparently, however, he completed his General Staff training. In late 1938, he was named adjutant of the 3rd Panzer Brigade of the 2nd Panzer Division. He served with this unit in Poland and was transferred to the 7th Panzer Division as Ic (chief of intelligence) in February 1940—at the same time Rommel arrived.

Rommel was pleased with Ziegler's performance in France and made him Ib (chief supply officer or quartermaster) of the division on July 29, 1940, after Joachim von Metzsch moved up to the staff of the XVI Panzer Corps. This was a promotion of sorts for Ziegler. The two, however, never developed a close relationship, which was typical for Rommel. Ziegler was transferred to the staff of the 20th Motorized Division in October, 1940, as Ib of that unit. He became Ia (chief operations officer) of the 20th on January 6, 1941.

The 20th Motorized was on occupation duty in France until April 1941, when it was transferred to East Prussia. It crossed the border into the Soviet Union with the first wave on June 22, 1941. Ziegler was 1st General Staff Officer (Ia) of the division in the massive battles of encirclement at Bialystok and Minsk, and in the drive on Leningrad. He also fought in the brutal winter battles of 1941–42. In May 1942, he was named acting chief of staff of the LVII Motorized Corps, which was then in the rear, rebuilding and reorganizing as a panzer corps. After this task was completed, Ziegler accompanied his unit to the Caucasus sector of the Eastern Front. On September 29, 1942, however, he was transferred back to the central sector of the Russian Front, as chief of staff of the XXXIX Panzer Corps, which was then nearly encircled in the Rzhev salient. He was promoted to colonel shortly thereafter.

Joachim Ziegler was an ambitious officer who had nothing against National Socialism. In June 1943, he was given what he considered an opportunity. It was the fourth year of the war, Adolf Hitler had lost confidence in the army and its generals, and the *Waffen-SS* (Armed SS) was expanding rapidly. Although the Waffen-SS had the best equipment Germany could produce, excellent human material (from the military point of view), and fine junior combat officers, it was short of competent General Staff officers. In June 1943, Ziegler was summoned to Berlin and offered the job of chief of staff of an SS panzer corps. He quickly accepted. He was given the temporary rank of *SS-Oberfuehrer* (roughly SS colonel, senior grade) and returned to the Eastern Front as chief of staff of the II SS Panzer Corps.[3] Soon, however, he was transferred to the III (*germanischen*) SS Panzer Corps, then operating on the northern sector of the Eastern Front, also as chief of staff. His commander was General of Waffen-SS Felix Steiner.[4]

Ziegler did a fine job as chief of staff of the III SS. He fought in the unsuccessful attempt to prevent the Soviets from breaking the Siege of Leningrad, in the retreat to the Luga River and then to the Panther Line, and in the battles of the Narva. Then, on July 28, 1944, SS Major General Fritz von Scholz, the commander of the 11th SS Volunteer Panzer Grenadier Division "Nordland" (*11 SS-Freiwilligen-Panzergrenadier-Division*

Nordland), a part of the III SS Panzer Corps, was killed in action while defending a sector on the Narva. Steiner posted his ambitious chief of staff to the vacant position. On August 1, 1944, Ziegler was promoted to *SS-Brigadefuehrer und Generalmajor der Waffen-SS*.

Ziegler's new command consisted of two infantry regiments, composed mainly of Norwegian and Danish volunteers. Although he lacked command experience, Ziegler led it well enough in the fierce fighting on the Narva and earned himself a Knight's Cross. He continued to direct his unit in the retreat through Estonia and eastern Latvia, the retreat into Courland, and the opening Battles of the Courland Pocket. By the end of 1944, however, the Soviets had effectively bypassed Courland, and Heinz Guderian (now acting chief of the General Staff of the High Command of the Army) managed to secure Hitler's permission to withdraw the 11th SS to Germany. It was evacuated by sea in January 1945 and was committed to the fighting in Pomerania. By April 1945, the seriously depleted division had been shifted south and stood directly in the Red Army's path to Berlin.

Stalin's last offensive began on April 16, 1945. His divisions soon breached the thin German line on the Oder, and the 11th SS—along with the LVI Panzer Corps—were forced back into the capital of the Reich, where they were encircled on April 25. By now, SS Major General Ziegler was in despair and was apparently suffering from combat fatigue. In any case, General of Artillery Helmuth Weidling, the LVI Panzer commander and battle commandant of Berlin, was far from satisfied with Ziegler's dispositions. On April 26, he relieved Ziegler of his command and replaced him with SS Major General Dr. jur Gustav Krukenberg.[5] To reward his previous services, Ziegler's friends at Fuehrer Headquarters prevailed upon Hitler to decorate him with the Oak Leaves to his Knight's Cross. This award was made on April 28. It did little, however, to brighten Ziegler's mood or improve the hopeless situation.

On the afternoon of April 30, 1945, with the Russians less than 300 yards away, Adolf Hitler committed suicide. The next night (May 1–2, 1945), the commandant of the Reichschancellery and SS Major General Wilhelm Mohnke led those who wanted to try to escape in a breakout attempt.[6] Among those who accompanied him was Martin Bormann and Joachim Ziegler. Soon the initial four groups of survivors broke into several smaller groups, most of which were run down by the Red Army. Bormann and Dr. Ludwig Stumpfegger (Hitler's personal physician) committed suicide after a brush with a Russian outpost.[7] Ziegler was not with this particular group, but he also lost hope of escaping—and perhaps the will to do so as well. Sometime the next morning, he also committed suicide.

Joachim Ziegler was a competent General Staff officer, but he lacked command experience. Before he assumed command of the 11th SS Panzer Grenadier Division, he had never commanded so much as a battalion. Certainly he would have done better to have remained with the army General Staff, although he probably would never have reached general officers' rank had he done so.

Rommel and Colonel Karl Rothenburg, the commander of his panzer regiment, France, 1940. Rothenburg would be killed in action in Russia, 1941.

Lieutenant Colonel Rudolf Sieckenius and Major Otto Heidkaemper, early 1940. Both of these officers became major generals during the war.

Dr. Paul Joseph Goebbels, the minister of propaganda. He helped Rommel's career and clashed with Hanke, his state secretary, who tried unsuccessfully to replace him—and steal his wife. (photo from a Nazi Party scrapbook, circa 1933)

Karl Hanke, secretary of state in the ministry of propaganda. He later served as an orderly officer to Rommel and a company commander in the 7th Panzer Division. He was the Gauleiter of Silesia and the last Reichsfuehrer-SS. He was shot by Czech guards during an unsuccessful prison escape in 1945. (photo from a Nazi Party scrapbook, circa 1934)

Major General Georg von Bismarck. After a successful tour as commander of the 7th Rifle Regiment in France, 1940, Rommel arranged for him to be appointed commander of the 21st Panzer Division. A division commander of the highest rank, he achieved great success in Africa until he was killed in action near Alma Halfa Ridge.

Johann Mickl, the Austrian who commanded Rommel's antitank battalion in France. Rommel arranged for him to be transferred to North Africa, where he commanded the 155th Rifle Regiment. He was captured by the British but led a daring prison break and escaped, along with 800 men. He went on to serve on the Russian Front and in the Balkans.

An infantryman in action on the first day of Operation Barbarossa, the invasion of the Soviet Union, June 22, 1941. Russia would be the graveyard of many of Rommel's former officers and most of the 7th Panzer Division.

Colonel General Heinz Guderian, the "father" of the Blitzkrieg.

Colonel Karl Rothenburg, shortly after he was awarded the Knight's Cross for bravery in France, 1940. His Pour le Merite is barely visible in this photograph, which was apparently taken by Rommel himself.

General of Panzer Troops Georg Stumme, who commanded the 7th Panzer Division before Rommel and later succeeded the Desert Fox as commander of Panzer Army Afrika. He died of a heart attack while under enemy attack at El Alamein on October 23, 1942. Stumme was a much more amicable commander than Rommel, whose methods came as quite a shock to the officers of the Ghost Division in early 1940.

The officers of the 7th Panzer Division, France, 1940. Colonel Rothenburg is on the left. Major Otto Heidkaemper is on the right. The officer in the right foreground appears to be Georg von Bismarck. Erwin Rommel was a "photo bug" and apparently took this photograph himself. His photo collection from the French campaign is located in the U.S. National Archives.

Major General Erwin Rommel in France, 1940.

Colonel General Ludwig Beck, chief of the General Staff from 1934 to 1938. An anti-Nazi, he opposed Hitler's aggressive policies, which he felt would lead to war. When Hitler did not relent, Beck resigned in protest—the only senior German officer to do so. He was later a leader in the July 20, 1944, anti-Hitler coup and was killed that same night. Unfortunately for Germany, his direction of the General Staff did not reach the level of his moral courage.

Frido von Senger und Etterlin, who commanded a two-battalion motorized brigade attached to the 7th Panzer Division in France, 1940. A bit of an aristocratic snob, he somewhat disliked Rommel, who was a commoner and somewhat abrasive.

SS-Obergruppenfuehrer Reinhard Heydrich, Himmler's deputy and a personal friend of Karl Hanke. Heydrich helped spy on Goebbels and assisted Hanke in his efforts to displace him as minister of propaganda.

Hans von Luck, who became commander of the 37th Panzer Reconnaissance Battalion of the 7th Panzer Division after its original commander was killed in action. Luck later led the 3rd Panzer Reconnaissance Battalion in Libya and Egypt, as well as a panzer grenadier regiment in Normandy and on the Russian Front.

Goebbels reporting to Hitler, circa 1933. Hitler apparently considered firing Goebbels over the Lida Baarova affair but did not do so.

Rommel and a group of his officers, France, 1940. This photograph was taken with Rommel's own camera. *First row, left to right:* 2nd Lieutenant Loh, 1st Lieutenant Seibold, Rommel, Lieutenant Colonel Sieckenius. *Second row, left to right:* Lieutenant Deichbaum and Lieutenant Karl Hanke. Siebold was a communications expert. Rommel arranged for him to be transferred to North Africa, where he did a brilliant job as commander of Rommel's Wireless Intercept Service. He was promoted to captain before he was killed in action in the 1st Battle of El Alamein.

General of Panzer Troops Hans von Funck, who succeeded Rommel as commander of the 7th Panzer Division, which he led in Russia from 1941 to 1943. Funck later commanded the XXXXVII Panzer Corps in Normandy. Ironically, Funck was earmarked to command the Afrika Korps instead of Rommel, but Hitler vetoed his appointment because of some derogatory remarks he made about the Italians during an interview with the Fuehrer. Instead, Hitler selected Rommel.

Frido von Senger und Etterlin, the commander of the XIV Panzer Corps in Italy.

Goebbels on the campaign trail, Berlin, circa 1932. (photo courtesy of Dr. Waldo Dahlstead)

Rommel accepting the surrender of a French corps. *Left to right:* Unknown, a Condor Legion veteran, possibly Captain Schraepler; Georg von Bismarck, Rommel, Heidkaemper, French General Ihler (*foreground*), a Wehrmacht beamte (warrant officer), a Luftwaffe lieutenant (probably a liaison officer), Hanke (*hands on hips*), British General Fortune.

Caen, France, after the Allied bombings. The rubble of this university city significantly delayed the counterattack of the 21st Panzer Division on D-Day, June 6, 1944.

Rommel and some of his officers, 1940. The officers of the 25th Panzer Regiment are dressed in black. Colonel Rothenburg is second from the left. The
officers on either side of the colonel are believed to be Major Franz von Linde-
nau and Major Casimir Kentel. The officer to Rommel's left is apparently Otto
Heidkaemper. The 7th Panzer was equipped with inferior Czech tanks, some
of which are seen to the rear.

A German self-propelled gun destroyed by an Allied fighter-bomber in Normandy.

A machine crew from the 7th Panzer Division in action in France, 1940.

Grenadiers in the attack.

German infantry continue the advance despite a destroyed bridge, France, 1940.

A German infantry unit attacks across a river despite French artillery fire, 1940. A shell burst can be seen to the rear of these men as another squad lands.

General der Panzertruppen
von SENGER und ETTERLIN

General of Panzer Troops Frido von Senger und Etterlin. (U.S. Army War College photo)

Allied fighter-bombers circle the battlefield in Normandy in the zone of Kampf-gruppe von Luck, June 6, 1944. The aircraft on the ground are British gliders.

The Red Army takes the Reichstag in Berlin, April 30, 1945. Major General Sieckenius was killed in a suicide attack not far from here the day before.

Colonel General Hermann Hoth (1885–1971), directing the 4th Panzer Army on the Eastern Front. In 1940, he commanded the XV Motorized Corps—including the 7th Panzer Division—in France. He backed Otto Heidkaemper, the chief of operations of the Ghost Division, in his dispute with Erwin Rommel. Later, on November 30, 1943, Hitler sacked Hoth. He was never reemployed. He was sentenced to 15 years in prison in 1948 but was released in 1954.

Hitler speaks with General Hans von Seeckt, the guiding light in the development of the Reichsheer and commander of the German Army, 1920–26. Seeckt played a major role in suppressing the Nazi Party in 1923. He and Hitler later made peace politically. In return for his support, Hitler made Seeckt's partially Jewish wife an "honorary Aryan." Seeckt died in 1936. (photo courtesy of Dr. Waldo Dahlstead)

German soldiers in action in Normandy, 1944. The men of Kampfgruppe von Luck had to become masters of camouflage to survive in the hedgerow fighting. The panzer in this photograph, for example, is barely visible. (photo courtesy of Bundesarchiv)

Another victory for Georg von Bismarck and Rommel's lieutenants in North Africa, 1942. These British and South African prisoners were captured near Ain el Gazala, when the Gazala Line was abandoned.

The Winter Battles, 1941–42. An Afrika Korps column advances.

Panzer Army Artillery blasts away at the British.

The desert in flames, Winter Battles of 1941–42.

CHAPTER IX

GOTTFRIED FROELICH: THE SAXON GUNNER

Rommel's artillery commander in France was Gottfried Froelich, who, like Bismarck, also went on to command a panzer division, but without Bismarck's success.

Froelich was born in the beautiful Saxon capital of Dresden on June 3, 1894. He entered the service as a Fahnenjunker on August 12, 1914, just as World War I was beginning. He was commissioned *Leutnant* in the Wuerttemberger 49th Field Artillery Regiment in March of the following year and fought on the Western Front. Froelich's unit was part of the 27th Infantry Division of the XIII (Royal Wuerttemberg) Corps, which fought in the Lorraine (1914), on the Meuse (1914), and in the Argonne (late 1914–December 1915). For six months (January–July 1916), the young lieutenant fought at Ypres, where the 27th suffered heavy losses against the Canadians at Observation Ridge and where Froelich himself was severely wounded on May 16. After he returned to duty late that summer, Froelich was named adjutant of the I Battalion, a post he held for the rest of the war. He fought in the Somme sector (August 1916–early 1917), east of Cambrai (early 1917), on the Artois near Arras (April–July 1917), and in Flanders (August–October 1917). The division was hurriedly sent to Alsace in November 1917. In the last year of the war, Lieutenant Froelich fought in the Schlettstadt region (north of Colmar), at Cambrai, and on the Meuse. He was still at the front when the war ended. Selected for the Reichsheer, Froelich served in the 12th Artillery Regiment (1919–20), the 4th Transportation Battalion (1921–22), the 4th Medical Battalion (1922–23), the 4th Engineer Battalion (1924), and the 4th Transportation again (this time as battalion adjutant) (1927–29).[1]

In 1929, Froelich returned to the artillery, serving on the staff of the 4th Artillery Regiment and as a battery commander (1931–34). He commanded the I Battalion/14th Artillery Regiment at Naumburg from October 1934 to July 1937. Then, after attending a course at the Artillery School at Jueterbog, he was promoted to lieutenant colonel on June 1, 1938, and was named commander of the II/76th Artillery Regiment at Wuppertal in November 1938. Before that time, the 76th was a nonmotorized General Headquarters (GHQ) artillery unit, not organic to any division. On November 11, however, it became part of the 1st Light Division. Froelich trained his battalion in Westphalia, deployed it to Silesia in the autumn of 1939, and led it in Poland in September 1939. As a part of the 10th Army, II/76th supported the main German spearhead in the Polish campaign. It then returned to Wuppetal, where the 1st Light was converted into the 6th Panzer Division. This process had hardly begun, however, when Gottfried Froelich was named commander of the 78th Motorized (later Panzer) Artillery Regiment of the 7th Panzer Division. He assumed command on November 1.

Froelich remained commander of the 78th for the next three-and-a-half years. He led it in France and Belgium (1940); in the preparations for the possible invasion of Great Britain (1940); in its redeployment to East Prussia (February 1941); in Operation Barbarossa, the invasion of the Soviet Union (1941); and for two years on the Eastern Front (1941–43).

Colonel Froelich and his regiment distinguished themselves by supporting the tanks and panzer grenadiers of the "Ghost Division" in the first campaign in Russia. They crossed the Soviet frontier on June 22, 1941, and fought in the battles of the Minsk Pocket, in the breaking of the Stalin Line, in the Dvina crossings, in the encirclement of Smolensk, in the Dnieper crossings, and at Vitebsk, Vyasma, Klim, and in the Battle of Moscow. By October 13, the 78th Panzer Artillery Regiment alone had destroyed 263 Soviet tanks, 124 guns, 69 antitank guns, 760 trucks, 48 bunkers, 4 airplanes, 5 ammunition depots, 6 locomotives, and an armored train. Losses in the regiment were not exceptionally heavy, however, until winter arrived.

During Stalin's winter offensive of 1941–42, Froelich's regiment (along with the rest of 9th Army) was locked in a life-and-death struggle in the Rzhev salient. Thanks in large part to the efforts of the 7th Panzer Division, the 9th Army held out, but losses were very high. The division started the campaign with about 14,000 men, but lost 9,203 officers and men from June 22, 1941, to January 23, 1942, and, at one time, had only five operational tanks left. It invaded Russia with just under 200 tanks. The 78th Panzer Artillery was similarly decimated.

As a result of its losses, the 7th Panzer Division was sent back to southern France in May 1942 to rebuild. In November, it took part in the occupation of Vichy France, driving all the way to Toulon and

Marseilles. Shortly thereafter, the Red Army encircled Stalingrad, and the 7th Panzer found itself en route back to the Eastern Front, this time on the southern sector. Arriving in December 1942, the division was involved in defending Rostov against heavy Soviet attacks. It destroyed more than 350 Russian tanks in six weeks but lost 100 of its own.

Froelich's last battle with the Ghost Division was Kursk—Hitler's last major offensive in the East—where it suffered heavy losses. After Kursk, the 7th Panzer Division was a kampfgruppe. It was reduced to a strength of about three infantry battalions, a battalion or so of artillery, and 15 tanks.

Gottfried Froelich, meanwhile, had served for more than two years on the Eastern Front and had nothing left to prove as a regimental commander. The HPA now at last decided to promote him. At first he was named acting commander of the 36th Infantry Division, a motorized unit then in the process of demotorizing and becoming a marching infantry unit. Froelich served in this post for a couple of weeks in September 1943; then, on September 20, he assumed command of the 8th Panzer Division.[2] This made him eligible for a promotion to major general, which he received on December 1, 1943.

The 8th Panzer had been serving on the central sector of the Eastern Front, but it was transferred to the southern sector after the Battle of Kursk. It was here that Stalin was launching his major offensive for 1943. The 8th Panzer was immediately swept up in the battle and suffered heavy losses in the withdrawal from Kiev. The division was in more or less continuous combat from the fall of 1943 until 1945, fighting at Zhitomir (in the northern Ukraine), at Tarnopol, in the Brody sector, in southern Poland, at Lemberg, in the Carpathian withdrawal, and in Slovakia. Froelich was not with the division in all of these battles, however. On March 31, 1944—after almost three years of continuous service on the Eastern Front—he fell ill. He was replaced by Colonel Werner Friebe, the former chief of staff of the XXXXVIII Panzer Corps, who was promoted to major general on June 1.

Friebe was an acting commander only and turned out to be a better staff officer than a battlefield leader. On July 15, 1944, the Reds were in the midst of a massive offensive and were trying to encircle General of Infantry Arthur Hauffe's XIII Corps near Brody. Fortunately for the XIII, General of Panzer Troops Hermann Balck's XXXXVIII Panzer Corps lay to the south, and he had the 1st and 8th Panzer Divisions in reserve.[3] Both divisions, however, were very much understrengthened, and the Reds had air superiority in the sector. Balck, a veteran tank officer, ordered both divisions to advance only through forests or along a road that went through forests—never down an open road—and to check the Soviet spearheads. The 1st Panzer did as it was told and brought the Soviet 38th Army to an abrupt halt. Friebe, however, ignored Balck's instructions and moved the division over an open road. The Red Air Force pounced on the 8th Panzer and flew almost 2,000 combat sorties against it on July 15 alone. The division was slaughtered.

Absolutely furious, Balck immediately relieved Friebe—his own former chief of staff—of his command. He replaced him with Colonel F. W. von Mellenthin, the current chief of staff of the XXXXVIII Panzer and Rommel's former intelligence officer in Libya and Egypt.[4] Balck told him to regroup, reinforced him with elements of the 20th Panzer Grenadier Regiment, and ordered him to attack against on July 19, in order to rescue the XIII Corps, which was now surrounded.

Mellenthin had been in more or less constant combat for three years and was not easily shocked. He was stunned on the morning of July 19, however, when he learned that several of his commanders had not advanced as ordered; instead, they took it upon themselves to retreat. Mellenthin immediately sacked all of these commanders, including the leader of the 10th Panzer Regiment.

Meanwhile, Gottfried Froelich returned to his HQ and reassumed command of the 8th Panzer Division on July 20. He quickly launched another attack but too much valuable time had been lost. The Soviet defenders were ready and the thrust gained little ground. Meanwhile, the XIII Corps was crushed. Between 25,000 and 30,000 German soldiers and their Ukrainian allies (from the 15th SS Volunteer Grenadier Division) were killed and 17,000 were captured. General Hauffe was among the dead.[5] Only 12,000 managed to break out, escape the Soviets, and reach the lines of the 1st Panzer Division. In July 1944, the 8th Panzer Division lost 2,361 men, 8 tanks, 77 armored personnel carriers, and 24 guns.[6] Its performance had not been impressive under Friebe, Foerlich, or von Mellenthin.[7]

General Froelich was not, in fact, a particularly good division commander and was much better suited to leading mobile artillery units, as opposed to tank units. In the German Army, major generals commanding divisions were often promoted to the rank of lieutenant general after only six months in grade, if they were rated highly by their corps commanders and army commanders, and if they were highly thought of by the powerful HPA. Nothing of the sort happened in the case of Gottfried Froelich. He was obviously considered a fair to mediocre commander but not a poor one.

During the Hungarian campaign of 1944–45, Froelich played a credible role in checking the Soviet 2nd Ukrainian Front's offensive northwest of Erd in December 1944, and in slowing the advance of the 6th Tank Army north of Budapest later that month. On New Years Day, 1945, along with the 6th Panzer Division, General Froelich managed to surprise and overrun the 34th Guards Rifle Division west of Budapest. His division was hurriedly sent north of the Danube, however, because the

Red Army was threatening the vital city of Komaron, the site of one of the few oil refineries still in German hands and the location of the only permanent bridge linking Slovakia to Hungary. East of the city, Froelich reinforced the 711th Volksgrenadier Division and the Hungarian St. Laszlo Division. They were quickly defeated by the Soviet 7th Guards and 6th Armies and were soon in rapid retreat. General of Infantry Otto Woehler, the commander of Army Group South, and General Balck, who was now commander of the 6th Army,[8] saved the city only by rapidly committing their few reserves: the 13th Tank Destroyer Battalion, the 286th Army Flak Battalion, the independent 208th Panzer Battalion (12 tanks), and several hastily organized emergency (Alarm) battalions.

General Balck held Froelich responsible for the near disaster and relieved him of his command for indecisive and slow leadership. This move effectively ruined Froelich's career and ended his chances of ever being promoted to lieutenant general.

General Froelich was unemployed until March 18, 1945, when he was given command of the ad hoc Korpsgruppe von Tettau.[9] As part of the 3rd Panzer Army, Army Group Vistula, he was charged with holding Belgard and Swinemuende in Pomerania. This he could not do because of the overwhelming superiority of the Red Army and because he had very few combat units. On April 10, however, he was given a promotion of sorts. The commander of the 3rd Panzer Army, General of Panzer Troops Baron Hasso von Manteuffel, was an old friend; they had, in fact, both been regimental commanders in the old Ghost Division at the same time.[10] Manteuffel remembered that Froelich was an excellent motorized artillery commander, so he named him Harko (Higher Artillery Commander), 3rd Panzer Army. He did as well in this post as anyone could have, under the circumstances.

Along with most of the 3rd Panzer Army, the 3rd Panzer Army Harko disengaged from the Russians in late April 1945 and headed west. Gottfried Froelich surrendered to the British on May 2, 1945. He remained a prisoner of war until 1948. Shortly after his release, he moved to Meisenheim. He died in Heidenheim on July 30, 1959.

CHAPTER **X**

GEORG VON BISMARCK: THE PRUSSIAN JUNKER

Georg von Bismarck was one of Rommel's leading commanders both in France and in North Africa. Like so many others, however, he did not survive his time with the Desert Fox.

The son of a distinguished Prussian Junker family, Georg was born at Neumuehl, the Bismarck estate near Kuestrin, Neumark province, Prussia, on February 15, 1891. He entered the service as a Fahnenjunker in the 6th Jaeger (Light Infantry) Battalion on June 13, 1910, and was commissioned second lieutenant on November 18, 1911. During World War I, young Bismarck served exclusively with the 6th Jaeger (later Reserve Jaeger) Battalion,[1] a unit which was used as stock troops on the Western Front.[2] He successively served as platoon leader, company commander, and battalion adjutant, and was promoted to *Oberleutnant* (first lieutenant) on January 27, 1917.

Lieutenant von Bismarck survived the war and applied for duty with the Reichsheer. He was accepted, and the fact that his last name was "Bismarck" did not hurt at all.

Promotions were slow in the 100,000-man "Treaty Army" (as they are in any small army), and Bismarck did not become a captain until 1924. He was not promoted to major until 10 years after that. In the meantime, he served with the 16th Infantry Regiment in Westphalia (western Germany), the 3rd (Prussian) Cavalry Regiment (where he commanded the regimental leadership training unit), and the 5th (Prussian) Infantry Regiment at Stettin. In October 1924 he became a company commander in *Kraftfahr-Abteilung 2* (the 2nd Motorized Battalion) in Stettin. Young von Bismarck quickly recognized the potential of highly mobile units in a future war and spent most of the rest of his career in motorized units. After spending several years in the 2nd

Motorized (1924–31), he served with the 6th Medical Battalion (1931–34), and then became commander of Motorized Battalion Koenigsburg in 1934. This unit became the 1st Reconnaissance Battalion of the 1st Infantry Division in the mid-1930s. Georg von Bismarck commanded the 1st Reconnaissance until November 1938. He was promoted to lieutenant colonel in 1936 and to full colonel on February 1, 1939.

On November 10, 1938, Bismarck assumed command of the 7th Cavalry Rifle Regiment (*Kavallerie-Schuetzen-Regiments 7*) of the 2nd Light Division. He led this regiment in Poland with considerable success. The division itself, however, proved too unwieldy in combat, so when it returned to Germany in October 1939 it was reorganized, given a panzer regiment (the 25th), and redesignated the 7th Panzer Division. Bismarck's regiment was redesignated the 7th Rifle.

Erwin Rommel replaced Georg Stumme as commander of the 7th Panzer in February 1940. Bismarck's initial reaction to the new, live-wire commander has not been recorded verbatim, but it was not positive. He was not one of Rommel's defenders at Bad Godesberg, and they never developed a close personal friendship. The two, however, definitely did establish a close professional relationship during the French campaign of 1940. Rommel even recommended him for the Knight's Cross, which Bismarck received on September 30, 1940. With high praise from a commander who was known to be very demanding, and Rommel's favorable comments on his fitness report, Bismarck had cleared the hurdles for his next promotion. As the winter of 1940–41 arrived in Europe, he left the Bordeaux region in southern France for east-central Germany as the first commander of the 20th Rifle Brigade of the recently formed 20th Panzer Division. He assumed his new command on December 10, 1940. The new brigade controlled the 59th and 112th Rifle Regiments. Bismarck's headquarters was in Jena.

The 20th controlled four former "marching infantry" battalions from the 59th and 74th Infantry Regiments. Bismarck's task was to oversee their motorization, train them in mobile warfare, and (although he did not know it yet) lead them in Operation Barbarossa.

The first commander of the 20th Panzer Division was the highly capable Lieutenant General Horst Stumpff. As part of Army Group Center, the 20th Panzer crossed into Russia on June 22, 1941, took part in the Minsk encirclement, took Vitebsk by *coup de main* on July 10, stormed Ulla on July 17, fought in the encirclement of Smolensk, checked several attempts by the Red Army to break the encirclement, and penetrated to the Dvina. Army Group Center probably could have launched a successful drive on Moscow at this point, but Hitler diverted most of the panzer divisions to Army Groups South and North, leaving Army Group Center to face a series of desperate Soviet offensives in the Vyasma area. Meanwhile, General Stumpff's health collapsed, cutting short a brilliant career. He was succeeded by Colonel Georg von Bismarck on September 10, 1941.[3]

Bismarck's new command included the 20th Rifle Brigade, the 21st Panzer Regiment (three battalions), the 92nd Panzer Artillery Regiment, and the 20th Motorcycle, 20th Panzer Reconnaissance, 92nd Tank Destroyer, 92nd Panzer Engineer, and 92nd Panzer Signal Battalions. Because Hitler had virtually stripped Army Group Center of armor, Bismarck's depleted division was used as a "fire brigade" to check the relentless Russian assaults hurled against Army Group Center. Although the Red Army managed to recapture Vyasma, they were not able to accomplish their true objective, which was to smash the army group. Meanwhile, Hitler's legions managed to capture Kiev (along with 667,000 prisoners), overrun the Ukraine and most of the Crimea, and push to the gates of Leningrad. Then, in yet another change of strategy, Hitler decided to capture Moscow before the onset of winter. Colonel von Bismarck pushed his unit to within 60 miles of the Kremlin, but here he was stopped. Beginning on December 6, the 20th Panzer faced the full fury of Stalin's winter offensive of 1941–42. By the time these battles were over, the division had suffered such heavy casualties that two of the three battalions of the 21st Panzer Regiment had been dissolved, along with the 20th Motorcycle Battalion and the II Battalion/121st Motorized Infantry Regiment. Bismarck was not on hand to see the successful end of the division's retreat, however. In a personnel move initiated by Erwin Rommel, he handed over command of the 20th Panzer to Major General Ritter Wilhelm von Thoma on December 18, 1941, and was soon on his way from the snowy wastelands of Russia to the deserts of North Africa.

After a brief leave, Bismarck joined the staff of Panzer Group Afrika on January 5, 1942. Here he learned that Rommel had earmarked him for command of the 21st Panzer Division. Its previous commander, Baron Johann von Ravenstein, had been captured during the Winter Battles, and his temporary replacement, Major General Karl Boettcher, was not a panzer officer and was in poor health. Boettcher, in fact, was not able to remain in command until Bismarck completed his orientation. He left Africa for treatment in Germany on February 9, 1941. Bismarck took command of the 21st Panzer on February 11, succeeding Lieutenant Colonel Gustav-Georg Knabe, who returned to his regular post as commander of the 104th Motorized Regiment.[4] Figure 10.1 shows the North African battlefields, 1941–1943.

Bismarck's first task was to reorganize the division. It consisted of the 5th Panzer Regiment, the 104th Rifle (later Panzer Grenadier) Regiment, the 155th Panzer Artillery Regiment, and the 15th Motorcycle, 3rd Panzer Reconnaissance, 39th Tank Destroyer, 200th Panzer Engineer, and 200th Panzer Signal Battalions. The 104th Rifle, however, had been smashed in Operation Crusader and the division was desperately short of motorized

Figure 10.1
The North African Battlegrounds, 1941–43

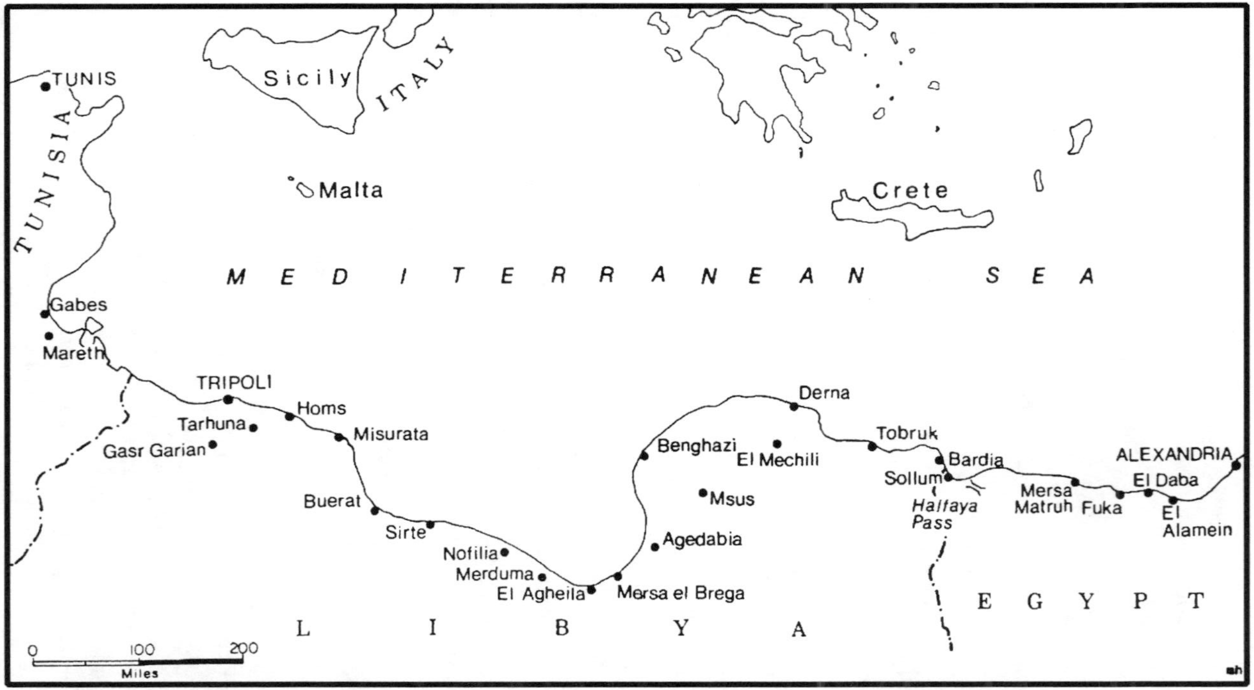

infantry. (The I Battalion/104th Rifle Regiment had been completely destroyed at Halfaya Pass in January 1942.) With the concurrence of higher headquarters, Bismarck transferred all of the survivors of the 104th to the II Battalion and converted the 15th Motorcycle Battalion into III/104th Rifle Regiment. He then set about the task of making the 21st Panzer Division as combat worthy as possible before Rommel launched his next offensive. He was, meanwhile, promoted to major general on April 1, 1942, with an effective date of rank of February 19. There was, however, little time to celebrate: Rommel launched his next offensive on May 26. Figure 10.2 shows the first phase of the Battle of the Gazala Line.

Figure 10.2
The Battle of the Gazala Line, Phase 1

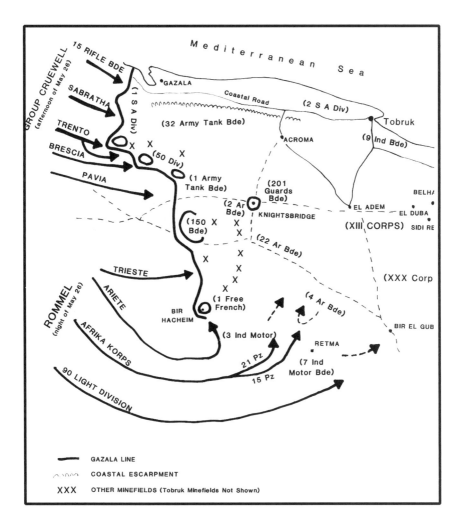

Georg von Bismarck distinguished himself in the Battle of the Gazala Line, which began during the night of May 26–27. On May 27, in a series of fierce engagements, Bismarck's 21st Panzer defeated the British 4th Armoured Brigade, helped smash the 3rd Indian Motor Brigade, and crushed the 3rd Royal Tank Regiment (RTR). The next day, however, a British counteroffensive completely isolated the Afrika Korps in the area soon known as "the Cauldron," and Bismarck's tank strength was down to 29 "runners." Despite the unfavorable situation, the Prussian Junker was not content to go over to the defensive. On May 28, he attacked again and scattered the British/South African "Stolcol" Force south of Elwet el Tamar, destroyed nine tanks from the 8th RTR, captured the British strongpoint called Commonwealth Keep, and pushed as far north as the Coastal Escarpment. Rommel, however, recalled Bismarck that evening because the Afrika Korps, along with the 90th Light Division, the Italian Ariete Armored Division, and most of the 104th Artillery Command, was completely cut off and trapped behind British lines. The Desert Fox decided to hedgehog in the Cauldron area, before breaking out to the west.

For the next few days, Bismarck's mechanics worked feverishly to repair damaged panzers, while the bulk of the division held Sidra Ridge and the British prepared to crush the Cauldron. By June 1, the Afrika Korps was down to a ration of only one cup of water per day and Rommel was desperately trying to destroy the British 150th Infantry Brigade in the Got el Ualeb Box, but he was unable to do so. The Desert Fox called on Bismarck to reinforce him. Gambling that the British would not attack, Bismarck virtually stripped Sidra Ridge of its infantry and sent the entire 104th Panzer Grenadier Regiment into the battle. Their attack led to the collapse of the British defenses, which had defied Rommel's strike force for five days. The British lost the 150th Brigade and the 44th RTR—a total of 3,000 men captured, 101 tanks and armored cars captured or destroyed, 124 guns captured or destroyed, and large quantities of supplies. Rommel now reestablished contact with the rest of Panzer Army Afrika to the west, while the 104th Panzer Grenadier Regiment hastily returned to Sidra Ridge. Bismarck immediately resumed his policy of launching sharp, local attacks, to keep the British off balance. On June 2, for example, he struck the 4th Armoured Brigade and destroyed 19 Grant tanks, 8 field guns, and 2 self-propelled artillery pieces. The 21st Panzer Division suffered no casualties.

On June 5, the British finally launched their long-delayed attack on the Cauldron (see Figure 10.3). It was poorly conceived. They struck Bismarck at Sidra Ridge with the 32nd Army Tank Brigade, which was equipped with heavy Matilda and Valentine infantry support or I-tanks, but it was supported by only a dozen field guns and a single battalion of infantry—which was hopelessly inadequate. Bismarck blasted the 32nd Tank as it approached Sidra Ridge and then, at just the right moment, launched a brilliant counterattack and forced it to retreat—into a minefield. The 32nd Tank lost 50 of its 70 tanks and was virtually eliminated as a combat force.

Rommel promptly capitalized on Bismarck's victory. He ordered the former Jaeger to attack to the north, through the gap in the British line caused by the destruction of the 32nd Tank. He was then to drive southeast, in an effort to double up the British right (northern) flank on its center. Simultaneously, to the south, Rommel would personally direct an attack by the 15th Panzer and Italian Ariete Armored Divisions, which were to double the British left flank on its center. The plan was executed just as Rommel outlined it. By nightfall, he and Bismarck had encircled the 9th and 10th Indian Brigades, a battalion of the 21st Indian Brigade, the Support Group of the British 7th Armoured Division (including the 107th Regiment, Royal Horse Artillery), as well as the 4th, 28th, and 157th Field Regiments, Royal Artillery.

Figure 10.3
The Cauldron, Dawn, June 5, 1942

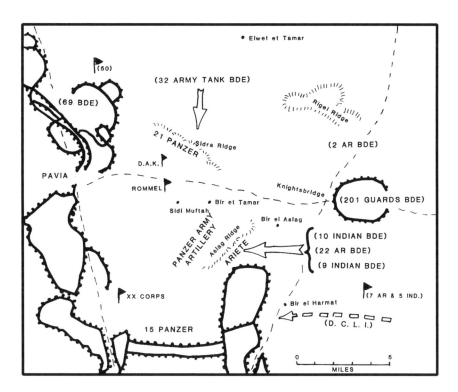

The next day, the main body of the 21st Panzer Division helped crush the British pocket, along with the 15th Panzer and Ariete. The British 2nd Armoured Brigade tried to rescue its trapped colleagues, but Bismarck checked their effort with elements of his division without seriously lessening the pressure on the pocket. One by one, the Allied units were smashed, destroyed, or forced to surrender. Then Bismarck and his division turned north, to deal with the rest of the British 8th Army.

The Desert Fox and his nearly exhausted veterans continued to fight the battered Allies until June 11, but neither side could deliver a knock-out blow. That evening, however, Rommel saw his chance. He ordered Bismarck to elude the British 1st Armoured Division and to attack the British 7th Armoured Division (2nd and 4th Armoured Brigades) in the rear, while General Walter Nehring, the Afrika Korps commander, pinned it down with frontal assaults. With any luck, the 7th Armoured would be destroyed.

Bismarck and Nehring struck on June 12 and their timing was perfect. The distinguished British historian Correlli Barnett called the ensuing battle the greatest defeat in the history of the British armor.[5]

When the British XIII Corps commander, General Norrie, realized what was happening, he sent the 22nd Armoured Brigade to rescue the trapped 7th Armoured. The 22nd, however, was pinned down by the Italian Trieste Motorized Division and was taken in the rear by Bismarck and the 21st Panzer. It retreated with heavy losses. Bismarck then returned to the Battle of Knightsbridge, where he, Nehring, and Rommel crushed the 7th Armoured. By dawn of the next day, June 13, the British 4th Armoured Brigade had only 15 runners, while the 2nd and 22nd Armoured had a combined total of only 50 operational tanks, and the partially reconstituted 32nd Army Tank Brigade had but 30. The British had lost 185 cruiser (main battle) tanks and 50 infantry tanks, and were no longer able to compete with the Afrika Korps, although they were slow to recognize that fact.

On June 13, Bismarck attacked again. Despite severe troop exhaustion, the 21st Panzer Division destroyed another 25 British tanks in the Battle of Maabus er Rigel (Rigel Ridge), overran part of the 2nd Scots Guards, and knocked out all eight guns of the 6th South African Anti-tank Battery. As a result, the British were forced to abandon the critical Knightsbridge Box and retreat to the northeast, in the direction of Tobruk.

The next day, Bismarck overran the Tamar Box (Best Point), while the British began abandoning the Gazala Line. Because of troop exhaustion, Rommel and Bismarck were unable to move rapidly enough to cut off the 1st South African Division, which retreated into Tobruk. The men of the British 50th Infantry Division, however, were forced to break through Italian lines and escape to the south across the open desert. They eventually reached friendly lines, but they lost all of their heavy weapons and most of their equipment in the process.

Meanwhile, Bismarck stormed the Sidi Rezegh Box, the southeastern cornerstone of the Tobruk defenses, on June 16, and captured most of the 1/6th Rajputana Rifle Battalion in the process.

The next day, June 17, the British armor made its last stand in the desert south of Sidi Rezegh against the 15th and 21st Panzer Divisions. In this battle, the 4th Armoured lost half its strength. The 9th Queen's Royal Lancers fought brilliantly but was reduced to a strength of nine Grant tanks. None of these, however, were battle-worthy, because of damage to their main battle guns.

On June 18, Rommel headed for the Egyptian frontier and deceived the British into thinking that he intended to drive on Alexandria; then, under the cover to darkness, he doubled back on Tobruk. Figure 10.4 shows Rommel's plan of attack against Tobruk, which he drew up on June 17. It worked exactly as he envisioned it. He unleashed the major assault on the fortress at 5:20 A.M. on June 20, and was inside the perimeter within two hours. After breaking through, Rommel ordered

Figure 10.4
Rommel's Plan of Attack, Tobruk, June 20, 1942

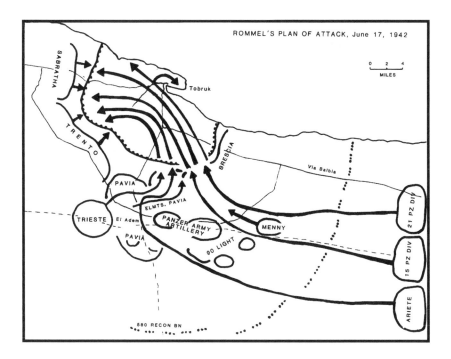

99

the 15th Panzer Division to turn west and dispose of the remaining British reserves. He gave Bismarck and the 21st Panzer Division the honor of capturing the town. Bismarck personally directed the attack from the sidecar of a motorcycle, riding right next to his panzers and giving orders constantly. Before nightfall, Tobruk was in German hands. The garrison surrendered the next day.

Rommel invaded Egypt with hardly a pause. When he crossed the Egyptian border on June 23, his two German panzer divisions could muster only 44 tanks between them. He nevertheless defeated the British 8th Army again at Mersa Matruh in a two-day battle on June 26–27. The next day, Bismarck pursued rapidly to the east, intercepted some British columns near Fuka, and took 1,600 more prisoners. He was, however, stopped near El Alamein—60 miles from Alexandria—on June 30.

From June 30 until July 27, Panzer Army Afrika and the British 8th Army fought the indecisive First Battle of El Alamein. Casualties were heavy on both sides, and, although the British suffered heavier losses, they could afford them; Rommel could not. He had to do something to break the stalemate.

During the month of August, Rommel's new opponent, General Sir Bernard Law Montgomery, built up his strength, while the Desert Fox did the same. Malta, however, had become active again, and the supply imbalance gave the British a major advantage, while Churchill flooded the desert with reinforcements and the Royal Air Force secured aerial superiority all across the front. Rommel knew that he must attack soon, or the odds would tilt irrevocably against him.

In the Battle of Alam Halfa Ridge, which began on August 30, 1942, the Afrika Korps attacked with 259 worn-out tanks. The British had more than 700—a clear 2.7 to 1 superiority. To make matters much worse, the Afrika Korps would have to breach several major minefields. Rommel gave the task of spearheading the attack to his best divisional commander—Georg von Bismarck.

Shortly after midnight on August 31, at the head of his division, Bismarck penetrated the first major minefield. Significantly, he directed this breakthrough from inside a command tank—not a motorcycle sidecar. Just as he cleared the minefield, the vehicle erupted. Did it hit a mine or was it struck by a round from a British tank or antitank gun? Sources differ, and we will never know for sure. One thing is certain, however: one of the best panzer division commanders ever was incinerated. He was temporarily replaced by Colonel Baron Kurt von Liebenstein.[6]

Georg von Bismarck did not look like a brilliant panzer commander and certainly was not an outstanding physical specimen. He was short, thin, small, and balding, and wore thick horn-rimmed glasses, which were among the ugliest spectacles anyone has ever seen. On the battlefield, however, he was quick, decisive, and almost always right. He never committed a major blunder, had an incredible sense of timing, and almost always smashed the units that opposed him, usually with a single blow. He certainly knew how to command a panzer division. Erwin Rommel understood this, which is why he arranged for Bismarck's transfer to Africa. During the critical battles of 1942, Rommel and General Nehring, the commander of the Afrika Korps, called on him repeatedly, and he never let them down. In addition, it was extremely rare for either of these generals to accompany the 21st Panzer Division. With Bismarck in command, it needed no further supervision. After General von Vaerst was wounded during the first day of the Battle of the Gazala Line, both Rommel and Nehring habitually traveled with the 15th Panzer Division.

Bismarck's death deprived Rommel of his best divisional commander. They recognized this, even at Fuehrer Headquarters. On November 16, 1942, they honored Georg von Bismarck with a posthumous promotion to lieutenant general, to date from August 1.

CHAPTER XI

FRIEDRICH FUERST: THE SECOND IN COMMAND

Friedrich Fuerst was a veteran infantry officer who served as Rommel's second in command in France, 1940.

A Bavarian, he was born in Munich on May 25, 1889. He entered the army as a Fahnenjunker on July 19, 1909, became a Faehnrich on March 7, 1910, and was commissioned Leutnant in the 10th Bavarian Infantry Regiment on October 26, 1911. He was the adjutant of the II Battalion of the 10th Bavarian Reserve Infantry when World War I broke out.[1]

Fuerst served with his unit on the Western Front throughout the war. He was severely wounded on November 5, 1914, and did not return to duty until January, when he was given command of his first company. Three months later, on April 4, 1915, he was transferred to the regimental staff as an orderly officer. In July, he served two weeks as acting commander of the regiment's engineer company, and then in rapid succession served as deputy adjutant of the regiment (July 19–August 8), deputy commander of the II Battalion (August), and deputy commander of the III Battalion (September–October). He was promoted to 1st lieutenant on July 9, 1915. Fuerst took a five-week officers' advanced training course at St. Thomas in October and November 1915. His records for 1916 are missing, but apparently he took an abbreviated General Staff course and then returned to his regiment. On January 10, 1917, he was named adjutant of the 10th Bavarian. He held this post until June 10, 1918, when he was critically wounded. He spent months in the hospital and did not return to active duty until after the armistice.

After six months of medical treatment and wounded leave, Friedrich Fuerst rejoined the replacement battalion of the 10th Bavarian Reserve on December 20, 1918. In early 1919, he became adjutant to *Bezirkskommando* Straubing. He was promoted to captain on August 19.

Fuerst was accepted into the Reichswehr in 1919. After briefly serving on the staff of the II Battalion of the 48th Infantry Regiment, he was named commander of a company in the training battalion of the 24th Reichswehr Infantry Brigade at Grafenwoehr. After a year in his post, he briefly commanded a company in the 48th Infantry Regiment (October 1920), before becoming regimental adjutant on October 13, 1920. On New Year's Day 1921, he became adjutant of the 20th Infantry. From October 1, 1923, to February 1, 1928, he served as a company commander in the 20th Infantry Regiment. He spent the next two years on the staff of the 20th Infantry. Finally assigned to the staff of the Bavarian 7th Infantry Division at Munich in 1930, he was promoted to major on February 1, 1931, after 12 years as a captain. After Hitler assumed power on January 20, 1933, Fuerst rose rapidly in rank, becoming a lieutenant colonel (July 1, 1934), a colonel (October 1, 1936), a major general (October 1, 1940), and a lieutenant general (October 1, 1942). During the process, he commanded the II/21st Infantry Regiment at Nuremberg (1933–37), the 103rd Infantry Regiment (1937–38), and the 6th Cavalry Rifle (later Rifle) Regiment (1938–39), which he led in the Polish campaign. He was named commander of the 7th Rifle Brigade on October 19, 1939, just after the 2nd Light Division returned from Poland.

Fuerst did a good job commanding the brigade during the French campaign. He was promoted to major general on October 1, 1940, and was given command of the 14th Infantry Division six days later.

The 14th had fought well in Poland, Belgium, and France, and had already been selected for upgrading to a motorized division. In the fall of 1940, it returned to its main base at Leipzig (as well as to its satellite bases of Naumburg and Leisnig). General Fuerst supervised the reorganization of the unit from a three regiment "marching" infantry division into a two regiment motorized unit. (He lost the 101st Infantry Regiment but was allowed to keep the I Battalion of the 101st and convert it into the 54th Motorcycle Battalion.) He also prepared his division for Operation Barbarossa.

The 14th Motorized took part in the invasion from the beginning. Initially, it fought in the huge battles of encirclement at Bialystok, Minsk, and Smolensk. Fuerst's superiors, however, were not satisfied with his performance in these operations. It is not clear whether he was sacked by Hermann Hoth, the commander of the 3rd Panzer Army, or by General of Panzer Troops Adolf Kuntzen, the commander of the LVII Panzer Corps; in any case, Friedrich Fuerst was relieved of his command on August 15, 1941.[2]

General Fuerst's career was damaged, but not completely ruined, by his perceived failure with the 14th Motorized. After he had been unemployed for two months, a vacancy opened as commander of the 34th Infantry Division, which was part of Colonel General Baron Maximilian von Weichs's 2nd Army.[3] Apparently, his fellow Bavarian asked that he be given the post. Although it was a definite demotion from his previous position, Fuerst led the 34th in the Battle of Gomel, in the advance on Moscow, and against Stalin's massive winter offensive of 1941–42. Facing almost overwhelming forces, Fuerst lost so many men that three of his nine infantry battalions had to be disbanded, but he held his unit together and finally stabilized his position near Juchnov. The 34th Infantry held this line more or less intact until 1943.

In the fall of 1942, General Fuerst was recalled to Germany and then sent to Arnhem in the Netherlands, where he assumed command of the 171st Reserve Division on September 20, 1942. He received his promotion to lieutenant general on October 1. This promotion was late and was to be his last, but most commanders who are relieved of their commands never receive another chance. Fuerst had done well and had made a good professional "comeback."

After engaging in training for six months, the 171st Reserve was sent to the south, where it prepared a section of the Belgian coast for the Allied invasion in March 1943. It established its headquarters in Ostend and remained there until January 5, 1944, when it was absorbed by the 48th Infantry Division. Fuerst, however, was only unemployed long enough to take a six-week leave. He assumed command of the 442nd Special Purposes Division (*Division z.b.V. 442*) in Russia on February 20, 1944.[4]

The 442nd was, in essence, a security and special administration division, composed of men from the older age-groups. It was by no means a first-rate combat unit. It was responsible for keeping installations running and guarding the lines of communications in the rear of Army Group Center, which was struck by a massive Soviet offensive on June 22, 1944. During this offensive, which was dubbed Operation Bagration, Germany lost more than 300,000 men, 4th and 9th Armies were virtually annihilated, and 3rd Panzer Army was crushed. Although they were hardly a match for the Russians, Fuerst's troops were used as replacements for decimated combat units. The division was finally dissolved on July 26.[5]

Following the defeat of Army Group Center, Friedrich Fuerst was sent to the Protectorate (formerly Czechoslovakia) in September, where he briefly engaged in helping organize and train Infantry Division Moravia. Then he returned to Germany, where he commanded POW camps in Wehrkreis IX (Hesse) and later XI (Brunswick, Anhalt, and most of Hanover). He surrendered to the Western Allies on May 9, 1945.

General Fuerst remained a prisoner of war until November 27, 1947, when he was released. No war crime charges were ever filed against him. He retired to Ruhpolding and died on April 10, 1956. Although commanding a motorized division proved too much for him, he was a good marching infantry commander and a competent administrator.

CHAPTER XII

FRIEDRICH-CARL VON STEINKELLER: THE MOTORCYCLE COMMANDER

Friedrich-Carl von Steinkeller, the motorcycle battalion commander of the 7th Panzer Division, was born in Deutsch Krone, in extreme eastern Germany, on March 28, 1896. He entered the Imperial Army as a Fahnenjunker in August 1914, when World War I broke out. He was commissioned second lieutenant in the 3rd Ulan Regiment, a cavalry unit, in 1915. Initially, he served on the Russian Front. After the Soviets surrendered, however, Steinkeller's regiment gave up its horses and was transferred to the Western Front, where it formed part of the 6th Cavalry Division (Dismounted). For all practical purposes, it was an infantry unit. It fought in the Alsace (April–June 1918), at Ypres (July–August), at Cambrai (August–September), and at Ypres again (October–November). Steinkeller was not selected for the Reichswehr and was discharged from the service in 1919, but he returned to active duty on July 1, 1934, as a *Rittmeister* (captain of cavalry).

Steinkeller transferred to the panzer branch in 1938 when he became adjutant of Hermann Hoth's XV Motorized (later Panzer) Corps. He was a major when World War II broke out. After the successful invasion of Poland, Steinkeller was given command of the 7th Motorcycle Battalion of the 2nd Light (soon to be 7th Panzer) Division on October 17, 1939.

Steinkeller commanded the motorcycle battalion in Belgium, France, and Russia, where it took heavy casualties in the drives on Leningrad and Moscow and in the battles of the Rzhev salient. He was promoted to lieutenant colonel on September 1, 1941, and assumed command of the 7th Rifle Regiment of the Ghost Division on May 1, 1942.[1]

Shortly after Colonel Steinkeller assumed command of the 7th, it was shipped back to France, where it was rebuilt and redesignated 7th Panzer Grenadier Regiment. In November 1942, it took part in the occupation of Vichy France, and then was hurriedly sent to the Eastern Front after the fall of Stalingrad. Steinkeller led his regiment with considerable success in the Donetz battles in the winter and spring of 1943. He was promoted to colonel on April 1, 1943, and in May took part in the heavy fighting around Kharkov. He also fought in the subsequent major battles of Belgorod, Kiev, and Zhitomir. By this time, OKH was convinced that Steinkeller was general officer material. He was recalled to Germany in January 1944, where he underwent a two-week Division Commanders' Course. After an extended leave, he returned to Russia and assumed command of the 60th Panzer Grenadier Division "Feldherrnhalle" (or FHH), which had recently transferred from Italy to the Eastern Front.[2]

The 60th fought on the northern sector of the Eastern Front in the spring of 1944, successfully covering Army Group North's retreat from Leningrad. It performed very well, despite a lack of training. With their confidence in him justified, the High Command promoted Friedrich-Carl von Steinkeller to major general on June 1, 1944. Later that month, however, FHH was rushed to the aid of Army Group Center, which had been crushed by Stalin's summer offensive, Operation Bagration. On the order of Fuehrer Headquarters and Army Group Center, the FHH Panzer Grenadier Division was committed too far forward and too quickly. It was unable to prevent a disaster of mammoth proportions and was itself soon cut off and surrounded, along with most of the 4th Army, which lost 130,000 of its 165,000 men. General Steinkeller tried to break out, but the situation was hopeless. He surrendered the remnants of his division on July 8, 1944.

Friedrich von Steinkeller spent the next 11 years in Soviet prisons. Finally released on October 9, 1955, he retired to Hanover. He died on October 19, 1981, at the age of 85.

CHAPTER XIII
HANS JOACHIM VON KRONHELM: THE HEAVY ARTILLERY COMMANDER

Hans Joachim von Kronhelm was born in Brieg, Silesia, on October 23, 1896.[1] Called "Joachim," he joined the Imperial Army on August 5, 1914, at the beginning of World War I and served in Field Artillery Regiment von Scharnhorst. He received a commission during the war but left the service in 1919. During the Weimar Republic era, he went to school and became a mechanical engineer. In 1934, he rejoined the army and the following year commanded a battery of the 47th Artillery Regiment in Koenigsberg. His son Eberhard von Kronheim was born on February 2, 1936.

Captain von Kronhelm was transferred to Neisse, Upper Silesia, at the end of 1936. He was given command of the II Battalion, 45th Motorized Artillery Regiment (II/45th Motorized Artillery), at Wetzlar in 1938. This unit was attached to the 7th Panzer Division at the end of the French campaign.

The II/45th was a three-battery heavy motorized GHQ artillery battalion without a regimental headquarters (i.e., no Staff, 45th Motorized Artillery Regiment existed).[2] It was formally absorbed by the 7th Panzer Division on February 4, 1941, when it became the III/78th Motorized Artillery Regiment.

Major von Kronhelm commanded the III Battalion in the Russian campaign of 1941–42, fighting at Vilna, in the huge battle of encirclement at Smolensk, at Vyasma, at Klim, and in the final thrusts on Moscow. He was promoted to lieutenant colonel by early 1942.

Kronhelm and his battalion were part of Model's 9th Army in the early battles of the Rzhev salient (January–May 1942), after which it was sent to France to rest and refit. Colonel von Kronhelm, however, was recalled to the Russian Front and ordered to report to 2nd Army Headquarters in the fall of 1942.

At that time, the 27th Panzer Division was being formed in southern Russia from Group Michalek of the 22nd Panzer Division. It was organized in the Voronezh sector under the general supervision of Headquarters, 2nd Army. It is a good example of how German divisions were sometimes created in the fourth year of the war. It included the 127th Panzer Battalion (formerly the III/204th Panzer Regiment) and the two-battalion 140th Panzer Grenadier Regiment, all from the 22nd Panzer Division; the Staff, I, and II Battalions of the 127th Panzer Artillery Regiment, which all came from the 677th Special Purposes Artillery Regiment (z.b.V.), a 2nd Army GHQ unit; the 127th (formerly 560th) Tank Destroyer Battalion, another GHQ unit; and the 127th (formerly the 260th) Engineer Battalion from the 260th Infantry Division. The 27th Panzer Division was also given the I/140th Panzer Artillery Regiment (from the 22nd Panzer Division), the I/51st Artillery Regiment (another army GHQ unit), and the newly created 27th Panzer Reconnaissance and 127th Panzer Signal Battalions. Colonel von Kronhelm was selected to be the commander the 127th Panzer Artillery Regiment. His title was more impressive than his command, however; his regiment had the strength of a battalion, and the entire division had a strength of slightly less than 3,000 men.[3] In the spring of 1940, most German panzer divisions had six times that number. It was, in fact, a *kampfgruppe*: a division with the strength of a regiment.

Initially, Colonel Helmut Michalik commanded the division, which was activated on October 1, 1942. He was soon replaced, however, by Major General Hans Troeger.[4]

The new division took part in the clearing of the Don region of Soviet forces and in the conquest of the Donetz. During the retreat from Stalingrad, however, it was broken up and scattered over the whole southern sector of the Eastern Front. Some parts were attached to the Italian 8th Army, while other elements fought at Voronezh and Voroshilovgrad under German command. Elements of the Kampfgruppe 27th Panzer Division took part in the retreat across the Donetz and in the fighting south of Kharkov, suffering heavy casualties in the process. At one point, the division had been broken up into seven battle groups. Kronhelm fought in several of these battles and was promoted to colonel on February 1, 1943.

The decision to disband the division was made after the Soviet Winter Offensive of 1942–43 had been stopped. Its commander, General Troeger, left for Germany, where he took a brief leave before assuming command of the School for Panzer Troops. Command devolved on Colonel von Kronhelm, who had very little to command. As of February

8, 1943, the division had a strength of 1,590 men and 11 tanks under its direct command, although another 20 of its tanks were on detached duty under Headquarters, 2nd Army.

Most of the equipment and survivors of the 27th Panzer Division were absorbed by the 7th Panzer Division. The 127th Panzer and the 127th Panzer Signal Battalions were sent to France, where they were absorbed by the 24th Panzer Division.[5] The 127th Panzer Engineer Battalion became the 127th Motorized Engineer Battalion and became a GHQ unit under III Panzer Corps and later 4th Panzer Army.

The details of the last year of Colonel von Kronhelm's military career are sketchy. He was assigned to the staff of the General of Artillery at OKH in March 1944. Later that year, he reportedly served as acting commander of the depleted 313th Higher Artillery Command (Harko 313) on the central sector of the Russian Front. Sometime thereafter, he was named commander of Arko 500 (the 500th Artillery Command), which was attached to the elite Grossdeutschland Panzer Corps, which fought in Poland, East Prussia, and Pomerania (1944–45). Some sources state that he was promoted to major general near the end of the war but, according to his son, was still a colonel when the war ended. This is a little strange, because he held positions normally reserved for general officers from early 1943 on. Apparently, he ran afoul of the Nazis or of someone in the powerful HPA, but this conclusion cannot be confirmed.

Colonel von Kronhelm managed to evade Allied captivity at the end of the war. A few months after the Reich surrendered, he turned up at Wetzlar and started working for the U.S. Army, in the same barracks he commanded in 1939. His son, meanwhile, emigrated to Sweden, where he still resides. While on a visit there, the former colonel died in Oxeloesund, Sweden, on June 3, 1971. He was 75 years of age.

CHAPTER **XIV**

EDUARD CRASEMANN: THE WAR CRIMINAL

Eduard Crasemann was born in Hamburg on March 5, 1891. He entered the service as a Fahnenjunker in the 46th Field Artillery Regiment on February 11, 1910, and received his commission on August 18, 1911. He was a battery commander when the war broke out.

The 46th Artillery was part of the 20th Infantry Division from Hanover and Brunswick. It crossed into Belgium on August 11, 1914, and, as part of the 2nd Army, fought at Charleroi, Guise, and St. Quentin. It also took part in the Battle of the Marne and the subsequent retreat to Rheims. It engaged in trench warfare on the Western Front until March 1915, when it was sent to the Eastern Front. Crasemann took part in the heavy fighting in Galacia, where his division suffered heavy casualties; meanwhile, he became adjutant of the II Battalion on November 11, 1914, regimental adjutant of the 46th Artillery on February 25, 1915, and was promoted to first lieutenant on August 18, 1915. Crasemann thus became a regimental adjutant while he was still a second lieutenant—a very high compliment indeed in the Imperial Army.

After fighting in the east (present-day Poland and Ukraine), Crasemann and his regiment were sent back to France, where they fought in the battles in Champagne in October. From November 1915 to June 1916, the division held a sector of the trench line north of the Aisne, and the 46th engaged in a great deal of firing. In June 1916, the division (along with the entire X Corps) was suddenly pulled out of the line and rushed to the Eastern Front, where the Russians were attacking. The entire move from France to Kovel took only four days. The Czar's offensive was brought to a bloody halt in short order. Casualties in the 20th Division were not light, however, and the division was pulled out of the line and rebuilt in September and October.[1]

In November 1916, Crasemann's regiment was sent to Camp Simonne, France, near Namur, where it underwent extensive training, mainly for the benefit of the many young recruits it had absorbed in the fall. At the end of December 1916 it took over a sector of the trenches near Moulin sous Touvent, Chevillecourt, where it remained until the end of January. Then, in anticipation of a new French offensive, it was transferred to Alsace. Here, it took part in the Battle of Chemin des Dames, a German defensive victory that cost both sides heavily. At one point during the offensive, Lieutenant Crasemann took charge of a battery and led it for a month, until a suitable replacement arrived.

Finally pulled out of the line, the 20th Division recuperated in the Champagne district for a few weeks, after which it was loaded back on trains and sent to the Russian Front in July. On its third trip to the east, the 20th fought in Galacia and Courland, after which it was again returned to France in September. It was sent into action in the Arras sector later that month. Crasemann, meanwhile, was given command of a company in the 77th Infantry Regiment, a post that he held for two months, fighting at Havrincourt (southwest of Cambrai), where his unit suffered heavy losses. Some of the division's infantry units lost 70 percent of their strength in these battles. Eduard Crasemann survived his introduction to infantry command, however, and returned to his parent unit, the 46th Artillery, on November 20, 1917, as regimental adjutant.

Crasemann had only been "back home" four days when his career took a giant leap forward: he was appointed directly to the General Staff of the Army as a probationary member and packed off to the headquarters of the Marine Corps, a naval infantry command fighting near the North Sea coast of Belgium. He remained with this unit until May 7, when he was appointed Ib (chief logistical officer) of the East Prussian 35th Infantry Division, which was also fighting in Flanders. The 35th had suffered a considerable number of casualties and its infantry companies were down to 50 men. Eduard Crasemann, meanwhile, was promoted to captain on August 18, 1918.

Crasemann's new unit received a considerable number of replacements and fought well in Flanders and Artois sectors until the armistice on November 11, 1918. It then returned to Germany and disbanded. Crasemann rejoined his old unit, the 46th Artillery, and was given command of a battery on December 11, 1918. The next day, he was named commander of the I Battalion. He held this post until April 7, 1919. On or about this date he received word that, despite a solid record of achievement, his application to be one of the 4,000 officers in General von Seeckt's new Reichsheer had been rejected. He was discharged from the service on April 30, 1919.

Edmund Crasemann spent the Weimar years in the private sector of the economy. When Hitler began his military buildup, Crasemann was in no hurry to return to active duty. When he did return (as a supplemental officer) on August 1, 1936, he was immediately assigned to the very important operations branch (*1. Abteilung* or Branch 1) of the High Command of the Army—a prime assignment for any General Staff officer.[2] A year later, on October 12, 1937, he was assigned to Branch 10, the maneuvers and operational planning branch.[3] He was promoted to major on June 1, 1936.

Crasemann returned to troop duty in November 1938 when he was attached to the II Battalion, 20th Artillery Regiment, a motorized unit that was an integral part of the 20th Motorized Infantry Division and that was stationed in his home town of Hamburg. After almost six months on the battalion staff, he was given command of a battery in the 73rd (Motorized) Artillery Regiment, which was part of the 1st Panzer Division and based at Weimar. The position was one grade below his rank, but it gave Eduard Crasemann a chance to "catch up" on the developments in his field and learn how to command motorized and self-propelled artillery in support of panzer operations. In September 1939, his battery took part in the Polish campaign as part of the armored spearhead, fighting in the decisive battle of Radom and in the subsequent drive on Warsaw. It then returned to Germany and was redeployed around Hunsrueck in the Eifel (the German Ardennes).

Although he had served almost a year in a post below his grade in rank, Major Crasemann had performed well and learned what he needed to know. On February 1, 1940, he was given command of the II Battalion of the 78th Motorized Artillery Regiment of the 7th Panzer Division—a major promotion. He arrived at about the same time as the new division commander, Erwin Rommel.

Crasemann did well in the French campaign and performed to Rommel's complete satisfaction. As a result, he was promoted to lieutenant colonel on August 1, 1940. He spent the next six months on occupation duty near Bordeaux. In February 1941, Erwin Rommel was given command of the Afrika Korps, which include the 5th Light (later 21st Panzer) and 15th Panzer Divisions. The 5th Light was transported to Libya in February and March, while the 15th Panzer did not begin to arrive until late March and was not fully disembarked until May. While this move was still taking place, Rommel requested that Eduard Crasemann be assigned to his new command. His request was approved, and Crasemann was named commander of the 33rd Motorized (later Panzer) Artillery Regiment on May 10, 1941. His new command was part of Major General Karl von Esebeck's 15th Panzer Division.[4]

As commander of the 33th Motorized Artillery, Crasemann supported the 15th Panzer Division in every major battle in the North African theater. These included the unsuccessful attacks on Tobruk in May 1941; the defeat of two British attempts to relieve the fortress that summer (Operations Brevity and Battleaxe), and in Operation Crusader (called "the Winter Battle" by the Germans), which lasted from November 18 to December 7, 1941, and ended with the rescue of the Tobruk garrison. Crasemann fought well in all of these battles and continued to do so during the retreat from Tobruk and Rommel's Second Cyrenaican campaign, during which the Germans captured Benghazi and the British 8th Army retreated to the Gazala Line. Crasemann, meanwhile, was promoted to full colonel on February 1, 1942, and decorated with the coveted Knight's Cross on December 26, 1941.

From February 6 to May 25, 1942, a lull descended on the North African Front as both sides prepared for the next battle. During this phase, the British completed construction of the Gazala Line—a huge series of minefields that extended 40 miles from the Mediterranean Sea to Bir Hacheim. It consisted of more than a million mines; in fact, General F. W. von Mellenthin later wrote that it was mined "on a scale never yet seen in war."[5] The line also included several isolated strongpoints, called "boxes," each garrisoned by a reinforced brigade. Behind the line lay the British strategic reserves: the 1st and 7th Armoured Divisions, the 1st and 32nd Army Tank Brigades, and the 29th Indian Motor Brigade. All totaled, the British outnumbered the Germans two to one in men and 849 to 332 in tanks. The Italians contributed another 228 tanks, but they were so inferior that they were nearly useless. Rommel nevertheless began his major offensive on May 26. He managed to get behind the Gazala Line, but then faced a series of fierce (although badly coordinated) counterattacks. The strike units of Panzer Army Afrika were soon fighting for their lives.

The leadership of the 15th Panzer Division, meanwhile, had changed rapidly. The original division commander in North Africa was Heinrich von Prittwitz und Gaffron, who was killed by an antitank shell near Tobruk on April 10, 1941. He was succeeded by Karl von Esebeck. On May 15, 1941, Esebeck caught a shell splinter at Tobruk and was seriously wounded. He was temporarily replaced by Maximilian von Herff, the senior regimental commander. Esebeck's permanent replacement was Major General Walter Neumann-Silkow, who arrived on May 26. He, in turn, was mortally wounded on December 7, 1941, and died on December 9. Colonel Erwin Menny succeeded Neumann-Silkow for three days until his permanent replacement, Major General Gustav von Vaerst, arrived. Vaerst, in turn, was seriously wounded on May 27, 1942, just as the Gazala offensive entered a critical phase. He was replaced by Edmund Crasemann.

When Crasemann assumed command, the 15th Panzer Division (along with the rest of the Afrika Korps, the 90th Light Division, the Italian Ariete Armored Division, and several Italian and GHQ units) was surrounded in "the Cauldron," facing east, with the Gazala Line to their backs. To make matters worse, the division was virtually out of gas. Crasemann dug in along the Maabus er Rigel Ridge and awaited a British attack that did not come until May 29. (The British obviously had no idea how vulnerable the 15th Panzer was on May 27.) By the time the British did attack, Rommel had gotten a supply column through the minefields and Crasemann had been able to partially refuel his panzers. He had about 35 tanks posted along a small ridge south of his main position when the British 2nd Armoured Brigade struck on the morning of the 29th.

Crasemann lured the British into a trap. As the British assumed, many of the panzers on Crasemann's front line were inoperable derelicts; behind the ridge, however, he had placed several powerful 88mm antitank guns, none of which were derelicts. The 9th Queen's Lancers, which spearheaded the charge, lost about 25 of its 45 tanks before it could extricate itself.

That afternoon, the British tried again. Their artillery covered the area with smoke, so that the British tanks could close with and destroy the 88mm guns and the operational German panzers. British coordination, however, was poor, and the artillery bombardment struck 10 minutes ahead of the tanks. By the time they arrived, the smoke screen had dissipated, and the Germans again blasted the British. By the time the fighting was over, the 9th Queen's Lancers had lost 10 more tanks and the 10th Hussars was down to three "runners."

While Crasemann was checking the British to the east, Rommel attacked through the west, destroyed the British 150th Infantry Brigade and 44th RTR, and pierced the Gazala Line. By June 1, supplies were flowing through unimpeded. With the 15th Panzer thus resupplied, Rommel ordered Crasemann to the south, where his division covered the southern face of the Cauldron. The northern face was held by Bismarck's 21st Panzer Division, while the Ariete Armored Division (backed by the Panzer Army Artillery) held the center. After the British launched several fruitless attacks on the Axis center on June 5, Bismarck and Crasemann launched a skillful double envelopment and trapped the 9th and 10th Indian Brigades, the Support Group of the British 22nd Armoured Brigade (which included the 107th Regiment, Royal Horse Artillery), and the 4th, 28th, and 157th Field Regiments, Royal Artillery. They were then crushed by the 21st Panzer and Ariete Divisions—well supported by the 104th Artillery Command—while Crasemann's division blocked any Allied relief effort from the east. The British lost 3,100 men captured, as well as 115 tanks and armored cars, 96 guns, and 37 antitank guns. Apparently, General of Panzer Troops Walter Nehring (the commander of the Afrika Korps and the man in charge of wiping out the pocket) did not bother to count the dead. Now Panzer Army Afrika took aim at Tobruk.

It should be noted here that Nehring habitually traveled with the 15th Panzer Division, and often Rommel did so as well. This is because the commander of the Afrika Korps' other division, the 21st Panzer, was General Georg von Bismarck, one of the best panzer division commanders in the German Army. Colonel Crasemann was also highly thought of, but not nearly as much so as von Bismarck; and he definitely lacked experience in divisional command. Nehring, for example, was with Crasemann all day on June 12, when the Afrika Korps and the Italian Trieste Motorized Division crushed the British 2nd and 4th Armoured Brigades south of Knightsbridge. Crasemann nevertheless performed well, and the 15th Panzer Division smashed the 4th Armoured Brigade. By 4 P.M., it was pursuing the survivors across the desert toward Tobruk. Agar-Hamilton later wrote, "The desert was strewn with the wrecks of Grants, Crusaders and Stuarts...."[6] Correlli Barnett called this battle the greatest defeat in the history of British armor.[7] By morning, the 4th Armoured had only 15 tanks left.

After the decisive victory of Knightsbridge, the British 8th Army hastily evacuated what was left of the Gazala Line. Crasemann led the 15th Panzer Division northward toward the Coastal Road, in a vain attempt to cut off the 1st South African Division and the 201st Guards Brigades before they could escape to the west. The men had been fighting for three weeks, almost without letup, and troop exhaustion had set in. The Afrika Korps was moving in a most unusually slow and sluggish manner. The 33rd Panzer Artillery did manage to shell the 2nd and 3rd South African Brigade Groups as they retreated along the Coastal Road, but the panzers and panzer grenadiers were not able to negotiate the steep coastal escarpment for some hours. By the time the III/115th Panzer Grenadier Regiment cut the road, most of the British forces had escaped. Crasemann only succeeded in capturing about 200 men from the rearguard, along with 13 guns. The Allies, however, had been forced to abandon a huge cache of supplies.

Crasemann's next major battle was the assault on Tobruk. Along with Bismarck's division, the 15th Panzer broke into the fortress shortly after dawn on June 20. Allied resistance crumbled quickly and, by June 22, it was all over. The garrison of 35,000 men had surrendered.

Following Tobruk, Panzer Army Afrika invaded Egypt. Crasemann's division fought in the indecisive victory at Mersa Matruh (where it garnered no particular laurels) and in the early stages of the 1st Battle of El Alamein (where it turned back several British attacks). On July 25, 1942, Vaerst's permanent replacement, Major General Heinz von Randow, arrived, and Crasemann returned to the command of the 33rd Panzer Artillery Regiment.[8]

Crasemann led the 33rd Panzer Artillery at Alma Halfa Ridge and during the 2nd Battle of El Alamein, during which it suffered heavy casualties. By the time the battle was over, the regiment had only seven guns left. Crasemann continued to lead the 33rd in the retreat from Egypt, in the evacuation of Tobruk, in the withdrawal across Cyrenaica, and into Tripolitania. Then, on January 17, 1943, he was sent back to Europe and was placed in Fuehrer Reserve. Why he was sent back to Germany is not made clear by the records, but the strenuous battles and the harsh desert climate was no doubt difficult on the health of a man now in his 50s. In any case, he did not return to active duty until April 20, 1943, when he assumed command of the 116th Panzer Artillery Regiment on the Eastern Front.

The 116th Panzer Artillery was part of Major General Ernst Faeckenstedt's 5th Panzer Division—one of the best units in the Wehrmacht. It was currently located near Orel, under the command of Army Group Center. It was not involved in the Battle of Kursk to the south (which began on July 5), but on July 12 the Soviets launched a major counteroffensive against Orel, pitting their Western and Bryansk Fronts (army groups) against elements of the German 9th and 2nd Panzer Armies, both under the command of Colonel General Walter Model. These attacks were a contributing factor in Hitler's decision to cancel the Kursk offensive the next day. For the next month, the Germans conducted a fighting withdrawal to the west. They halted in the Hagen Line in mid-August.

The "powers that be" were satisfied with Crasemann's performance in these battles and, on September 1, 1943, named him commander of the 143rd Artillery Command (Arko 143), which was part of General of Panzer Troops Walter Nehring's XXIV Panzer Corps. This represented a significant promotion for the cigar-smoking Hamburger colonel. Crasemann had previously worked for the general, who had commanded the Afrika Korps in Libya and Egypt. Now the pair fought together on the Mius, in the retreat to the Dnieper, in the Battles of Kiev and Zhitomir, and at Winniza, Luzh, and Kamenez-Podolsk.[9]

Eduard Crasemann did an excellent job in Russia. On April 5, 1944, he gave up command of Arko 143 and went on leave. He had, however, at last been earmarked to become a general. Three weeks later, from May 1 to June 5, he attended the Division Commanders' Course at Hirschberg, Silesia, which was now the home of the War Academy. Then he was sent to Italy, where he replaced Lieutenant General Smilo von Luettwitz as commander of the 26th Panzer Division. He was, however, an acting commander only. On July 18, he handed command over to Major General Dr. rer. Dr. jur. Hans Boelsen, but stayed on as deputy commander. On August 27, Boelsen assumed command of the 18th Panzer Grenadier Division, and Crasemann again took command of the 26th Panzer. This time, it was a permanent appointment.[10]

Crasemann led his division in the heavy defensive fighting against the British 8th Army as it pushed its way up the Adriatic coast. In late

August, it fought in the Battle of Coriano Ridge, west of Rimini, and played a major role in checking the initial British attacks on the Gothic Line. The 8th Army finally stormed the ridge on September 12, so Crasemann conducted a fighting retreat to the Cesena. When this line was breached, the 26th Panzer fought a delaying action to the Savio River. Another delaying action followed, across the Romagna Plain, until the retreat was at last halted in the German winter positions south of Bologna. The division was at last pulled out of the line for a much-needed rest. Crasemann, meanwhile, had been promoted to major general (October 1, 1944), had distinguished himself as a division commander, and had convinced his superiors that he was capable of greater things.

Figure 14.1
The Battle of the Ruhr Pocket, 1945

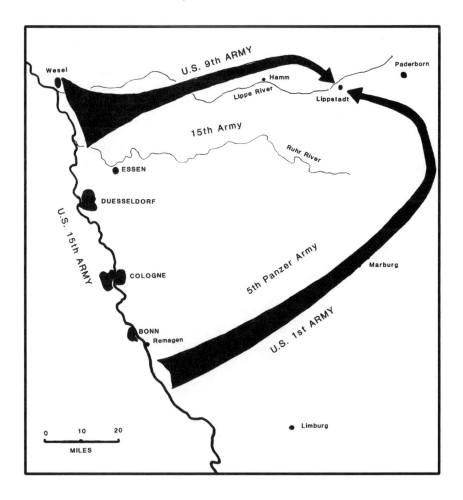

In early 1945, Eduard Crasemann was again recalled to Germany. On January 29, he replaced General of Infantry Guenther Blumentritt as commander of the XII SS Corps. Most of the staff, however, were actually army officers, and Crasemann never held SS rank. He was promoted to lieutenant general on February 25, 1945. The XII SS was on the Western Front, holding a sector along the Roer River, on the northern wing of the 15th Army. Its task was to defend the Rhineland against an expected offensive by Lieutenant General William H. Simpson's U.S. 9th Army. The offensive began on February 23. By early March, the XII SS was forced back across the Rhine. Then, on March 7, the Americans seized the Ludendorff Bridge at Remagen. Almost paralyzed by a lack of fuel and total Allied domination of the air, the Germans were unable to prevent the Anglo-Saxons from encircling Army Group B (the 5th Panzer and 15th Armies) in the Ruhr Industrial Area by April 1, as Figure 14.1 shows. On April 17, Field Marshal Model disbanded the remnants of the army group and committed suicide near Duisburg on April 21. Meanwhile, Crasemann's command had already been destroyed, and he had been captured by the Americans on April 16.

Eduard Crasemann was sent to Special Camp 11 (the "Island Farm" POW camp), along with dozens of other generals and admirals.[11] In the spring of 1947, he was sent to Padua, Italy, where he was tried by a British War Crimes Tribunal for his complicity in the mass execution of 162 Italians (including 26 children) in the Fucecchio Marshes (*Padule di Fucecchio*) near Florence in late August 1944. The 26th Panzer Division had been involved in an antipartisan operation in the marshes at the time. Crasemann's defense—that the atrocity was a reprisal—was rejected by the court, and he was sentenced to 10 years' imprisonment. The commander of the division's reconnaissance battalion, Captain of Cavalry Joseph Strauch, was also convicted.

General Crasemann spent the rest of his life in prison. He died at Werl on April 28, 1950, at the age of 59.

CHAPTER XV

FRIDO VON SENGER UND ETTERLIN: THE SNOBBISH ARISTOCRAT

Frido von Senger und Etterlin was born in the beautiful medieval town of Waldshut, Baden (on the Upper Rhine, within sight of the Alps) on September 4, 1891.[1] His aristocratic ancestors came from Bamberg, between the Black Forest and Lake Constance, where they served as ministers and advisors to the princes and dukes who ran the various states in the region (principally Baden) before Bismarck unified Germany.

Senger grew up in a family of wealth and prestige. His mother was a fervent Roman Catholic, and she helped imbue him with a strong religious faith, which he held throughout his life and which, along with his sense of class and education, formed the bedrock of his character.

With no need to settle down or engage in a profession, and with the means to do what he wished, young Senger devoted the early years of his adulthood working on his higher education. He attended the University of Freiburg, became fluent in English and French and—although his studies seem somewhat unfocused—grew into a sophisticated, cosmopolitan gentleman of impeccable manners. In 1911, Senger entered the 76th (5th Baden) Field Artillery Regiment for a year's compulsory military service. (He had no thoughts of becoming a professional soldier at this point.) As soon as he was discharged, Senger resumed his education, which included two years as a Rhodes Scholar at St. John's College, Oxford. He read history and political economy, became thoroughly familiar with art in its various forms, and generally studied whatever interested him. By 1914, Senger had a world view that was much broader than the average German's.

The outbreak of World War I shattered Senger's idyllic world forever. He spent virtually the entire war with the 76th Field Artillery on the Western Front, although he did serve as adjutant of the XIV Reserve Corps from the summer of 1918 until the end of the conflict in November 1918.

The young second lieutenant's unit was part of the Baden 29th Infantry Division, which fought in Alsace-Lorraine, in the Artois battles (where it suffered heavy casualties), in the Champagne District (1915–16), on the Somme, in the Hindenburg Line, and at Verdun (1917), where it again was decimated. After this battle, the division was never the same. It nevertheless returned to the line in 1918 and fought at Verdun, at Lys, and on the Aisne.[2]

For Senger, two major events occurred in the last year of the war. On November 30, 1917, his younger brother, 2nd Lieutenant Johann-Gustav von Senger und Etterlin, a fighter pilot whom he dearly loved, was shot down and killed. As the tank Battle of Cambrai (the first tank battle in history) raged about him, Frido von Senger and two enlisted men from the 76th Artillery dug in a German mass grave for the body. At times they had to dive for cover in the grave, to avoid British artillery fire. Finally, in the lowest of three layers of bodies, they found Johann. At this point, the enlisted men refused to help carry the corpse through heavy Allied artillery fire. (Senger later admitted that they were right to refuse.) Frido thereupon grabbed his brother's legs and dragged him through the fire to his car and finally propped the lifeless body up next to him.[3]

A much more positive event occurred at Jenlain, France, where Senger met Hilda Margaretha von Kracht, a Bavarian Red Cross nurse whom he called "P." They fell in love and were married on December 2, 1919.

After the war, General Ludwig Maercker, the former commander of the 214th Infantry Division, began recruiting the volunteer *Landesjaeger-korps* (Provincial Light Infantry Corps) in a Franciscan convent near Salzkotten, Westphal, not far from Baden. It was the first Freikorps formation and was the best of them all; in fact, it formed the model for all others. Lieutenant von Senger joined it almost immediately.

Germany had deteriorated to near civil war conditions in late 1918 and early 1919, and the government relied on the Freikorps to suppress Communist insurrections. Along with other Freikorps, the "Maercker Volunteer Rifles" put down rebellions in Berlin, Bremen, Halle, Saxony, Magdeburg, Berlin again, Dachau, Munich, and others. The Maercker Rifles were so efficient that they were incorporated into the regular army en masse as the 16th Reichswehr Brigade. Frido von Senger thus did not have to apply for a position in the 4,000-man army—the appointment fell into his lap. It was a good thing for him, too, because (despite a solid record) he would probably not have survived the incredibly tough Reichsheer selection process. As we have seen, a great many other gifted and capable officers did not.

Horses were one of the loves of von Senger's life. He was delighted when he was able to transfer from the artillery to the cavalry and when he was assigned to the Cavalry School at Hanover in 1920. Later that year, he was posted to the 18th Cavalry Regiment at Stuttgart-Cannstatt and remained there very happily for 13 years. He had no desire to transfer elsewhere or to join the General Staff, or even to advance in rank. He was promoted to *Rittmeister* (captain of cavalry) on May 1, 1924, and he was content with that. He took the mandatory Wehrkreis War Academy entry exam and passed (when 85 percent of his contemporaries did not), but was passed over for General Staff training because he was considered to be too old. Many officers would have been furious or at least would have protested, but not Senger. In his memoirs, *Neither Fear Nor Hope*, he admits to being very happy with the army's decision, because he was delighted to remain at home with his family and his horses.[4] He frankly enjoyed the quiet, unhurried life of a backwater cavalry garrison. His whole attitude was, "If you are happy where you are, why move?" He bought a house near Cannstatt and enjoyed more than a decade of peaceful years. During this time his children, a son and a daughter, were born.[5]

The second idyllic phase of Senger's life ended in 1934. He was promoted to major and, after a brief interlude as adjutant of the cavalry brigade at Hanover, was transferred to Berlin as chief of staff of the Cavalry Inspectorate in the Army High Command.

In 1938, after four years in Berlin, Senger (who had been promoted to lieutenant colonel in 1936) was given command of the 3rd Cavalry Regiment at Goettingen. He was happy to be back with the troops and his horses, and Goettingen remained his family's home until 1948. He was promoted to colonel on March 1, 1939.

Upon mobilization, Senger's headquarters was dissolved and his subordinate units were assigned to infantry divisions, primarily for use as reconnaissance battalions during the invasion of Poland. Senger himself remained at Goettingen. He was unemployed until November 1939, when he was given command of the 22nd Cavalry Regiment. It was part of the 1st Cavalry Division—the only cavalry division the German Army had until 1942, when it was converted into the 24th Panzer Division.

The 22nd Cavalry was posted along the Dutch border in the winter of 1939–40, preparing for the campaign against France. On February 1, 1940, Senger's brigade commander, Baron Wolfgang von Waldenfels, died suddenly, and Senger was promoted to brigade command. He led the 2nd Cavalry Brigade (a two-battalion unit) in the invasion of the

Netherlands (May 10–16, 1940). Then it was sent to Cambrai, reorganized as a motorized brigade, and temporarily redesignated Motorized Brigade von Senger. It took part in the breaking of the Weygand Line, after which it was attached to the 7th Panzer Division. It covered Rommel's left flank in the Rouen operation and in the subsequent pursuit of the defeated French. At one point, the brigade covered 120 miles in 25 hours.

During the pursuit, Senger's adjutant, the son of Major General Kurt Feldt, the 1st Cavalry Division commander, drove his tracked vehicle over a land mine, killing everyone inside. His only brother had been killed in action in Poland the year before. Senger therefore had the bitter duty of writing Feldt and informing him that he had no sons.[6]

The aristocratic and somewhat snobbish von Senger did not like Erwin Rommel and, in fact, looked down on him. He, von Senger, was after all the descendant of a long line of aristocrats; Rommel was a mere commoner and the son and grandson of school teachers. In addition, at this point in his career, Rommel admired Hitler, and Senger had detested the Nazi regime from its beginning. For his part, Rommel apparently had no feelings for von Senger one way or the other. He was just another horse in his stable, another tool to be used in the accomplishment of his military objectives. They were, in fact, completely different people. To Senger, life outside the battlefield was poetry, something to be savored and appreciated; Rommel, on the other hand, did not stop to smell the roses. To him, life was strictly prose.

Senger nevertheless had no choice but to work under the future Desert Fox, although he clearly found that distasteful. Along with the Ghost Division, he took part in the capture of Le Havre and Cherbourg. Reading Senger's memoirs, one gets the impression that Motorized Brigade von Senger beat 7th Panzer Division to Cherbourg, and that Rommel was very upset by this development. In reality, the motorized brigade was *part* of the 7th Panzer Division and was also under Rommel's command. This brings out another point that should be addressed: Senger's memoir, *Neither Fear Nor Hope*, like Guderian's *Panzer Leader* and Rommel's *Papers*, should be handled with care by professional histories and laypeople alike (although not nearly to the extent of *Panzer Leader*). They are both valuable but also, at least to a degree, are self-serving (especially Guderian's). In his book, Senger portrays himself as a military genius who never made a mistake and also as an outspoken opponent of the Fuehrer. It is true that Senger was an outstanding commander; he was just not *that* outstanding. Germany, in fact, had a great many outstanding commanders during World War II, and some of them stand a little taller than Senger, morally and professionally. To Senger's disgust, one of them was named Rommel, but (professionally speaking) there was also Manstein, Hube, Guderian, and Nehring, to name a few. Also, while it is true that he detested Hitler and recognized the evil of the regime long before many of his peers, he did not actively oppose it. It was Rommel, Beck, von Stauffenberg and others who gave their lives in the attempt to rid Germany of Adolf Hitler. Senger had ample opportunity to join the anti-Hitler conspiracy, but he did not. (I do not wish to appear too critical of Senger for this; after all, he did have a family to protect, but then so did most of the others.) Like many people in that era, however, he was more of an opponent to Hitler after the fact than before it.

Immediately after the French campaign, Colonel von Senger was in charge of the administration of the Department of Rennes. From July 1940 to July 1942, he was liaison officer between the Franco-German Armistice Commission at Wiesbaden and Franco-Italian Armistice Commission at Turin. The cosmopolitan Senger was an excellent choice for this post, and he loved Italy, a country with which he was already familiar. He was also an excellent diplomat, and General of Infantry Heinrich von Stuelpnagel, the head of the German Armistice Commission, soon named Senger chief of the liaison staff.[7] Partially as a result, he was promoted to major general on September 1, 1941. But Senger felt somewhat uncomfortable in his rather luxurious post after Germany invaded Russia on June 22, 1941. "I was impatient to be 'in the fray,'" he recalled. "There is something that compels the military man ... into the adventure of war."[8]

In July 1942, he was named commander of the 10th Panzer Grenadier Brigade in Artois, France. Because he had commanded a motorized brigade in the French campaign and had done well, Senger was already earmarked to command a panzer division. His appointment in Artois was therefore regarded by both commander and subordinates alike as transitory, and he had many days with nothing to do. He spent his afternoons hunting and had a thoroughly enjoyable summer.

In early October, the pleasant interlude ended. His wife drove him to Berlin, and he boarded a train at the Zoo Station. "As the train drew out of the station it seemed to me that I was falling into a huge dark chasm," Senger wrote later.[9]

He had indeed. After a visit to the Headquarters of the 2nd Panzer Army at Orel, he assumed command of the Bavarian-Swabian 17th Panzer Division on the Eastern Front.

Senger's new division was a bit of a mess. It had been formed in late 1940 and had fought in the battles of encirclement at Smolensk, Kiev, and Bryansk, among others. With the 2nd Panzer Army (then under Guderian), it had fought in the bitter Battle of Tula (southeast of Moscow) and in the winter battles of 1941–42. It had held a sector near Orel since January 1942. It had started Operation Barbarossa with more than 200 tanks; now it had 30 left. All of its armored cars had been destroyed, and only one or two reconnaissance vehicles were still operational. Between 30 and 40 percent of its trucks were also unserviceable, which meant that one company from each panzer grenadier battalion had to follow on foot as "marching infantry." (They were later temporarily organized as a single marching battalion.) The German Army, however, had neither the time nor the material available to rebuild the 17th Panzer. On November 19, 1942, the Red Army launched a huge offensive northeast and southeast of Stalingrad. By November 23, the 230,000 men of the 6th Army were trapped inside the fortress. Field Marshal Erich von Manstein, the commander-in-chief of newly created Army Group Don, was given the task of rescuing the trapped garrison. Despite its depleted condition, Senger's division was earmarked to take part in the relief operation.

For the counteroffensive, the 17th Panzer redeployed by rail far to the south. It was attached to Lieutenant General Baron Hans-Karl von Esebeck's LVII Panzer Corps of Hoth's 4th Panzer Army. It crossed the Don at Tsymlianskaya and, in cold and muddy conditions, formed up for the drive to Stalingrad, which was 60 miles away.

LVII Panzer included the 6th Panzer Division, the 17th Panzer, and the 23rd Panzer Division, which was in even worse shape than the 17th.

Although one would never know it from reading Senger's memoirs, Major General Erhard Raus's 6th Panzer Division played the primary role in the relief attempt. This was only natural, because it had just returned from being rebuilt in France and had more than 150 tanks when the offensive began. In the end it would lose half of its tanks and be stopped at Bolwassiljewka, 29 miles south of the city. Senger and the 17th Panzer, however, did a fine job under incredibly difficult circumstances—snow, temperatures as low as −10°F, and a sun setting at 3 P.M. The division even managed to cross the Myschkova River, but, by Christmas Day, it had only 180 to 200 riflemen in each of its two panzer grenadier regiments and only 23 serviceable tanks in the panzer regiment. By December 27, the Rumanian forces on Senger's left flank had collapsed and the 17th and 23rd Panzer Divisions were fighting for their lives.[10] Senger and his comrades nevertheless managed to extract their divisions and conducted a difficult retreat behind the Don and then the Donetz. Then, in March 1943, the spring thaw imposed a stalemate on the Eastern Front. During this break, Senger was promoted to lieutenant general on May 1, 1943.

In June 1943, as the German Army prepared to launch Operation Citadel, its final major offensive in the East, Frido von Senger was ordered to report to Fuehrer Headquarters, which was then at the Obersalzberg. Here Field Marshal Wilhelm Keitel, the commander-in-chief of OKW, appointed him German liaison officer to the Italian 6th Army. Senger would spend the rest of the war in the Mediterranean theater of operations—primarily in Italy.

Although he did as well as anyone could have done, because of his subordinate position and the fact that he did not have direct command of troop units, Senger had little influence on the Sicilian campaign. He, for example, correctly opposed the dispersion of the 15th Panzer Grenadier Division (as did General d'Armata Alfredo Guzzoni, the commander of the Italian 6th Army), but Field Marshal Albert Kesselring, the OB South, ordered it broken into combat groups and scattered it anyway. As a result, the Axis lost its only chance of launching an effective counterattack and throwing Patton's U.S. 7th Army back into the sea. This and other issues led to friction between Senger and Kesselring. When General of Panzer Troops Hans Valentin Hube arrived with his Headquarters, XIV Panzer Corps, to take charge of all German forces on the island, Senger's position became superfluous. He was recalled to the mainland on August 8.[11] After a visit to the monastery at Cassino, Senger met with Kesselring in Rome on August 11, where the marshal treated him with considerable respect. Then the former cavalryman was sent on leave to Goettingen.

Obviously, despite the friction between them, the OB South appreciated Senger's performance in Sicily, because in early September he placed the general from Baden in charge of all Wehrmacht and SS forces in Sardinia and Corsica, with orders to evacuate the former and defend the latter. Here he faced an extremely difficult situation. The Allies had complete control of the air and sea, the Italians were preparing to defect and were showing as much of an inclination to fight against the Germans as the Anglo-Saxons, and the French population of Corsica was threatening to rebel against the Italians and the Germans. Senger arrived in Ajaccio with an ad hoc staff on September 7.

In Sardinia, Senger had at his disposal the newly organized 90th Panzer Grenadier Division, which was the descendent of the 90th Light Division that had been destroyed in Tunisia. In Corsica, he had the SS Assault Brigade "Reichsfuehrer-SS" (SS Lieutenant Colonel Karl Gesele), which had only two battalions of infantry but did have an antitank battalion and strong artillery detachments.[12] Also on the island was General Giovanni Magli's Italian VII Corps with four divisions. Magli was not informed of Senger's true missions; the German general's official position was "liaison officer."

The Italian forces were disposed so that they could defend the west coast but not the east, which was the most likely site of an Allied landing. The SS brigade was in a position to defend the southern coast, but the important northeast port of Bastia was weakly held by the Italians. Senger therefore decided to bring the 90th Panzer Grenadier from

Sardinia to Corsica, to establish a link between Bastia and the southern coast. He was only just beginning to carry out this plan on September 8, however, when the government of anti-Nazi Marshal Pietro Badoglio attempted to defect from the Axis. Kesselring had ordered that all Italian forces in Corsica be disarmed if Italy attempted to defect, but Senger realized immediately that this order would be impossible to execute. Fortunately for him, General Magli continued to cooperate with him while the 90th Panzer Grenadiers arrived. Their relationship became more strained, however, as the German forces on the mainland disarmed their former allies. Magli agreed to keep his forces in the center of the island but refused to abandon Bastia, on the grounds that the loss of the port would sever his line of communications to the mainland. By the evening of September 12, Senger had concluded that he would have to resort to force of arms to secure the port.

Meanwhile, in Sardinia, Lieutenant General Carl-Hans Lungershausen, the commander of the 90th Panzer Grenadier, persuaded the island commander and his personal friend, General Basso, to allow his division to leave unmolested.[13] Elements of the 90th, therefore, were able to link up with the Reichsfuehrer-SS Brigade and launch an attack on Bastia during the night of September 13–14.[14] They took the city quickly, along with thousands of Italian prisoners, more than 200 of whom were officers. The rest of the Italian VII Corps in the Bastia area retreated into the mountainous interior.

On September 14, an order arrived from Hitler, instructing Senger to shoot all of his officer prisoners and to forward the names of the murdered victims to Fuehrer Headquarters that same evening. With considerable moral courage, Senger spoke to Kesselring by radio-telephone and refused to obey the order. Kesselring accepted his decision without comment but obviously intervened on Senger's behalf with Fuehrer HQ, for there were no repercussions.

Meanwhile, on September 13, Major General Siegfried Westphal, Kesselring's chief of staff, visited the island and ordered Senger to evacuate all German forces to the mainland. He had 30,000 men, 10,000 of whom were Luftwaffe personnel. Using the good airfield at Ghisonaccia and the much poorer one at Borgo-Bastia, as well as the port of Bastia and the smaller ports of Bonifacio and Porto Vecchio, he could evacuate a theoretical maximum of 3,000 men per day, with most of the heavy equipment leaving via Bastia. It would take several days to complete the preparations for the evacuation.

In the meantime, regular French troops under General Henri Honore Giraud landed near Ajaccio (on the west coast), seized the city, and began preparing to complete the conquest of the island. Soon they totaled 23 battalions of infantry (mainly Moroccan and Senegalese troops), well supported by American tanks and well equipped with mules, provided by the Italian VII Corps. Senger was thus forced to engage the French and simultaneously evacuate his forces, while the Allies—aided by native insurgents—tried to cut off his forces before they could be evacuated.

General von Senger was able to form a perimeter around Bastia and simultaneously delayed the Free French forces by blowing up roads and bridges in the mountainous terrain. Meanwhile, however, the airfields and the port of Bastia were pounded by British and American bombers, which slowed the evacuation considerably. Allied fighter-bombers, meanwhile, attacked most German troop daylight movements. Several German transport ships were also torpedoed by Allied submarines, while Allied fighters shot down up to 11 Junkers Ju-52 transports a day.

During the night of September 20–21, General Lungenshausen successfully evacuated the bridgehead at Bonifacio, and (after blowing up the port) the last elements of the 90th Panzer Grenadier were evacuated from the island.[15] Porto Vecchio was rendered unusable and abandoned on September 22, and two days later General von Senger was forced to abandon his command post at Ghisonaccia and retreated to the Bastia perimeter. The Ghisonaccia airfield was captured by the French on September 25, again significantly slowing the pace of the evacuation. The Luftwaffe then opened another airstrip at Poretta, but it was quite poor. Finally, during the last phases of the evacuation, German air operations could only be carried out at night, further slowing the process. The last airfield at Borgo fell on October 2. Nevertheless, Senger had succeeded in his mission. It was now a matter of getting the rearguards out, for they were the last troops on the island.

Allied submarines now prevented him from using ships, so the last troops were evacuated during the night of October 3–4, using shallow-draft lighters and Siebel ferries, which were not particularly seaworthy. Fortunately for the Germans, the weather held. Several hundred trucks had to be abandoned (after they were set on fire), but the 88mm flak batteries, which had done such an excellent job of defending Bastia, were taken out in the last ferries. General Senger was in the last boat, which left Sicily shortly before midnight on October 3. He arrived in Leghorn the following morning, where the German naval officers involved in the operation threw him a victory celebration. The next day, Hitler sent him a telegram of congratulations in which he admitted that he did not expect such a successful evacuation.

With the Nazis, of course, General von Senger was not dealing with people who forgave easily, and his refusal to commit an atrocity ordered by the Fuehrer left a permanent black mark next to his name. Almost certainly for this reason, he was never given the opportunity to command an army, except for a few days as an acting commander. He was later told by General of SS Karl Wolff, the higher SS and police commander in Italy, that Himmler demanded his dismissal several times and that his career was saved only because of the intervention of Wolff and Kesselring.[16]

Senger's reward for this brilliant operation was not slow in coming. On October 8, 1943, he was named commander of the XIV Panzer Corps, then headquartered at Roccasecca in southern Italy. Its strategic mission was to delay the Allied advance up the Italian peninsula. Specifically, it was to conduct a staged retreat under enemy pressure to the Bernhard Line. It was then to hold the Bernhard Line until the construction of the Gustav Line (along the Garigliano, Gari, and Rapido Rivers) was completed. Initially, Senger's command consisted of the 94th Infantry Division (Major General Hellmuth Pfeiffer), the 15th Panzer Grenadier (Major General Eberhard Rodt), the 3rd Panzer Grenadier (Lieutenant General Fritz-Hubert Graeser), and the Wuertemberg-Baden 305th Infantry Division (Major General Friedrich-Wilhelm Hauck). Senger had a high opinion of all of his subordinate commanders except Hauck, although General Graeser had been seriously wounded on a number of occasions and now walked only with the aid of sticks.[17]

Later, the 26th Panzer, 29th Panzer Grenadier, and 1st Parachute Divisions would also come under Senger's command. They were commanded by Major General Baron Smilo von Luettwitz, Major General Walther Fries, and Luftwaffe Lieutenant General Richard Heidrich, respectively.[18] Later, the 26th Panzer was commanded by Eduard Crasemann, and Major General Bernhard Steinmetz assumed command of the 94th Infantry.[19]

Like Rommel in France in 1940, Senger was aided in Italy by the excellence of his commanders. (Unlike Rommel, however, Senger often praised them in his writings.)

- Hellmuth Pfeffer was a Prussian whom Senger praised highly as "a soldierly personality who inspired confidence." He was an infantry battalion commander when the war began but by 1943 was commanding a division on the Eastern Front. He was promoted to lieutenant general on June 1, 1944, but was killed in action in northern Italy on April 22, 1945.
- Eberhard Rodt (1895–1979) was a Bavarian. He would be promoted to lieutenant general on March 1, 1944. He commanded the 15th Panzer Grenadier with great success for the rest of the war. As commander of the 22nd Panzer Division on the Russian Front (1942–43), he had been less successful, but had redeemed his career during the Battle of Sicily.
- Friedrich-Wilhelm Hauck (1897–1979) was a Silesian who entered the army as a war volunteer in 1914. He won a commission in 1917 and remained in the Reichsheer. He would end the war as a general of artillery (April 20, 1945), commanding the LI Corps.

- Fritz-Hubert Graeser (1888–1968) would rise higher than any of them, including Senger, ending the war as commander of the 4th Panzer Army on the Eastern Front (September 1944–end). As commander of the 29th Infantry Regiment, Graeser had been critically wounded in Russia on July 11, 1941, and had not returned to active duty until March 1, 1943, when he assumed command of the 3rd Panzer Grenadier. He was promoted to general of panzer troops on September 1, 1944.

- Smilo von Luettwitz (1895–1975), who would be promoted to lieutenant general on October 1 and to general of panzer troops the same day as Graeser, later commanded the XXXXVI Panzer Corps and 9th Army on the Eastern Front. He was sacked by General Schoerner for abandoning Warsaw in January 1945, but nevertheless he was given command of the LXXXV Corps on the Western Front on March 31, 1945.[20] In 1958, as a lieutenant general in the West German Army (equivalent to a three-star general in the new rank structure), Luettwitz was given command of the III Corps.

- As commander of the 87th Motorized Infantry Regiment on the Eastern Front, Walter Fries (1894–1982) lost an arm and a leg when his command post was leveled by a Soviet artillery salvo at Rzhev in early 1942. He nevertheless assumed command of the 29th Panzer Grenadier in the spring of 1943 and led it brilliantly in Sicily, three times evading Patton's attempts to encircle him. Fries was promoted to general of panzer troops in December 1944 and was given command of the XXXXVI Panzer Corps on the Eastern Front.

- General Heidrich later commanded the I Parachute Corps in Italy. British Field Marshal Alexander called his 1st Parachute the best division to fight in World War II.

General von Senger retreated into the Gustav Line in January 1944, which he held against large elements of the U.S. 5th Army, the British X Corps, and the New Zealand Corps. The focal point of his defense was Monte Cassino, which he held against six Allied divisions. The details of these battles have been well recounted in a number of books and so will not be rehashed here. Suffice it to say that the XIV Panzer Corps did very well. The lion's share of the credit for the defense of Cassino must go to the 1st Parachute Division. Senger did his best work in extracting his corps from an impending encirclement by the U.S. 5th Army and the U.S. VI Corps, which broke out of the Anzio beachhead and struck into the rear of the XIV Panzer Corps.

The major Allied offensive began on May 12. Unfortunately, Senger had handed over command of the XIV Panzer to his deputy on April 12 and had gone to Fuehrer Headquarters to receive the Oak Leaves to his Knights' Cross. He then attended a corps commanders' course at

Sonthofen and went on leave. Colonel General Heinrich von Vietingh-off, the commander of the 10th Army, had received the Oak Leaves on the same day as Senger and was also on leave, as was Senger's chief of staff.[21] Senger did not return to his headquarters until May 17, by which time the situation was desperate. He nevertheless managed to extract seven divisions over a single mountain road in five days and nights, despite the Allied dominance of the air.

On June 12, Headquarters, XIV Panzer Corps was shifted to the east and placed under HQ, 14th Army. This change Senger welcomed not at all. His old divisions were now placed under I Parachute Corps, and he had to direct third-class units. He led them in the retreats from the Trasimene and Arno lines, in the Battle of Tuscany, and in the retreats from the Gothic Line and through the Apennines (see Figure 15.1). He became acting commander of the 14th Army on October 15, 1944, but only held this post for nine days.[22] At the end of the month, he switched sectors with Headquarters, LI Mountain Corps, and was charged with the defense of Bologna. He held this sector until the next major Allied attack, which began on April 14, 1945.

Senger was very concerned that the beautiful and historic renaissance city of Bologna not be destroyed in the fighting, so he pursued a policy of pacification. The general went so far as to meet with anti-Fascists to ensure that heavy fighting would not break out in the city. Senger was highly relieved when he was able to evacuate the city without fighting for it.

The area between Bologna and the Po is flat, with little cover for about 10 miles. As the XIV Panzer Corps retreated toward the Po, it was subjected to heavy Anglo-American fighter-bomber attack. Sergeant Feuerstak, who had served as Senger's batman and constant companion since before the war, was one of the victims. He was pushing a dogcart, gathering provisions for the corps staff, when a fighter-bomber strafed him. He was critically wounded and one of his legs had to be amputated. Senger immediately visited him in the field hospital and held his hand for a long time. As Senger feared, he never saw him again. Feuerstak ended up living the rest of his life as a peasant in East Germany.

As it fell back to the Po, the units of the XIV Panzer Corps were smashed. By the time they reached the river, the 65th Infantry, 305th Infantry, and 5th Mountain Divisions were disorganized remnants, and the 94th Infantry had disappeared altogether. General Pfeffer was killed at the bridge at Finale, which eliminated any hope Senger may have had of establishing serious resistance south of the river. On the night of April 22–23, Senger faced a choice: let the HQ be captured by the Americans or cross the river and try to continue resisting. Senger chose the second option and escaped via raft. Major General Friedrich

Figure 15.1
Northern Italy, 1944–45

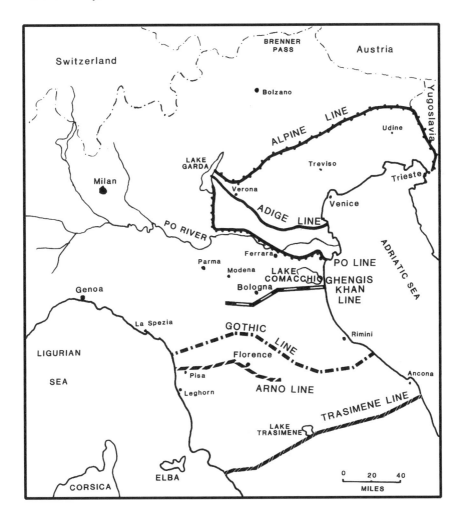

von Schellwitz, the commander of the 305th Infantry Division, took charge of the remnants of the 65th Infantry as well as his own division, but he was captured south of the Po on April 23.

Senger and his staff finally reached the remote mountain village of Ronchi on April 25. Here the staffs of the 94th Infantry and 8th Mountain Divisions turned up again, and Senger reinforced them with replacements from the Parachute Officers' School and an SS Mountain Troops School. He was thus able to establish a thin, isolated defensive line. He still had no artillery but did manage to impress several anti-aircraft batteries from the Luftwaffe. Fortunately for both sides, Senger was not attacked before Hitler committed suicide on April 30, 1945.

Because of his command of the English language, his sophistication, and his diplomatic background, Senger was chosen on May 7 to negotiate the details of the surrender of Army Group C, which was now commanded by General of Infantry Friedrich Schulz.[23] He showed great diplomacy, even after General Clark's pit bulldog bit him in the leg and drew blood, leaving holes in his boot.

Senger completed his task on May 22, and then went into Allied captivity. Initially, he was held in the huge POW camp at Ghedi, Italy. After that he was sent to Rome, to testify on behalf of General of Infantry Anton Dostler, who was being tried for murder for obeying one of Hitler's orders to shoot commandos. Despite Senger's testimony, Dostler was convicted and was shot on December 1, 1945. Senger himself was handed over to the British and was imprisoned at the Central District Cage in Kensington and Bridgend, among other places. He was released in May 1948 and returned to Goettingen.

P., Senger's wife, had kept her head above water financially by becoming an antique dealer. With the help of a friend of the former general, he secured an appointment as headmaster of Spetzgart, a branch of the famous Salem Castle School near Lake Constance. In the 1950s, he became involved in journalism as the military correspondent for the Suedwestfunk Broadcasting Service ("South West German Radio") and the *Deutsche Zeitung*. From 1952, he served on a secret committee appointed by West German Chancellor Konrad Adenauer, which was charged with setting up guidelines for the new West German Armed Forces (*Bundeswehr*). He also sat on the screening committee that was responsible for keeping good officers who were too closely associated with Hitler from joining the Bundeswehr. He himself did not join the new army, although his son became one of its generals. Frido von Senger died in Freiburg on January 4, 1963.[24]

CHAPTER XVI

OTTO HEIDKAEMPER: THE CHIEF OF STAFF

Rommel's chief of operations or Ia during the campaign in the West was Major i.G. (major of the General Staff) Otto Heidkaemper, who also was in effect his chief of staff, because German units below corps level had no chief of staff per se. (See appendix 2 for a listing of German staff positions.) Not a War Academy graduate himself, Rommel was generally suspicious of General Staff officers (especially early in the war), and Heidkaemper was a General Staff officer from his monocle to his highly polished boots. Naturally, no personal friendship developed between the two men, and a considerable amount of evidence suggests that they did not like each other. Rommel, however, believed in the technique of leading from the front, and he had no choice but to trust Heidkaemper during his frequent and lengthy absences from headquarters or to transfer him out of the 7th Panzer Division. He would do both. From February until November 1940, however, Heidkaemper was often the man in de facto charge of the Staff, 7th Panzer Division.

Rommel could hardly have left his headquarters in more capable hands. In many ways, Heidkaemper embodied the ideal of his class and breed: "Great achievement, small display. More reality than appearance." "General Staff officers," as General Hans von Seeckt liked to observe, "have no faces." Otto Heidkaemper was a case in point. Although he played a significant role in several major campaigns during World War II, few people today know his name, even among professional military historians.

He was born in Lauenhagen district of Stadthagen, Lower Saxony (*Niedersachsen*), on March 13, 1901, and entered the Imperial Army as a Fahnenjunker in the 10th Engineer Replacement Battalion on July 9, 1918. After a quick basic training, he was sent to the 10th Engineer

Battalion in September 1918 and spent the closing weeks of World War I on the Western Front with the 10th Engineers. After the armistice, he returned to the Fatherland with his unit and was accepted into the Reichswehr, where he served with various engineer units. He completed his officer training at the Engineer School at Munich and was commissioned *Leutnant* (second lieutenant) on April 1, 1922.[1]

Promotions were slow in the 100,000-man army and Heidkaemper did not reach the rank of captain until 1934. In the meantime, he served almost exclusively in engineer units, including bridging columns. His education was more diverse than his troop duty, however, and included training in mobile operations. He also served a tour as an instructor at the Engineer Officers' School in Munich. He was adjutant to the higher engineer officer of Army Group 1 in Berlin when Hitler took power on January 30, 1933. Shortly thereafter, Heidkaemper was selected for General Staff training, which he began on October 1, 1933.

General Staff training was the highest the army conducted. Most of Heidkaemper's classes were held at the Kriegsakademie in Berlin—the famous War Academy, which was reopened on August 1, 1934. Because of the rich tradition and place in Prussian history that the General Staff occupied, the War Academy had a special place in the hearts of German military leaders and (to a lesser extent) the general public as well, and was considered almost sacred ground to the German Officers' Corps.

Because the chief of the General Staff was responsible for the education of all General Staff officers, the guiding hand behind the resurrected War Academy was that of Colonel General Ludwig Beck, who gave considerable thought to the selection of students, the selection of instructors, the courses of instruction, and all other matters related to the Academy.[2] Unfortunately, despite his intelligence, lofty ideals, and high morals, General Beck was an officer of limited vision. "Whenever something new had to be done," his staff historian recalled, "he asked himself what had been done in the past."[3] This statement goes far toward explaining both Beck's opposition to the panzer branch and the deficiencies of the German General Staff during the Nazi era, for the curriculum of the War Academy stressed tactical proficiency, to the neglect (and virtual exclusion) of the larger, strategic questions. In other words, the course of study was very similar to that Beck underwent when he was a student. Colonel Count Claus von Stauffenberg, one of its graduates in the early Nazi era, later said that too much emphasis was placed on tactical instruction and not enough on technical difficulties (especially logistics) and problems related to the war economy. There were also no required courses in philosophy, the philosophy of warfare, or strategy. Geography, general history (as separated from military history), and economics were only touched on, and even Clausewitz was neglected; in fact, the only nonmilitary subject stressed under Beck's administration was the study of foreign languages. These facts are peculiar when one considers that Beck himself was no simple soldier who grew up in the army and knew nothing else; he was the son of a professor and was himself broadly and well educated, as well as intelligent and scholarly. He spoke excellent French, understood other languages, and was nationally recognized for his proficiency in higher mathematics, which was one of his hobbies. Ludwig Beck both knew and understood the literature of philosophy and war, and recognized its value and importance; nevertheless, he produced narrowly educated officers. This fact is partially (but not wholly) explained by the fact that the pressure of rearmament and the high demand for General Staff officers forced Beck to shorten the course from four years to three (and later it was reduced to two), followed by the traditional staff ride under Beck's personal supervision.

Despite its drawbacks, in the 1930s, the War Academy offered the best military training in the world at the tactical and operational levels. In 1935, American Lieutenant Colonel Alfred C. Wedemeyer graduated from the U.S. Army's Command and General Staff College at Fort Leavenworth, Kansas. At that time, the U.S. and German governments had just concluded a reciprocal exchange agreement that, among other things, allowed two students from each country to attend the other nation's war academy. Wedemeyer was offered the opportunity to go to Berlin, and he jumped at the chance. In his excellent book (*Wedemeyer Reports!*), he has left a magnificent account of his thoughts and experiences at the Kriegsakademie and of the friends and acquaintants he made in Germany, including classmates such as Lieutenant Colonel Alfred Jodl and Captain Claus von Stauffenberg.[4] Wedemeyer's War Academy training is one of the major reasons he became chief of the War Plans Department of the U.S. General Staff and advanced from "light" colonel to four-star general in less than 10 years. (How this great strategic thinker and authority on the German Army ended up commanding U.S. forces in China is a story that, unfortunately, is beyond the scope of this book.) On the other hand, the Germans did not exercise their option of sending students to Kansas and tactfully implied that they did not think too highly of the U.S. General Staff course. Wedemeyer would have agreed with this assessment. "The German pedagogy and curriculum were, in my judgment, superior to our own," he wrote after the war.[5]

Wedemeyer found that the German War Academy was located in Moabit, an unattractive industrial section of Berlin. Each class began with 100 students, and was divided into five "study halls" of 20 members each. Because the Prussian and other provincial General Staffs had been merged under the Reichsheer, the old instructional methods of Prussian authoritarianism had been discarded in favor of techniques more closely associated with south Germany. Most of the instruction was in the hands of south Germans (who had not been educated in the more rigid Prussian manner) and the encouragement of uninhibited exchanges of views among students and between students and their instructors was certainly more liberal and less dogmatic than would have been the case had the Prussian model been adopted. Here, relationships between junior and senior officers were much closer than outside of the General Staff, and young officers felt free to disagree with older officers who were often two or more grades their superiors in rank, although the proprieties were always observed. This atmosphere, established under Beck (a Hessian), was continued under his successor, Franz Halder, who was a Bavarian. Even criticism of National Socialism was permitted.[6]

Unfortunately for Germany, the General Staff course, which flourished in this climate of mutual confidence, consisted of only two parts: the first dealt with command through the regimental level, and the second with command and staff problems at the divisional level and above. During the first year, the students received six hours of lecture each week on tactics, plus four on military history, one in engineering, one on panzer forces, and another on air forces. The rest of the students' time was taken up by group study hall sessions, homework, and individual study. The second year the course remained the same, except an hours' lecture on logistics was added. Finally, in the third year, the student received an entire day's worth of lectures on tactics, plus another six hours each week. He also attended four hours of lectures on military history, plus an hour on logistics and another hour on air forces. Each winter, the officers underwent a block of special tactical instruction (called the "winter study") and each summer he was assigned to a combat arms branch other than his own, to broaden his base of experience.[7] The student was also expected to pursue a program of study and reading at home. During the third year of his General Staff course, the officer-student was assigned to a higher staff. Shortly before the outbreak of the war, the General Staff course was shortened to two years, because of the desperate need for General Staff officers. By the second half of 1944, the War Academy had been moved from Berlin to Hirschberg, in the Sudeten Mountains of Silesia, to escape Allied bombers, and the course of study was only a few months long.

Largely because of this course, German mastery of tactical and operational arts on the battlefields of World War II is a generally accepted fact. Had there been a fourth year, dealing with strategy, international relations, geopolitical questions, and the problems of industrial and economic warfare and related issues—or perhaps less tactics and more of these other things in the first three years—events might have worked out much differently than they did—assuming, of course, that Hitler let his generals practice the strategic art, which is a very big assumption indeed.

Captain Heidkaemper graduated from the War Academy on January 8, 1937, and for the next eight years wore the red trouser stripes of a General Staff officer. His first postgraduate assignment was with the General Staff of the Army at Zossen, but he was soon named commander of the 3rd Company, 19th Engineer Battalion at Holzminden (1937–38), no doubt because he lacked experience in commanding troops. With this deficiency remedied, he was assigned to the General Staff of the 9th Army Service Depot. Then, as the Third Reich neared a showdown with France, Britain, and Czechoslovakia over the Sudetenland, Heidkaemper was sent to the Reich's western frontier and served on the General Staffs of Fortress Command Aachen, Corps Staff Eifel, and the Eifel Frontier Guard Command. He was promoted to major on August 1, 1938, and had successfully completed his apprenticeship. On May 1, 1939, Heidkaemper was given his own staff when he was named Ia (chief of operations) of the 2nd Light Division, then headquartered at Gera, Thuringia, in Wehrkreis IX. The division included the 66th Panzer Battalion, the 6th and 7th Mechanized Cavalry (*Kavallerie-Schuetzen*) Regiments, the 7th Reconnaissance Regiment, the 78th Artillery Regiment, the 58th Engineer Battalion, and the 42nd Antitank Battalion.[8] The divisional commander was Lieutenant General Georg Stumme, an amiable cavalry officer.

When World War II began on September 1, 1939, the 66th Panzer Battalion was equipped only with very poor Panzer Mark I (PzKw I) and Panzer Mark II light tanks. (See appendix 3 for a description of German tanks in World War II.) The rest of the division, however, was much better equipped. As part of the main German strike force—General of Artillery Walter von Reichenau's 10th Army—the 2nd Light fought its way through the Polish frontier defenses, helped overrun the Warta district, and pushed all the way to the suburbs of Warsaw, before doubling back to help smash the better part of the Polish Army in the Radom encirclement. It then pushed on to the Vistula and took part in the Siege of Warsaw, which ended with the Polish capitulation on September 27.

Heidkaemper returned to Germany with his unit and helped Stumme convert it into a panzer unit during the winter of 1939–40. During the French campaign of 1940, he supervised the administration, supply, and logistics of the 7th Panzer, while Rommel led it in combat. The two very different men made an effective team—as long as they were separated and did not have to talk to each other very often.

During the campaign, the 7th Panzer's adjacent unit, the SS Panzer Grenadier Division "Totenkopf," developed serious supply problems because of bad staff work. (Poor staff work and a severe shortage of qualified staff officers in general and General Staff officers in particular plagued the Waffen-SS throughout its existence.) The "Death's Head" division had only one really qualified staff officer, SS Colonel Baron

Cassius von Montigny. He had served in the U-Boat branch in World War I and had earned the Iron Cross, 1st Class. After fighting as part of the Freikorps in 1919 and 1920, he joined the police and served until 1935, when he joined the army. Eventually he served on the staffs of the 31st and 102nd Infantry Regiments. He was forced to resign from the service by the war minister, Field Marshal Werner von Blomberg, because of his pro-Nazi political activities. Montigny wrote to Heinrich Himmler about his perceived mistreatment and Himmler—who was always on the lookout for qualified staff officers—invited him to join the SS as a lieutenant colonel. After entering the SS on April 1, 1938, as an instructor at the SS Junker School at Bad Toelz, he became the Ia of the SS "Death's Head" Division in October 1939.[9]

Montigny was already overworked when the French campaign began and, within two weeks of the beginning of the invasion, he collapsed because of stress and nervous exhaustion. The fact that Totenkopf's commander, SS Lieutenant General Theodor Eicke, was in no way qualified for his post further exacerbated an already difficult situation. Eicke had contributed to Montigny's collapse by constantly berating him and screaming at him.[10] Rommel offered to help his floundering neighbor, in part because, if Eicke's failed to keep up, Rommel's own flank would be exposed. After Eicke accepted the offer, the future Desert Fox handed the problem to Heidkaemper and Joachim von Metzsch, the Ib, who handled it flawlessly.[11] They even ran SS convoys over 7th Panzer's main supply route without any particular difficulties.

Rommel and Heidkaemper generally worked well together in Belgium and France because the general directed the battle from the front or from his command post, while the major handled secondary operations, coordination, supply and logistical issues, and myriad other staff problems from the main headquarters. There was friction between the two, however, and it was sometimes serious. During the drive to the English Channel, for example, Rommel was in his typical position at the spearhead of the division, advancing on Cambrai, and Heidkaemper had no idea where he was or what he was up to. Nervous and annoyed, the young Ia wrote a memorandum on the staff difficulties caused by Rommel's methods of command and forwarded it to the future Desert Fox, who reacted with fury. He blamed poor staff work and a lack of initiative in the rear areas for the supply difficulties experienced by the 25th Panzer Regiment in the drive to the sea—not his own bold leadership style. He also denounced his chief of operations for failing to anticipate his requirements.

It is difficult not to sympathize with Heidkaemper—and not with Rommel—in this controversy. Heidkaemper, after all, was not clairvoyant and could hardly be blamed for being nervous. In my opinion, Rommel should have kept him better informed. Instead, he left young

Heidkaemper (a very junior officer) with great responsibility but without commensurate authority. Moreover, Rommel's very fair and even tempered corps commander—General of Panzer Troops Hermann Hoth—generally agreed with Heidkaemper, who had taken out a professional insurance policy by forwarding a copy of his memo to Hoth. Sacking the young General Staff officer—a typical Rommel response—was therefore out of the question. Given this development, the impetuous division commander had little choice but to meet with his Ia and make peace with him, which is exactly what he did.[12] This incident, however, was not forgotten.

The Rommel-Heidkaemper team clearly worked best when one or the other was not present. During the fighting phases of the French campaign, this was no problem. When the division was on occupation duty in southwestern France, however, and Rommel was not busy in the combat zone, their relationship became increasingly strained. (Rommel was often difficult for his subordinates to deal with—especially General Staff officers, whom he neither fully trusted nor appreciated. This gradually changed over time. Later, Rommel grew to both rely on and respect his General Staff officers, but this was certainly not the case in 1940.) In any case, by mutual consent, Otto Heidkaemper transferred to the 4th Panzer Division on November 15, 1940, 15 days after his promotion to lieutenant colonel was confirmed by OKH.

As Ia of the 4th Panzer, Heidkaemper's transfer did not represent a promotion. His new division, however, had just been sent back to Germany, so that was probably a plus. He also got along well with his new commander, Major General Baron Willibald von Langermann und Erlenkamp.[13] Heidkaemper was soon deeply involved in the reorganization of the division, much of which was used to form the 14th Panzer Division. In May 1941, the 4th Panzer was sent to East Prussia. It invaded the Soviet Union on June 22, 1941.

The 4th was an outstanding unit even by German Army standards. At the end of the war, it would be the most heavily decorated of all the Wehrmacht divisions. In 1941, it fought at Minsk, Gomel, Bryansk, Vyasma, and several other bitterly contested battles on the road to Moscow. By mid-November 1941, it had only 50 tanks left. (It had about 180 when the invasion began.) It nevertheless attempted to encircle the strategic city of Tula (southeast of Moscow) but failed, and suffered heavy losses in the process. On December 6, 1941, Stalin launched his winter offensive, and the 4th Panzer Division was heavily engaged in the exceptionally bitter fighting. Well led by Langermann and Major General Dietrich von Saucken, who replaced Langermann on December 24, the unit repulsed every attack. Saucken was seriously wounded on January 2, 1942, and was replaced by the equally capable Major General Heinrich Eberbach.[14] The 4th remained with Army Group Center until 1944.

After the Soviet attempt to smash the army group was thwarted, Eberbach went on leave for a month, beginning on March 2, 1942. Instead of following the normal practice of getting a temporary divisional commander or leaving the senior regimental commander in charge, Eberbach turned the command of the division over to Heidkaemper. This was a tremendous vote of confidence in the young officer—lieutenant colonels almost never served as divisional commanders, even on a temporary basis. He held the post until Eberbach returned in early April; then he went on leave himself. When he returned to duty on May 13, 1942, he was given another career advancement: he was named chief of staff of the XXIV Panzer Corps. His commander was his old friend, Baron Willibald von Langermann und Erlenkamp. Heidkaemper was promoted to colonel on June 1, 1942.

The next campaign was Otto Heidkaemper's most difficult and ended in the Battle of Stalingrad. Although the XXIV Panzer was not encircled in the city, it suffered heavy losses in the drive on the Volga and faced the full fury of the Soviet offensive. This is reflected in the loss of commanders: Langermann (killed in action, October 3, 1942); General of Artillery Martin Wandel (missing in action, January 14, 1943); Lieutenant General Arno Jahr (killed in action, January 20, 1943); and Lieutenant General Karl Eibl (assumed command on January 20 and killed in action near the Don River the next day).[15] Some Italian soldiers mistook his command car for a Russian vehicle and blew it up with hand grenades. Although only a colonel, Otto Heidkaemper assumed command of what was left of the corps. OKH pulled the battered headquarters out of the line to reorganize and left Heidkaemper in charge until February 12, 1943, when General of Panzer Troops Walter Nehring arrived to supersede him.[16] In recognition for his services, Heidkaemper was decorated with the Knight's Cross on February 8.

Shortly after Nehring arrived, Heidkaemper went on an extended leave. When he returned to the Eastern Front on May 5, 1943, he was promoted to major general (effective May 1) and was named chief of staff, 3rd Panzer Army. His commander was now Colonel General Georg-Hans Reinhardt.[17]

As was the case throughout the war, Heidkaemper and his commander made an extremely effective team. Third Panzer Army won several defensive victories in 1943 but, in June 1944, along with Army Group Center, it fell victim to one of the Fuehrer's "not one step back" orders. At Vitebsk, the entire LIII Corps was sacrificed on the altar of Hitler's inflexible strategy. By August, only two of Reinhardt's nine divisions remained more or less intact, although 3rd Panzer had come out better than the 4th or 9th Armies. Hitler blamed the army group commander, Field Marshal Ernst Busch, for this defeat and sacked him on June 28. He was replaced by Field Marshal Walter Model.[18] In mid-August 1944, however, with the Western Front on the verge of collapse, Hitler learned that the commander-in-chief of OB West and Army Group B, Field Marshal Guenther von Kluge, had known about the conspiracy to assassinate him and had given it cautious support. By now seeing treason in every event, the paranoid dictator replaced Kluge with Walter Model.[19] As the senior army commander in Army Group Center, Reinhardt succeeded Model on August 16, 1944. As was common practice in the German Wehrmacht, Model carried his chief of staff, Lieutenant General Hans Krebs, with him to Army Group B.[20] Reinhardt, in turn, named Heidkaemper chief of staff of the army group. Heidkaemper helped Colonel General Edhard Raus, the new commander of the 3rd Panzer Army, transition into his new job for two weeks and then joined Reinhardt in Poland on September 1.

General Reinhardt directed the retreat across eastern Poland and into East Prussia. In January 1945, in another desperate tactical situation, Hitler issued a typically irrational order and instructed the 4th Army to hold at all costs. Reinhardt appealed to him to allow a retreat, but the dictator refused. Reinhardt authorized a retreat anyway. As a result, both Reinhardt and General of Infantry Friedrich Hossbach, the commander of the 4th Army, were relieved of their commands. (Reinhardt would have had to be replaced in any case; he had been hit in the head by a Soviet bullet on January 25 and only barely survived. He would be in the hospital for months. News of his wound had not yet reached Fuehrer Headquarters when he was relieved.)[21]

Reinhardt was succeeded by Colonel General Ferdinand Schoerner, a brutal Nazi.[22] As soon as he arrived at headquarters, he sacked Otto Heidkaemper, because of his lack of enthusiasm for National Socialism and because of his involvement in Reinhardt's unauthorized retreat.

Heidkaemper remained unemployed until April 15, 1945, when he assumed command of a rear-area sector. On April 27, he was given command of the recently activated 464th Infantry Division, which was made up of former members of the Replacement Army—mostly old men and boys.[23] It had been given a defensive sector on the Eastern Front near Dresden. After Hitler committed suicide on April 30, Heidkaemper and much of his command disengaged from the Russians and headed west, where they surrendered to the Americans. Heidkaemper was only held for about two weeks, from May 9 to 24, when he was released from prison and allowed to go home.

Heidkaemper was an excellent officer and a fairly typical example of the level of officer produced by the German General Staff during World War II. He settled in Bueckeburg, West Germany, and wrote a book about the Battle of Vitebsk. He died in Bueckeburg on February 16, 1969.

CHAPTER XVII

JOHANN MICKL: THE AUSTRIAN MOUNTAINEER

Johann Mikl was born in the small village of Zelting, a border area between Slovenia and Styria (Austria), on April 18, 1893.[1] Today it is a suburb of Ralkersburg, Slovenia, but at the time it was part of the Austro-Hungarian Empire. His father was a German and his mother (whose maiden name was Derwaritsch) was at least partially Slovene. Johann, however, grew up speaking German and later changed his name to Mickl, which was considered a more Germanized form of Mikl. He clearly considered himself to be an Austrian (i.e., German), although he mastered both the Slovenian and Hungarian languages as a child and remained fluent in them throughout his life. He also gained some command of other Balkan languages as well.

Mickl's father was a small farmer, and Johann grew up in meager circumstances. He entered the Austrian service as a Fahnenjunker in the cadet school at Vienna in 1908, but as a member of the *Landwehr* (Defense Force), rather than the Regular Army, suggesting that he was not well connected. Certainly there was nothing glamorous about Mickl's pre-1939 career; he owed his advancements to natural ability (improved by education, physical courage, endurance, and hard work). Three years later, in 1911, he was transferred to the Maria Theresa Military Academy at Wiener Neustadt (which Erwin Rommel later commanded), where his basic education was completed. He graduated three years later and was commissioned Leutnant in the 4th Landwehr Infantry Regiment at Klagenfurt on August 1, 1914. The 4th had been mobilized for action in World War I three days before.

Mickl's regiment was initially sent by railroad to Galicia (which is now part of Poland and Ukraine), where the Austro-Hungarian Empire was defending itself against a Russian invasion. Mickl's first battle was on the Zlota Lipa River, where the 4th Landwehr suffered heavy casualties. Young Mickl was among them. He sustained a serious chest wound and spent the next several months in the hospital. It was the first of six serious wounds the brave lieutenant would receive during his career.

Johann Mickl was discharged from the hospital on April 15, 1915, and was assigned to the regiment's replacement battalion at Klagenfurt, to complete his convalescence. He was promoted to 1st lieutenant (Oberleutnant) on May 1 and returned to the front later that month, fighting in the Pruth sector as a company commander. He was wounded again on June 3, but he remained with his command and personally covered its withdrawal. For his courage under fire, he was awarded the Military Merit Cross, 3rd Class, shortly thereafter. Meanwhile, Italy entered the war on the side of the Western Allies.

During World War II, the Italian soldiers proved very reluctant to die for Benito Mussolini and his corrupt and largely inefficient Fascist regime. Italy thus acquired a false reputation as a country whose soldiers were inept and unwilling to fight. This unfair and unjust reputation has, at least to a degree, persisted to this day. Their reticence to die for Mussolini, however, merely shows good sense and should not be confused with national ineptitude or widespread cowardice. Certainly their military performance in World War I did not rise to the high standards of the Germans, but it did equal (and sometimes exceeded) that of the Austrians, who were themselves a Germanic people. Italian courage in World War I, on the other hand, equaled that of any other major power. No doubt Johann Mickl would agree with this assessment. The Italians, in fact, came very close to killing him on a number of occasions.

With Italy's entry into the war, the Austro-Hungarian Empire's southern flank was threatened and experienced units were needed to the south. Mickl's regiment was assigned to the 44th Landwehr Infantry Division and was sent to the upper reaches of the Isonzo River, to face the Italians. Eleven major battles were fought in this mountainous sector, and they were fierce. Mickl continued to distinguish himself in these battles, recapturing the tactically important Cukla position in a counterattack on February 12, 1916, for which he was awarded the Order of the Iron Cross, 3rd Class.

Perhaps his most difficult operation of the war occurred at Mount Tschukla (near Rombon), where he led his company in a daring night attack. All of Mickl's 220 men were dressed in white camouflage and had to trudge through deep snow in extreme weather conditions to launch a surprise attack against an important Italian position. The plan worked, but the Italians counterattacked several times and the close-quarter fighting was heavy. After they failed to retake the position with their infantry, the Italians plastered it with artillery fire from their heavy guns. When Mickl's company was finally relieved two days later, only 40 men were able to walk down the mountain. The rest were dead or seriously wounded.

That summer, Mickl again distinguished himself by playing a major role in the capturing of Hill 1363 on Monte Cengio, earning for himself the Bronze Military Merit Medal in the process.

With Italy temporarily checked in the summer of 1916, Mickl's division was sent back to Galicia in June. Then Italy struck again, and the 44th Landwehr was rushed back to the southwest, where it fought in the 8th, 9th, 10th, and 11th Battles of the Isonzo. Mickl again fought well and was once more seriously wounded on October 10. He received two Silver Military Medals in the hospital. After he recovered, he was reassigned to the 4th Landwehr's replacement battalion.

In the summer of 1917, Mickl attended a three-month course at the VI Corps Reserve Officers' School. Meanwhile, the 4th Landwehr Infantry Regiment was reorganized and redesignated the 1st Mountain Rifle Regiment in the spring of 1917. Johann Mickl rejoined this unit in the autumn of 1917 and fought in the Caporetto offensive and in the subsequent pursuit to the Piave River. In May 1918, he attended a staff course and was reassigned to the Ukraine as an officer on the supply staff. He was still there when the war ended.

Following the collapse of the monarchy, there was chaos everywhere. Mickl was named officer-in-charge (OIC) of the border area around Bad Radkersburg and his home town in 1919; unfortunately, the entire area was in the hands of Slovene insurgents. Using local and ad hoc Austrian volunteers, Mickl liberated the entire area by 1920. Bad Radkersburg later honored him for this achievement by making him an honorary citizen in 1930. He was also awarded the Carinthian Cross for Bravery and the Special Carinthian Cross for Bravery by a grateful Austrian government. Later in 1920, the new Austrian Army (the *Bundesheer*) was created. Johann Mickl was naturally selected as one of the junior officers. He was initially assigned to the 11th Alpine Rifle Regiment (*Alpenjaegerregiment Nr. 11*).

In the fall of 1920, Mickl transferred to the 5th Bicycle Battalion (*Radfahrbataillon Nr. 5*), where he was finally promoted to captain on January 1, 1921. He was promoted to major on September 25, 1928. He spent 15 years with the same battalion and did not leave the 5th Bicycle until 1935, when he was attached to the staff of the 3rd Brigade at St. Poelten, where he underwent an abbreviated General Staff training course. He was admitted to the Austrian General Staff on August 14, 1935, and was assigned to the Headquarters, 3rd Infantry Division. He was promoted to lieutenant colonel on January 4, 1936. He was there when Germany annexed Austria in March 1938.

Like most Austrian officers, Mickl was allowed to transfer to the German Wehrmacht, where he found a greater scope for advancement. From mid-May until mid-August, he attended a course at the Panzer Troop School at Wunstorf. After a short tour of duty with the 41st Antitank Battalion, he was given command of the 42nd Antitank (later Tank Destroyer) Battalion of the 2nd Light Division, which he led in the Polish campaign.

Mickl was one of the few senior officers of the 7th Panzer Division who got along well with Erwin Rommel, but he would not get along with his successor, Baron Hans von Funck. In the French campaign, Mickl's battalion performed to Rommel's satisfaction, despite suffering severe losses in the Battle of Arras, where its small 37mm guns proved to be no match for the British Matilda heavy tanks. The 42nd did, however, fight with death-defying courage; several of its guns remained in action until the heavily armored Matildas crushed them beneath their treads. The British assault was finally stopped by a combination of artillery fire, Rothenburg's tanks, and the German anti-aircraft batteries. Mickl was awarded the Iron Cross, 1st Class, after the fall of Paris. On June 1, 1940, with Rommel's endorsement, he was promoted to full colonel.

After the French surrender, Colonel Mickl was temporarily attached to Rothenburg's 25th Panzer Regiment, where he learned more about armored operations. He succeeded Colonel Friedrich Fuerst as commander of the 7th Rifle Regiment on December 10, 1940.

Mickl commanded the 7th Rifle on occupation duty in southwestern France, in its redeployment back to Germany, and its preparations for the invasion of the Soviet Union. Then, in late May, he was suddenly sent to Libya, because Erwin Rommel had requested him for Panzer Army Afrika. Unlike the case with Hans von Luck, General von Funck offered no objections and he was quickly on his way. As soon as the Austrian colonel arrived, he was given command of the 155th Rifle Regiment of the 21st Panzer Division.

Mickl led the 155th Rifle with his typical bravery. He fought in the Siege of Tobruk and the first two British attempts to relieve the fortress, Operations Brevity and Battleaxe. He also played a significant role in the Battle of Sidi Rezegh and the blunting of the 8th Army's initial attempts to lift the Siege of Tobruk during the Winter Battles; then, on November 26, 1941, he was captured by New Zealand forces. For him, the war seemed over.

It was not. Colonel Mickl was thrown into a temporary POW collection center, along with 800 other tough veterans of the Afrika Korps. Before the disorganized British command could send them to the rear, Mickl organized his unarmed comrades and, in one daring rush, overwhelmed the guards, captured the commandant, took the camp, and headed west across the desert. They somehow managed to reach German lines before the Allies could run them down. Rommel was, of course, delighted. He immediately recommended Mickl for the Knight's Cross, which he received on December 13, 1941.

The harsh desert climate, the poor and irregular rations, the strain of fighting in temperatures of 120°F and greater, and the exertions of a three-week battle (not to mention being captured and leading a bold escape) had a negative effect on Mickl's health. He was, after all, now 48 years old, which was considered very old for desert warfare. After the Germans evacuated Cyrenica in December, he was sent back to Europe. After several weeks of rest and recuperation, he was given command of the 12th Rifle Brigade of the 12th Panzer Division on March 25, 1942.

In the spring of 1942, the 12th Panzer was in Estonia, recovering from Stalin's Winter Offensive of 1941–42. Under the command of Baron Erpo von Bodenhausen, the division returned to action south of Leningrad that spring, fighting at Volchov, Lake Ladoga, and Nevel, and acting as a fire brigade for Army Group North, which had relatively little armor. Thanks to the 12th Panzer, the army group was able to maintain the Siege of Leningrad, despite serious odds against it.[2] The cost, however, was very high. By January 1943, the division had shrunk to the size at which it no longer needed a rifle brigade headquarters; accordingly, Mickl's HQ was dissolved on January 26, and he was sent home and placed in Fuehrer Reserve. OKH and the HPA, however, had not failed to notice his performance. On March 1, he was promoted to major general; five days later, Hitler personally decorated him with the Oak Leaves to the Knight's Cross.

After a leave of three months, Johann Mickl was named commander of the 11th Panzer Division on May 11, 1943. He led this partially built unit in the huge tank battle at Kursk, where it suffered heavy losses in unsuccessful frontal assaults. His division was then taken out of the line and shifted north, where it fought in the Battle of Belgorod. Mickl, however, only fought in the earliest stages of this operation. He was replaced by Colonel Wend von Wietersheim on August 8. After a three-week leave, he was sent to Yugoslavia to organize and command the Croatian 392nd Infantry Division.

It is unclear whether Mickl ran afoul of Colonel General Walter Model, the commander of the 9th Army, or some other senior commander, or whether someone at OKH or OKW thought Mickl might be better employed in his native Balkans, where his command of the languages would serve him well. The first possibility seems most likely. On the other hand, Mickl's relief does not seem to be justified, based on his performance. Given the entire German military situation in the Kurst-Belgorod battles, Mickl performed about as well as any other

German commander. The HPA understood this and did not freeze Mickl's promotions. He became a lieutenant general on April 1, 1944. Fair or not, however, Mickl's career as a panzer officer was over.

Johann Mickl spent the rest of his career in a purely secondary theater. He organized the 392nd Infantry and spent the next year and a half fighting Yugoslavian partisans—mainly Tito's Communists—in Croatia and along the Dalmatian coast. Typically, he performed well. By January 1945, he was fighting Red Army units as well. On April 9, 1945, he was involved in the Battle of Vratnik Pass near Fiume (Rijeka) in Croatia, when a bullet fired by a Yugoslavian partisan struck him in the head. He was quickly rushed to the military hospital at Rijeka, but the doctors were unable to save his life. He died on April 10, 1945—less than a month before the end of the war.

APPENDIX 1: TABLE OF COMPARATIVE RANKS

U.S. Army	German Army
General of the Army	Field Marshal (Generalfeldmarschall)
General	Colonel General (Generaloberst)
Lieutenant General	General of Infantry, General of Panzer Troops (General der Infanterie, General der Panzertruppen), etc.
Major General	Lieutenant General (Generalleutnant)
Brigadier General[a]	Major General (Generalmajor)
Colonel	Colonel (Oberst)
Lieutenant Colonel	Lieutenant Colonel (Oberstleutnant)
Major	Major (Major)
Captain	Captain (Hauptmann)
First Lieutenant	First Lieutenant (Oberleutnant)
Second Lieutenant	Second Lieutenant (Leutnant)
None	Senior Officer Cadet or Ensign (Faehnrich)
Officer Candidate	Fahnenjunker (Officer-Cadet)

[a]Brigadier in British Army.

APPENDIX 2: GERMAN STAFF POSITIONS

	Chief of Staff (not present below the corps level)
Ia	Chief of Operations
Ib	Quartermaster (Chief Supply Officer)
Ic	Staff Officer, Intelligence (subordinate to Ia)
IIa	Chief Personnel Officer (Adjutant)
IIb	Second Personnel Officer (subordinate to IIa)
III	Chief Judge Advocate (subordinate to IIa)
IVa	Chief Administrative Officer (subordinate to Ib)
IVb	Chief Medical Officer (subordinate to Ib)
IVc	Chief Veterinary Officer (subordinate to Ib)
IVd	Chaplain (subordinate to IIa)
V	Motor Transport Officer (subordinate to Ib)
	National Socialist Guidance Officer (added in 1944)
	Special Staff Officers (Chief of Artillery, Chief of Projectors [Rocket Launchers], etc.)

APPENDIX 3: CHARACTERISTICS OF SELECTED GERMAN AND ALLIED TANKS OF WORLD WAR II

Model	Weight (tons)	Speed (mph)	Range (miles)	Main Armament	Crew
British					
Mark IV "Churchill"	43.1	15	120	16-pounder	5
Mark VI "Crusader"	22.1	27	200	12-pounder	5
Mark VIII "Cromwell"	30.8	38	174	175 mm	5
American[a]					
M3A1 "Stuart"	14.3	36	60	137 mm	4
M4A3 "Sherman"[b]	37.1	30	120	176 mm	5
German[a]					
PzKw II	9.3	25	118	120 mm	3
PzKw III	24.5	25	160	150 mm	5
PzKw IV	19.7	26	125	175 mm	5
PzKw V "Panther"	49.3	25	125	175 mm	5
PzKw VI "Tiger"	62.0	23	73	188 mm	5
Russian					
T34/Model 76	29.7	32	250	176 mm	4
T34/Model 85	34.4	32	250	185 mm	5
KV 1	52	25	208	176.2 mm	5
JSII "Joseph Stalin"	45.5	23	150	122 mm	4

[a]Characteristics of each tank varied somewhat from model to model.
[b]All American tanks were also in the British inventory. The British Shermans were sometimes outfitted with a heavier main battle gun. These Shermans were called "Fireflies."

NOTES

PREFACE

1. According to David Irving, *Trail of the Fox* (New York: 1977).
2. Erwin Rommel, *The Rommel Papers*, B. H. Liddell Hart, ed. (New York: 1953), pp. 82–84; Desmond Young, *Rommel: The Desert Fox* (New York: 1965), pp. 76–77. The tank loss figures exclude tanks of Czechoslovakian manufacture, which were apparently not reported. The 7th Panzer Division may have lost as many as 40 of these tanks during the French campaign.
3. Young, pp. 76–77.

CHAPTER I: THE SOURCES OF ROMMEL'S OFFICERS

1. T. N. Dupuy, *A Genius for War* (Fairfax, VA: 1984), pp. 47–48.
2. Ibid.
3. Charles de Gaulle, *The Army of the Future* (London: 1940), p. 47.
4. This figure excludes 300 medical and 200 veterinary officers, who were allowed by the Allies.
5. For the best English language books on the Reichswehr during the Seeckt era, see James S. Corum, *The Roots of the Blitzkrieg: Hans von Seeckt and German Military Reform* (Lawrence, KS: 1992) and Harold J. Gordon, Jr., *The Reichswehr and the German Republic, 1919–1926* (Princeton, NJ: 1957). For his discussion on sergeant-lieutenants and the establishment of the Provisional Reichswehr, see ff. 53.
6. W. E. Hart (pseudo.), *Hitler's Generals* (New York: 1944), p. 8; Richard Grunberger, *The Twelve-Year Reich: A Social History of Nazi Germany, 1933–1945* (New York: 1971), p. 22.
7. Joachim Kramarz, *Stauffenberg: The Life and Death of an Officer, 15 November 1907–20 July 1940* (London: 1967), p. 38.
8. W. E. Hart, *Hitler's Generals*, pp. 164–65.

9. One of the major flaws in the Treaty of Versailles from the Allied point of view was that the number of German NCOs was not restricted. By 1922, the Reichswehr had 48,680 NCOs (including corporals). This figure had increased in 1926, to the point that there were only 36,500 privates in the army—only about 35 percent of its total strength. See Corum, p. 47.

10. Ibid, p. 82.

11. Ibid, pp. 82–84.

12. Ibid, pp. 85–86.

13. Schleicher became chancellor of Germany in late 1932, but his tenure lasted only 57 days. He and his wife were murdered by the Gestapo on June 30, 1934.

14. Wiener-Neustadt is located south of Vienna in present-day Austria.

15. This section is based primarily on Siegfried Knappe, "Soldaten," an unpublished manuscript in the possession of the author. It was later published by Crown Publishers, New York.

16. Wolf Keilig, *Die Generale des Heeres* (Friedberg: 1986), p. 164 (hereafter cited as "Keilig").

CHAPTER II: KARL ROTHENBURG

1. Keilig, p. 285.

2. Georg Stumme died of a heart attack while serving as acting commander of Panzer Army Afrika during the 2nd Battle of El Alamein in October 1942. A full biography of him will appear in the author's forthcoming book, *Rommel's Captains: The Men Who Served the Desert Fox, North Africa, 1941–1942.*

3. Rommel's book, *Infantry Greift Au*, was essentially a rewrite of some of his lecture notes, which were based on his experiences in World War I. It was published by the Ludwig Voggenreiter publishing house in Potsdam in 1935. Hitler read it and named Rommel acting commander of his ad hoc bodyguard battalion during the Sudetenland, Czechoslovakian, and Polish crises in 1938 and 1939.

4. According to General of Panzer Troops Baron Hasso von Manteuffel, *Die 7. Panzer-Division, 1935–1945: Die "Gespenster-Division"* (Friedberg: 1978), p. 52. Other authors state that he was mortally wounded on June 28 and died the next day or believe that he was killed on June 28. Manteuffel (then a lieutenant colonel) was commanding the I/7th Rifle Regiment of the Ghost Division at the time and was involved in this battle; for this reason, his dates have been used here.

CHAPTER III: RUDOLF SIECKENIUS

1. Friedrich von Stauffenberg, "Panzer Commanders of the Western Front," unpublished manuscript in the possession of the author.

2. Oswald Lutz, the first German general of panzer troops (November 1, 1935), was born in Oehringen on November 6, 1876. He entered the Bavarian Army as a Fahnenjunker in a railroad battalion in 1894 and was commissioned

second lieutenant in the Bavarian 1st Engineer Battalion in 1896. After a long and distinguished career as an engineer and General Staff officer (he became a major general in 1931 and a lieutenant general on February 1, 1933), Lutz was named inspector of mobile troops in 1934, and commander of the panzer forces in 1935; simultaneously, he was inspector of mobile forces and army motorization. A true military pioneer and genius of organization and innovation, he was to some extent overshadowed by his more dynamic chief of staff, Heinz Guderian. When Hitler purged the army of conservative and anti-Nazi elements on February 4, 1938, Lutz was among those forced into retirement. He learned of his dismissal in a particularly tactless manner: he heard about it on the radio.

Lutz was briefly recalled to duty to head a special transport staff at Frankfurt/Oder in September 1941. He was retired again at the end of May 1942 and died in Munich on February 26, 1944.

Heinz Guderian (1888–1954) is known as "the Father of the Blitzkrieg." He was Germany's leading advocate of mobile warfare in the 1930s and greatly influenced Hitler in that direction. He commanded the 2nd Panzer Division (1935–38), XVI Motorized Corps (1938–39), XIX Motorized (later Panzer) Corps (1939–40), Panzer Group Guderian (1940), and 2nd Panzer Group (later Army) (1940–41). Relieved of command by Hitler in December 1941, for the German failure to take Moscow and for ordering an unauthorized retreat, he held no further commands, but he was recalled to active duty as inspector general of panzer troops (1943–44) and acting chief of the General Staff (July 21, 1944–March 1945). An outspoken leader, he was again relieved by Hitler after a bitter exchange and surrendered to the Western Allies in northern Italy in April 1945. He later wrote a book, *Panzer Leader*, which has been translated into many languages. Despite the fact that it is an invaluable historical document, it should be handled with care and not every word should be accepted at face value—especially concerning his alleged opposition to Hitler and the Nazis. His first order as chief of the General Staff, for example, was to outlaw the traditional army salute and replace it with the Nazi (Hitler) salute. He was, however, a brilliant tactician and field commander. He was promoted to colonel general on July 19, 1940.

3. Baron Maximilian von Weichs (1881–1954) was a cautious and conservative Bavarian who joined the Bavarian Army as a Fahnenjunker in 1900. He spent much of his pre–World War II career in the cavalry. He was given command of the 1st Panzer Division in 1935 because General Beck thought his conservative nature would be an effective counterweight to Guderian's blitzkrieg theories, which Beck considered impractical and too revolutionary. Weichs was never an effective panzer commander, but he proved to be a capable commander of marching infantry and horse-drawn formations. During World War II, he rose to the rank of field marshal and commanded the XIII Corps (1937–40) in Poland, 2nd Army (1940–42) and Army Group B on the Eastern Front (1942–43), and OB Southeast in the Balkans (1943–45). He was retired by Hitler

on March 25, 1945, because the Fuehrer distrusted his strong Catholic convictions. Almost alone of Hitler's marshals, he was not tried as a war criminal.

4. Johannes Streich later led the 5th Light Division in North Africa in 1941 before Erwin Rommel—who had a natural distaste for him—relieved him of his command for his failure to take Tobruk.

5. Paul Goerbig (1895–1974) was born in Hamburg and died in Saarbruecken. He joined the army as a Fahnenjunker when World War I broke out and was commissioned in the 30th Engineer Battalion the following year. He served in the Reichswehr and commanded the 67th Panzer Battalion in Poland. In late 1939, he was appointed a branch chief in OKH and spent most of the war there. From May 1943 to June 1944, he was in charge of the 509th Field Area Command (FK 509); then he commanded Maneuver Area Commands at Wischau, Bergen, and Sennelager. Promoted to major general in 1944, he led an ad hoc battle group from April 1, 1945. He was in American captivity from April 11, 1945, until 1947.

6. Stauffenberg MS.

7. Ibid. Neumann-Silkow was later killed in action in North Africa in December 1941. He was a major general commanding the 15th Panzer Division at the time.

8. Hans von Funck (1891–1979) was a former cavalry officer who turned out to be a very capable armored commander. He was military attaché to Lisbon when the war began but insisted on returning to Germany as the commander of a combat unit. He became commander of the 5th Panzer Regiment in October 1939 and took command of the 3rd Panzer Brigade a month later. On January 1, 1941, he was promoted to major general and was given command of the 5th Light Division. Earmarked by OKH to be the German commander in Africa, he made an unfavorable impression on Hitler, who opted for Erwin Rommel instead. (In an interview with the Fuehrer, the baron made some very unflattering comments about the Italians.) Funck was then given command of the 7th Panzer Division instead of the Afrika Korps, as sort of a consolation prize. (He did have friends at OKH.) Funck led the Ghost Division on the Eastern Front from June 1941 until early 1944. He was named commander of the XXXXVII Panzer Corps on March 5, 1944, led it with considerable success in Normandy, and was promoted to general of panzer troops. He was relieved of his command on September 3, 1944, because Hitler still disliked him and because the Fuehrer remembered a messy divorce Funck had gone through more than a decade before. Funck was never reemployed. He spent 10 years in Soviet prison camps after the war.

9. Hero Breusing's career never recovered from this incident. He was later given command of an independent panzer regiment in Russia (1941), commanded Panzer Troop Command XIII, a training brigade in Franconia (1941–44), and commanded the 122th Infantry Division on the Eastern Front (1944). He was commandant of Litzmannstadt (now Lodz, Poland) from September 1944 to January 1945 and ended the war as garrison commander at Stralsung.

His talents were totally wasted after 1940. Breusing, who was born in Berlin in 1894, died in Koblenz in 1973. He was belatedly promoted to major general on May 1, 1944.

10. Hans Valentin Hube was one of the best commanders in an army that had many excellent commanders; his talents, however, have generally been overlooked by historians. Born in 1890, he was a lieutenant in 1916 when he lost an arm at Verdun. He rehabilitated himself and was commanding an infantry company in the trenches when the war ended in 1918. The only handicapped officer selected for retention in the Reichsheer, he never allowed his handicap to get in his way and, in fact, became an excellent skier. He commanded the Infantry School at Doeberlitz (1935–39), the 3rd Infantry Regiment (1939–40) and the 16th Motorized (later Panzer) Division (1940–42), and the XIV Panzer Corps (1942–43). Ordered out of the Stalingrad pocket, Hube refused to go, and Hitler had to send in Gestapo agents, who literally forced him onto the airplane at gunpoint. Later he oversaw the reconstitution of the XIV Panzer Corps and led it brilliantly in the Sicilian campaign. After that, as a colonel general, he commanded the 1st Panzer Army in Russia with equal brilliance (November 1943–1944). Hitler decorated him with the Knight's Cross with Oak Leaves and Swords on April 20, 1944. The next day, Hube boarded an airplane heading back to the Eastern Front. It crashed within five miles of Berchtesgaden, killing everyone on board.

Hube was known throughout the German Army as *der Mensch*—the Man.

11. Count Hyazinth Strachwitz was a legendary figure in Hitler's Army. He was the descendent of a family of wealthy Silesian landowners. Born in 1893, he was educated at Gross-Lichterfelde (Germany's West Point) and was commissioned in the elite Guards Cavalry Corps in 1914. During the drive on Paris later that year, he led a number of bold cavalry raids—the last of which ended in his capture, 80 miles behind enemy lines. He remained in prison until 1919. He joined the Freikorps later that year and fought in the famous (and successful) Battle of Annaberg against the Polish Army. He managed the family estate until 1934, when he was accepted into the 2nd Panzer Regiment. This was much more suitable to his bold and restless nature. He fought in Poland (1939) and France (1940), where his daring raids earned him the nickname "the Panzer Count." In 1941, he commanded a battalion in the 18th Panzer. He and his men destroyed 300 Russian soft-skinned vehicles and several artillery battalions on the first day of Operation Barbarossa, the invasion of the Soviet Union. At one point during the invasion, a Russian bullet lodged in Strachwitz' body. Realizing that the wound was not life threatening, he cut it out himself and continued fighting. After he was promoted to lieutenant colonel and transferred to the 16th Panzer Division, he launched another raid and destroyed 158 Russian airplanes in an airport north of Stalingrad.

12. Gerd von Rundstedt (1875–1953) was educated in various cadet schools and entered the service in 1892, the year after Erwin Rommel was born. He spent more than 50 years in the German Army. During World War II, he commanded

Notes

Army Group South (1939), OB East (1939), Army Group A (1939–40), OB West (1940–41), Army Group South (1941), and OB West (1942–July 1944 and August 1944–March 1945). Hitler relieved him or forced him into retirement three times between 1938 and 1945. He was promoted to field marshal on July 19, 1940.

Ewald von Kleist was a cavalryman by profession. Born in 1881, he joined the army as a Fahnenjunker in 1901 and fought in World War I. He later commanded the 9th Infantry Regiment (1931–32), 2nd Cavalry Division (1932–35), and Wehrkreis VIII (1935–38). Forced into retirement by Hitler in 1938, he was recalled to active duty on the eve of World War II. He then led XXII Corps (1939), Panzer Group von Kleist (1940), 1st Panzer Group (later Army) (1940–42), Army Group A (1942–43), and Army Group South Ukraine (1943–44). He was relieved of his command by Adolf Hitler on March 31, 1944, and never reemployed. He died in a Soviet prison on October 15, 1954. A general of cavalry when the war began, he was promoted to colonel general on July 19, 1940, and to field marshal on February 1, 1943.

13. Gunther Angern was born in Kolberg, East Prussia, in 1892. He entered the Imperial Army as a Fahnenjunker in the 6th Jaeger Regiment in 1911 and was commissioned the following year. He spent all of World War I in the 6th Jaeger, serving as regimental adjutant for the last three years of the conflict. He later spent four years as a squadron commander in the 8th Cavalry Regiment (1924–28) and, after serving on the staff of the 1st Cavalry Division, commanded the 9th Cavalry Regiment (1935–38). He later commanded the 3rd Rifle Brigade (1938–39), which he led in Poland, and the 11th Rifle Brigade (1939–41), which he led in France and Russia. He assumed command of the 11th Panzer Division on August 15, 1941, but was seriously wounded nine days later. He did not return to active duty until September 25, 1942, when he took charge of the 16th Panzer Division. He committed suicide on February 2, 1943, to avoid Russian captivity. Angern was promoted to major general on September 1, 1941, and to lieutenant general on January 21, 1943. Dermot Bradley, Karl-Friedrich Hildebrand, and Markus Brockmann, *Die Generale des Heeres, 1921– 1945*, 7 vols. (Osnabrueck: 1993–2004), vol. 1, pp. 75–76.

14. Friedrich Paulus (1890–1957) was an excellent General Staff officer but an indecisive field commander. He entered the service as a Fahnenjunker in 1910, fought in World War I, and served in the Reichswehr. He was chief of staff of the XVI Motorized Corps (1938–39), chief of staff of Army Group 4 (1939), chief of staff of 10th Army (1939), chief of staff of 6th Army (1939–40), deputy chief of operations of OKH (1940–42), and commander of the 6th Army (1942–43). He was promoted rapidly under the Nazis: major general (1939), lieutenant general (1940), general of panzer troops (1942), colonel general (1942), and field marshal (February 1, 1943). Much to Hitler's disgust, he surrendered to the Soviets the next day, rather than commit suicide. He died in Dresden, East Germany. Paulus is often incorrectly referred to as "von Paulus." He did marry into the aristocracy and had an aristocratic air about him, but Paulus himself was not an aristocrat; his father, in fact, was a bookkeeper.

15. Curt von Burgsdorff was born on December 16, 1886. For his actions in the Stalingrad campaign, Burgsdorff was decorated with the Knight's Cross in April 1943 and was given command of the 580th Grenadier Regiment. Later promoted to lieutenant colonel of reserves, he survived the war and died on February 26, 1962.

16. Hans Adolf von Arenstoff was born in 1895 and entered the army as a Fahnenjunker when World War I broke out. Commissioned in the dragoons in 1915, he was selected for the Reichswehr and was a lieutenant colonel commanding the 152nd Reconnaissance Battalion when World War II began. He joined the panzer branch as a member of the staff of the 5th Panzer Brigade in late 1940 and assumed command of the 16th Rifle Brigade on January 14, 1942. He became acting commander of the 60th Motorized Infantry Division in the Stalingrad Pocket in November 1942 and surrendered on February 1, 1943. He died in the Soviet prison at Brjanka-Krasnopole on May 5, 1952.

17. After he was wounded, Strachwitz was evacuated to a military hospital in Breslau, where he recovered. He was then promoted to colonel and given command of a Tiger battalion in the Grossdeutschland Panzer Grenadier Division. After fighting at Kharkov and several other battles, he was again wounded. He was promoted to major general on April 1, 1944, and was named senior panzer officer of Army Group North. With 10 panzers and about 150 panzer grenadiers, and with the support of the naval cruiser *Luetzow* with its 280mm guns, he led a bold raid against a Soviet assembly area at Tuccum, where he captured 18,000 Russian soldiers and destroyed or captured 48 tanks and about 100 guns. He was decorated with the Knight's Cross with Oak Leaves, Swords, and Diamonds for this incredible victory. Again wounded shortly thereafter, he recovered in time to fight in the last battles on the Eastern Front. After Hitler committed suicide, he led an ad hoc formation from Czechoslovakia to Bavaria, to surrender to the Americans in May 1945. When he was released from the POW camps, he found that his estates had been confiscated by the Communists and his wife and younger son were dead. He went to work for Syria and reorganized that country's agriculture and army. When a coup overthrew that country's government, Strachwitz was a wanted man. He and his new (young) wife escaped a manhunt and returned to Germany in 1951. He died in poverty shortly thereafter. See James Lucas, *Hitler's Enforcers* (London: 1966), p. 17. Also see Samuel W. Mitcham, Jr., *Crumbling Empire: The German Defeat in the East, 1944* (Westport, CT: 2001), pp. 134–36, 140–42, 156, 160.

18. On rare occasions, there was an exception to this rule. A soldier who was critically wounded and for whom the doctors saw no chance for recovery could be awarded the Wounded Badge in Silver, even if he was suffering from his first wound.

19. Burkhart Muller-Hildebrand (born 1904) joined the army as a Fahnenjunker in 1923. He was commissioned into the 16th Cavalry Regiment in 1926, was admitted into the General Staff in the 1930s, and served on the staff of

OKH (1938–39). A major when the war broke out, he was named Ia of the 93rd Infantry Division on September 25, 1939. Later he served on the staff of the XVII Corps (1940), as adjutant to the chief of the General Staff of the Army (1940–42), chief of the Organizational Branch of the army (1942), acting commander of the 16th Panzer Division (early 1943), commander of the 24th Panzer Regiment (March 1, 1943–January 1, 1944), chief of staff of the XXXXVI Panzer Corps (April–August 1944), and chief of staff of the 3rd Panzer Army (September 1, 1944–end). He became a general in the West German Army (the Bundesheer) in 1956 and died in retirement on February 16, 1987.

20. OB South is the abbreviation for *Oberbefehlshaber* South. The term refers to the commander-in-chief of OB South or his headquarters. It has no exact English equivalent. An Oberbefehlshaber normally commanded at least two armies but not always. The OB West in 1944 commanded three army groups and several armies.

Albert Kesselring was born in Marktsheet, Bavaria, on November 20, 1885, the son of a local school teacher who saw to it that his son received an excellent education. Young Albert graduated from the Latin School at Bayreuth. He joined the 2nd Bavarian Foot Artillery Regiment as a Fahnenjunker in 1904, was commissioned in 1906, and was stationed at Metz for eight years, where he developed an interest in flying, and became a balloon observer and adjutant of the balloon battalion. During World War I, he fought on the Western Front, served on the staff of the 6th Army, and was appointed directly to the General Staff without having to attend even an abbreviated course—a rare mark of distinction. By 1932 he was a colonel in command of the 4th Artillery Regiment in Dresden. In 1933, somewhat against his will, Kesselring was transferred to the clandestine Luftwaffe. After that he was promoted rapidly and became a field marshal in 1940. In the meantime, he served as chief of staff of the Luftwaffe (1936–37) and built the Luftwaffe's ground establishment. He then commanded Luftkreis III (III Air District) and later Luftgau IV at Dresden, and Luftwaffe Group 1 and 1st Air Fleet in the Polish campaign. He commanded the 2nd Air Fleet in France, Russia, and the Mediterranean, all with great success. He was less successful in the Battle of Britain. Field Marshal Kesselring became the OB South in late 1941. He was the Axis commander-in-chief for much of the Italian campaign (1943–45), during which he simultaneously commanded Army Group C. After the war, he was tried by a British military court for his part in the execution of 335 Italian civilians in the Ardentine catacombs on March 24, 1944. He was convicted and condemned to death, but his sentence was commuted to life imprisonment in 1947. After he developed throat cancer in 1952, he was released as an act of clemency. His last years were plagued by ill-health. He died of heart failure at Bad Nauheim in 1960 and is buried in a small cemetery at Bad Wiessee, near Munich. All that appears on his tombstone is his name and rank.

Kesselring was a diplomat, a strong right-wing nationalist, a highly competent organizer, and an inveterate optimist—which sometimes had a negative impact on his campaigns.

21. Stauffenberg MS.

22. Konrad Heinrichs was born in 1890, joined the army as an infantry officer-cadet in 1911, received his commission in 1913, and fought in World War I. Selected for retention in the Reichswehr, he was a colonel on the staff of the 59th Infantry Regiment when World War II broke out. He assumed command of the regiment on November 1, 1939, and led it for more than two years. He took command of the 290th Infantry Division on May 6, 1942, and led it until February 2, 1944, when he assumed command of the 89th Infantry Division. Promoted to major general on July 1, 1942, and to lieutenant general on February 1, 1943, General Heinrichs was killed in action near Luettich on August 8, 1944.

23. Werner Richter was born in Zittau, Saxony, on October 21, 1893. He was educated at various cadet schools and entered the army as a Fahnenjunker in 1912. Commissioned in the infantry in 1913, he had served as chief of operations of the 4th Army (1939–40), chief of staff of 7th Army (1940–42), and commander of the 87th Infantry Division (1942–43) before assuming command of the 263rd on April 1, 1943. He died of his wounds in a Riga hospital on June 3, 1944.

24. Adolf Hemmann was born in 1895 and joined the Imperial Army as a Fahnenjunker in October 1914. Commissioned in the infantry in 1915, he fought in World War I but was not selected for the Reichswehr. He became a police officer in 1920 and returned to the army as a captain in 1935. He was a major in late 1937 when he assumed command of the I Battalion, 51st Infantry Regiment, which he led in the first year of the war. Later he was named adjutant of the XXVIII Corps (August 1940), commander of the 426th Infantry Regiment (June 17, 1941), course commander at the Infantry School at Doeberlitz (November 2, 1942), and commander of the 263rd Infantry Division (August 14, 1944). He surrendered the division to the Russians on May 9, 1945, and spent more than 10 years in Soviet prisons. Finally released in October 1955, his health was broken and he died at Friedberg/Hesse in 1957. He was promoted to lieutenant colonel (1939), colonel (1942), major general (October 1, 1944), and lieutenant general (April 20, 1945).

25. Hubert Lendle (born 1892) entered the army as a Fahnenjunker in 1911. Commissioned in the 126th Infantry Regiment in 1913, he fought in World War I, served in the Reichsheer, and commanded the V Antitank Troop in 1938. Promoted to colonel in 1938, he commanded the 26th Replacement Regiment (1939), the 345th Infantry Regiment (late 1939–1940), Maneuver Area Veldahorn (1940), and the 576th Infantry Regiment (1940–42). He assumed command of the 221st Security Division on July 5, 1942, and commanded it until August 1944. He was later recalled from retirement and commanded Division Staff 610 (January 28, 1945–end). He was promoted to major general in 1942 and to lieutenant general on June 1, 1943.

26. Baron Albert Digeon von Monteton entered the service as a Fahnenjunker in the cavalry in 1911. By 1938, he was a colonel, commanding the 15th Cavalry Regiment. Later he led the 167th Infantry Regiment (1939–42) and was acting commander of the 342nd Infantry Division (May–July 1942). He assumed

command of the 391st Field Training Division on September 10, 1942. He was promoted to major general in 1942 and to lieutenant general in 1943. He surrendered to the Soviets in May 1945 and was hanged in Libau on February 3, 1946, for alleged war crimes he committed as commandant. His older brother, Constantin, commanded the 3rd Panzer Army's Weapons School. He was killed in action on June 27, 1944, and was posthumously promoted to major general.

27. Friedrich Jeckeln was born in 1895, the son of a factory worker. He served in the artillery in World War I, became a pilot, earned a commission, and was discharged as a second lieutenant in 1920. He fathered three children, abandoned his wife (allegedly because she had Jewish blood), then remarried and fathered six more by his second wife. Short-tempered, cruel, and an extremist, he joined the Nazi Party in the 1920s and made a name for himself as a street fighter and brawler. Hitler named him a Reichstag delegate in 1932. He joined the Allgemeine-SS (the General SS) and rose rapidly, reached the rank of *SS-Obergruppenfuehrer* (General of SS) in 1936, but, because of his lack of education and training, was only offered command of a battalion in the *SS-Totenkopf* (Death's Head) Division in 1940. Named Higher SS and Police Commander West after France fell, he commanded an infamous *Einsatzgruppen* (murder squad) in Russia and, as Higher SS and Police Leader for South Russia (and later Higher SS and Police Leader for the Baltic States and Northern Russia) (1941–45), was responsible for the mass murder of tens of thousands of Jews and Slavs. He also combined mass murder with antipartisan operations. In the summer of 1944, he was given command of an ad hoc battle group and actually did well in battles with regular Soviet troops. This led to his appointment as commander of the V SS Volunteer Mountain Corps (1945). He was hanged in Riga on February 3, 1946.

28. Major General Emmo von Roden was born in 1892 and joined the army as a cavalry Fahnenjunker in 1912. He fought in World War I, served in the Reichsheer, and was commander of the II Battalion, 84th Infantry Regiment in 1937. He commanded three infantry and replacement regiments between 1939 and 1943. Promoted to major general in 1943, he held a minor rear-area post in the East until January 1945, when he was given command of the 286th Security Division. He fought in the Battle of Berlin and, after the city fell, disappeared on May 3, 1945. He was never heard from again.

29. Helmuth Weidling was born in 1891 and was educated in various cadet schools. He joined the army in 1911 and, by 1938, was a colonel commanding the 56th Artillery Regiment. Later he commanded the 20th Artillery Regiment (1939–40), Arko 128 (1940–41), 86th Infantry Division (1942–43), XXXXI Panzer Corps (1943–44), and LVI Panzer Corps (1945). He was promoted to general of artillery on January 1, 1944. Weidling surrendered Berlin to the Russians on May 2, 1945, and went into Soviet captivity, where he died in Vladimir Prison (southeast of Moscow) on November 17, 1955.

30. SS Major General Gustav Krukenberg was the son of a highly respected professor of medicine. Born in Bonn on March 8, 1888, he joined the army at an

early age and was a lieutenant in the Demonstration Regiment of the Artillery Gunnery School by 1909. He served in an artillery regiment in World War I, became a General Staff officer, and ended the war as a captain on the staff of the LVIII Corps. Not selected for the Reichswehr, he earned a law degree and joined the civil service, working for the Reichs Archives (as an assistant) and for the defense ministry (as a press representative). He was also the leading German delegate to the German-French *Studienkomittee* in Paris from 1921 to 1926. He received an SS commission in 1936. By 1939, he was an SS captain, commanding a battalion. He fought on the Eastern Front, served a tour of duty at SS Headquarters, and in January 1944 became chief of staff of the V SS Mountain Corps. That fall, Krukenberg became commander of Waffen-SS in Ostland, with headquarters in Riga. He was promoted to SS major general on September 23, 1944. At the end of September, he became de facto commander of French SS formations.

CHAPTER IV: KARL AUGUST HANKE

1. The first Reichsfuehrer-SS was Joseph Berchtold. Born in Ingolstadt, Bavaria, on March 6, 1897, he joined the Imperial Army in 1915 and fought on the Western Front, where he earned a commission as a second lieutenant. He settled in Munich after the war, where he owned a stationery shop and was active in the tobacco business. He joined the Nazi Party in 1920 and was commander of Storm Troop (Stosstrupp) Hitler during the Beer Hall Putsch in November 1923. After the coup collapsed, Berchtold (now a wanted criminal) fled to Austria, where he became regional business leader of the Nazi Party in Carinthia (Kaernten). He returned to Germany after he was amnestied in 1926. He became Fuehrer of the Schutzstaffel (SS) on or about June 9, 1926, but resigned the following year because of a conflict with Pfeffer von Salomon, the chief of staff of the SA (Brownshirts). Later, Berchtold served as chief writer for the *Voelkischer Beobachter* (the Nazi Party's official newspaper) and was deputy chief editor of the paper from 1938 until February 1943. He was also a member of the Reichstag (German parliament) from 1936 to 1945 and was a member of the Reich Senate of Culture. He remained active in the Brownshirts and, during the Night of the Long Knives, accompanied Hitler to Bad Wiessee and was involved in the arrest of Ernst Roehm and the purge of the SA. Berchtold was promoted to SA-Obergruppenfuehrer (General of Storm Troops) in 1942. He also served in the army as a reserve officer early in the war and was promoted to captain of reserves in 1940. After the war, Berchtold was convicted as a minor war criminal and served a brief prison term. He died in Herrsching am Ammersee, near Munich, on August 23, 1962.

Erhard Heiden was a police officer in Bavaria who joined the Stosstrupp Hitler in 1922. He became Reichsfuehrer-SS when Berchtold resigned in 1927. He was replaced by Himmler on January 6, 1929.

2. The rank *SS-Oberfuehrer* had no direct English equivalent. It falls between colonel (*SS-Standartenfuehrer*) and major general (*Brigadefuehrer*).

Notes

3. David Irving, *The War Path* (New York: 1979), p. 159.

4. Hans-Otto Meissner, *Magda Goebbels*, translated by Gwendolen Mary Keeble (New York: 1980), pp. 175–76.

5. Born in Prague on September 14, 1914, Lida Baarova attended a Czech conservatory for actors and actresses in Prague and appeared in her first film as a professional actress in 1931, at the age of 17. She became a star after appearing in the movie *Barcarole* in 1934. She was living with her costar, Gustav Froehlich, when she met Goebbels at a party. She appeared in several propaganda movies in quick order thereafter. She soon broke up with the jealous Froehlich, who cursed Goebbels to his face. (Some sources even say that Froehlich challenged Goebbels to a duel.) In any case, the propaganda minister had Froehlich's military deferment cancelled and the jilted lover was soon drafted into the army.

Lida's real name was Lidmila Babkova, but it was Germanized to Lida Baarova.

6. See http://www.mishalv.com/Baarova.html.

7. Irving, *War Path*, p. 159.

8. Ibid, pp. 192–94.

9. After her affair with Goebbels, Lida Baarova found it increasingly difficult to work. The Gestapo called her in and informed her that she was officially blacklisted in Germany and was forbidden to attend public events, including movie premieres. When she violated the order, they arranged for a group of hecklers to harass her, shouting "Whore! Whore!" when she attended the premiere of her own movie, *Der Spieler* (*The Player*). She returned to Czechoslovakia but then moved to Rome in 1943.

After the war, Baarova was imprisoned by the Americans for 16 months for collaborating with the Third Reich and possibly spying for the Nazis. Her acting career, of course, was ruined, and she died in poverty. In her later years she lived in Salzburg, where she developed a drug and drinking problem. She remarked in an interview that Goebbels loved her, but she did not love him. She was, however, afraid of him, which is why she had an affair with him. She wrote a memoir, *The Sweet Bitterness of My Life*, which was published posthumously in Czech and German. She died of Parkinson's disease in Salzburg on October 31, 2000, at the age of 86. She was married twice—in 1949 (divorced in 1956) and in 1970 (to a gynecologist 20 years her senior). This marriage also ended in divorce.

10. Grynszpan fired five shots, two of which hit Rath in the abdomen. Grynszpan was not tried for his crime but remained in a Paris juvenile penal facility until Germany overran the country in 1940. He was placed on a train heading south and escaped when it was strafed by a German airplane. He thus temporarily regained his freedom. For reasons not made clear by the records, however, he turned himself in to officials at the prison in Bourges a few days later. He was extradited to Germany in July 1940 and died in a German prison (apparently of illness) in late 1942 or 1943. His parents survived the Holocaust.

11. Bernt Engelmann, *In Hitler's Germany*, translated by Krishna Winston (New York: 1986; reprint, New York: 1986), p. 125.

12. John Toland, *Adolf Hitler* (New York: 1976; reprint, New York: 1977), p. 688.

13. Lionel Kochan, *Pogrom: 10 November 1938* (London: 1957): pp. 71–72.

14. Rita Thalmann and Emmanuel Feinermann, *Crystal Night*, translated by Gilles Cremonesi (London, 1974; reprint, Washington, DC: 1980), pp. 70–71.

15. Count von der Schulenburg left the police shortly thereafter and joined the army, where he became a leader in anti-Hitler conspiracy. He was hanged in 1944.

16. Alfons Heck, *A Child of Hitler* (Frederick, CO: 1985), pp. 27–28.

17. Werner Maser, *Hitler: Legend, Myth and Reality*, translated by Peter and Betty Ross (New York: 1973), p. 198.

18. Toland, p. 689.

19. Meissner, pp. 203–5.

20. In his Last Will and Testament, Adolf Hitler named Goebbels his successor as chancellor of Germany. On May 1, 1945—the day after Hitler committed suicide—both Joseph and Magda Goebbels killed themselves. They had murdered their own six children while they slept the night before.

21. After Hanke's death, Freda remarried and took the name Roessler.

22. Spielhagen was executed on January 30, 1945.

23. Hugh R. Trevor-Roper, *Hitler's Table Talk* (London: 1973), April 25, 1945.

24. Joseph Goebbels, *Final Entries, 1945: The Diaries of Joseph Goebbels*, Hugh Trevor-Roper, ed. (New York: 1978; reprint, New York: 1979), March 3, 1945.

25. Ibid, March 20, 1945.

CHAPTER V: JOACHIM VON METZSCH

1. Christian Zweng, ed., *Die Dienstlaufbahnen der Offiziere des Generalstabes des deutschen Heeres, 1935–1945* (Osnabrueck: 1995 and 1998), vol. 2, p. 64.

2. Erich Hoepner was born in East Prussia in 1905 and joined the army as a Faehnrich in the dragoons in 1905. He fought in World War I, served in the Reichswehr, and commanded the XVI Motorized Corps in Poland (1939) and France (1940). He was promoted to lieutenant general in 1938 and to general of cavalry in 1939. He commanded the 4th Panzer Group (later Army) in Russia 1941. Hoepner was an early member of the anti-Hitler resistance and, in 1938, actively planned to use the 1st Light Division against Hitler and the SS during the Sudetenland Crisis.

3. After Hitler relieved him of his command for ordering an unauthorized retreat in Russia in 1942, Hoepner remained active in the anti-Hitler conspiracy. His former Ib (chief supply officer) Colonel Claus von Stauffenberg, placed the bomb under Hitler's table and narrowly missed assassinating him on July 20, 1944. Hoepner was hanged for his part in the conspiracy on August 6, 1944.

4. Ernst-Guenther Baade was a cavalry officer and one of the mavericks of the German Army. His biography will be covered in the author's forthcoming book, *Rommel's Captains: The Men Who Served the Desert Fox, North Africa, 1941–1942*.

Notes

CHAPTER VI: DR. WILHELM BAUMEISTER

1. Keilig, p. 388.

CHAPTER VII: HANS VON LUCK

1. Hans von Luck, *Panzer Commanders* (New York: 1989), p. 5. Colonel von Luck's memoirs are the source of much of this essay.

2. Ibid.

3. Ibid, p. 32.

4. Ibid, p. 33.

5. Colonel Irmfried von Wechmar (1899–1959) was a Berliner. He later commanded the 147th Panzer Grenadier Regiment on the Eastern Front (1943–44). His son—also a member of the 3rd Panzer Recon—later served as German ambassador to London.

Captain Wolfgang-Dieter Everth joined the 3rd Panzer Reconnaissance Battalion (then the 3rd Reconnaissance Battalion) in 1935 and served as interim commander and later commander of the unit. He was severely wounded in 1943. Later, he served in the Bundesheer and retired as a full colonel.

6. Gustav von Vaerst later led the 5th Panzer Army in Tunisia from March 9, 1943, until it surrendered on May 12, 1943.

7. Rudolf Schmundt was born in Metz, Alsace, in 1896. An infantry Fahnen-junker in 1914, he became chief adjutant to the Fuehrer in early 1938, and rose from major to general of infantry between 1938 and 1944. He became chief of the Army Personnel Office on October 2, 1942. Considered decent but rather slow and politically naive by most of the other generals, Schmundt nevertheless did a good job as chief of the Army Personnel Office. On July 20, 1944, he was blinded by Colonel von Stauffenberg's bomb during the unsuccessful anti-Hitler putsch. He died of his wounds in the hospital at Ratsenburg on October 1, 1944.

8. Dagmar's mother was one-fourth Jewish but was tolerated by the Nazis because she was the wife of a prominent businessman. She judged the situation correctly, however, and realized that this toleration would not continue indefinitely. Accordingly, she went to Switzerland on a vacation and never returned.

9. Luck succeeded Colonel Rolf Maempel (1895–1955), a Knight's Cross holder from the Eastern Front, who had returned to Germany because of illness.

10. Edgar Feuchtinger, who was born in Metz in 1894, was an artillery officer and had commanded a horse-drawn artillery regiment on the northern sector of the Eastern Front. He had no experience whatsoever in commanding armored units. He had, however, organized the military parts of the Nuremberg rallies, so he had many friends in the Nazi Party, including Adolf Hitler. He used this influence to obtain command of the 21st Panzer Division and to pirate von Luck away from the Panzer Lehr Division.

11. General Feuchtinger did a poor job commanding the 21st Panzer Division in Normandy and in the subsequent retreat from France. During the night of June 5–6, as British paratroopers landed in his zone in preparation for the

D-Day landings, Feuchtinger could not be found. He was eventually located in a Paris nightclub. On Christmas Eve, 1944, while his troops were fighting the Americans, a German investigator found that Feuchtinger was away without leave (AWOL). He was arrested, demoted to the rank of private, and condemned to death, but his Nazi friends obtained a reprieve for him. He later worked for the U.S. Army in Krefeld and was under investigation for corruption when he died in Berlin on January 21, 1960.

12. One of only two men to reach the rank of *SS-Oberstgruppenfuehrer und Generaloberst der Waffen-SS* (colonel general of Waffen-SS), Sepp Dietrich was born in the village of Hawangen, Swabia, in 1892, the son of a master meat packer. He dropped out of school after eight years and was employed as an agricultural driver and an apprentice in the hotel business before serving four years on the Western Front, mainly in the artillery. He was wounded twice and, in 1918, served in an elite *Sturm* (assault) battalion and in one of Germany's few tank units. He later served in the Freikorps and in the Bavarian Provincial Police, but he was dismissed for marching with Hitler in the Beer Hall Putsch of 1923. A tough, burly brawler, he was Hitler's constant companion in the "years of struggle." He was rewarded with a promotion to *SS-Gruppenfuehrer* (lieutenant general of SS) in 1931 and the command of the Leibstandarte Adolf Hitler, the Fuehrer's personal bodyguard. This unit later grew into the 1st SS Panzer Division "Leibstandarte Adolf Hitler." Dietrich led it until 1943, when he assumed command of the I SS Panzer Corps. In August 1944, he became commander of the 6th (later 6th SS) Panzer Army, which he led until the end of the war. He was sentenced to 25 years imprisonment for his part in the Malmedy massacre (although he was nowhere near Malmedy at the time and knew nothing about the atrocity). After passions cooled, Dietrich was released in 1958. The West German government, however, sentenced him to 18 months imprisonment for his part in the Blood Purge of 1934. He was released after five months because of failing health. He died (perhaps in his sleep) of a massive heart attack in 1966.

13. Luck, p. 154.

14. Joseph Rauch (born 1902) had joined the army as a volunteer in the 7th Engineer Battalion in 1919. He was discharged as a sergeant in 1931, after his twelve-year enlistment expired. He returned to active duty as a reserve lieutenant in 1935. After World War II began, he rose rapidly in rank, successively commanding an engineer company, an engineer replacement battalion, and an engineer battalion and a panzer grenadier regiment on the Eastern Front. He assumed command of the 192nd Panzer Grenadier Regiment when it was rebuilt in May 1943.

15. In late November 1944, after he recovered from his illness, Joseph Rauch attended a brief Division Commanders' Course and, on January 1, 1945, assumed command of the 18th Panzer Grenadier Division on the Eastern Front. He was promoted to major general on April 20, 1945—Hitler's last birthday. He surrendered to the Russians at the end of the war and remained in Soviet prisons until 1955. He resided in Landsberg after the war and died in 1984.

16. Luck, pp. 262–63.

17. "Colonel Hans von Luck," *London Times*, Obituary, August 1997, kindly supplied to the author by Mr. Hardy of the Axis History Forum, August 28, 2001.

CHAPTER VIII: JOACHIM ZIEGLER

1. Ernst-Guenther Kraetschmer, *Die Ritterkreuztraeger der Waffen-SS* (Oldendorf: 1982), p. 609.

2. Ritter Wilhelm von Thoma later commanded the Afrika Korps and, as a general of panzer troops, was captured by the British at El Alamein on November 4, 1942.

3. According to Nikolaus von Preradovich, *Die Generale der Waffen-SS* (Berg am See: 1985), p. 217.

4. General of SS Felix Steiner was born in 1896, the son of an East Prussian school teacher. He joined the army as a Fahnenjunker in the 41st (5th East Prussian) Infantry Regiment in March 1914. He was severely wounded in the Battle of Tannenberg on the Russian Front, where he received the Iron Cross. He was commissioned in January 1915 and assigned to a machine gun battalion. After three years on the Eastern Front, he fought in France in 1918 and was promoted to first lieutenant in October. Steiner was discharged in January 1919 and immediately joined an East Prussian Freikorps and fought in the Baltic States. He was allowed to rejoin the Reichsheer in 1921 and underwent General Staff training. In 1930, he was a captain with the 1st Infantry Regiment in Koenigsburg, East Prussia. Promoted to major in 1933, he resigned from the army and joined the Waffen-SS later that same year. By 1935, he was an SS lieutenant colonel, commanding the III Battalion of the SS *Standarte* (regiment) "Deutschland." Later he commanded the regiment, the motorized SS Division "Viking" (later the 5th SS Panzer Division "Viking") (late 1940–1943), and the III SS Panzer Corps (1943–45). His service from 1941 to 1945 was exclusively on the Eastern Front, where he performed in a competent manner. During the Battle of Berlin, he commanded the ad hoc Armeegruppe Steiner. He surrendered to the Anglo-Americans in May 1945. A prisoner of war until 1948, he died in Munich in 1966.

5. Krukenberg surrendered to the Russians on May 8, 1945, and spent more than 10 years as a prisoner of war. Released in 1955, he died on October 23, 1980, at the age of 92.

6. Mohnke was born in Luebeck in 1911; he enlisted in the SS Leibstandarte in 1933. Mohnke, who spent most of the war with the 1st SS Panzer Division "Leibstandarte Adolf Hitler" and eventually became its commander, was apparently responsible for a number of atrocities on the Eastern Front. He also shot Canadian prisoners in Normandy and, as division commander, was linked to the murders of American prisoners during the Battle of the Bulge. He was captured by the Soviets on May 2, 1945, and spent 10 years in Russian prison camps. Released in 1955, he moved to a suburb of Hamburg and became a wealthy businessman. He died of natural causes on August 6, 2001.

7. See Jochen von Lang, *The Secretary*, translated by Christa Armstrong and Peter White (Athens, OH: 1979), p. 243. Lang succeeded in unearthing Bormann's body in 1972, within 15 meters of where he predicted it would be.

CHAPTER IX: GOTTFRIED FROELICH

1. Bradley et al., vol. 4, pp. 119–20.

2. The 8th Panzer Division was formed from the 3rd Light Division (which had fought in Poland) in October 1939. It fought in Belgium and France in 1940 and spent the period from 1941–45 on the Eastern Front. It surrendered to the Russians in Moravia at the end of the war.

3. Hermann Balck was born in Danzig, East Prussia, in 1893. He entered the army as a Fahnenjunker in 1913, fought in World War I, served in the Reichswehr, and distinguished himself as commander of the 1st Rifle Regiment in France in 1940. Later he commanded the 3rd Panzer Regiment (1940–41) and the 2nd Panzer Brigade (1941). After a tour of duty with the Office of Mobile Troops at OKH, he led the 11th Panzer Division (1942–43) and was commander of the Grossdeutschland Panzer Grenadier Division (1943), XXXX Panzer Corps (1943), and XXXXVIII Panzer Corps (1943–44).

4. F. W. von Mellenthin later served as Ic of Panzer Army Afrika in 1942.

5. See Samuel W. Mitcham, Jr., *The Crumbling Empire* (Westport, CT: 2001).

6. Alex Buchner, *Ostfront 1944*, translated by David Johnston (West Chester, PA: 1991), p. 222.

7. Friebe was unemployed until September 1, 1944, when he was named chief of staff of Wehrkreis III in Berlin. When the city became part of the combat zone, he handed his duties over to the chief of staff of the LVI Panzer Corps and fled the city, thus escaping Russian captivity. He died in Stuttgart in 1962. He had been born in Silesia in 1897 and had been Ia of the 20th Infantry Division (1938–40) before becoming chief of staff of the XXXXVIII Motorized (later Panzer) Corps at the beginning of 1941.

8. Hermann Balck led the 4th Panzer Army (1944), Army Group G on the Western Front (1944), and the 6th Army (late 1944–end). He was promoted to general of panzer troops on November 1, 1944. He moved to Stuttgart after the war and died at Erbenbach-Rockenau on November 29, 1982, less than two weeks before his 89th birthday. He is buried at Asperg, near Ludwigsburg.

9. Corps Group von Tettau had been formed from the 604th Special Purposes Division Staff (*Div. Stab z.b.V. 604*) on February 4, 1945. It consisted largely of Volkssturm and replacement and training units.

10. Hasso von Manteuffel (1897–1978) was an East Prussian cavalry officer who rose rapidly in the tank branch, from major in 1939 to general of panzer troops in 1944, despite missing both the Polish and French campaigns. He commanded the 3rd Motorcycle Battalion (1940), I/7th Rifle Regiment (of the 7th Panzer Division) (1941), 6th Rifle Regiment (1941–42), and the 7th Rifle (later Panzer Grenadier) Brigade (1942). Later he commanded the ad hoc Division

Manteuffel in Tunisia (1943) until he was wounded and had to be evacuated. After he recovered, Manteuffel commanded the 7th Panzer Division (1943–44) and the Grossdeutschland Panzer Grenadier Division (1944) on the Russian Front. In 1944, he led the 5th Panzer Army in France and the Battle of the Bulge (1944–45) and ended the war commanding the 3rd Panzer Army on the Eastern Front. One of the best commanders in the Wehrmacht, he was only 48 years old in 1945. He was later highly successful in private business in West Germany.

CHAPTER X: GEORG VON BISMARCK

1. Bradley et al., vol. 1, p. 417.

2. In 1916, for example, the 6th Jaeger Battalion was attached to the 2nd Landwehr Division on the Western Front and fought in the Argonne. See U.S. War Department, "Histories of 251 Divisions of the German Army Which Participated in the War (1914–1918)," Document No. 905. (Washington, DC: 1920), pp. 131–32.

3. See Rolf O. G. Stoves, *Die Gepanzerten und Motorisierten deutschen Grossverbaende (Divisionen und selbstaendige Brigaden, 1935–1945)* (Friedberg: 1986), p. 132; Andris J. Kursietis, *The Wehrmacht at War* (Soesterberg, The Netherlands: 1999), p. 103; and Samuel W. Mitcham, Jr., *The Panzer Legions: A Guide to the German Army Tank Divisions of World War II and Their Commanders* (Westport, CT: 2001), pp. 153–56.

Horst Stumpff (1887–1958) was not able to return to active duty for six months. He was initially assigned to a post as an inspector for Recruiting Area Koenigsburg. In 1944, he became General Inspector of Panzer Troops in the Replacement Army. He had joined the army as a Fahnenjunker in 1907 and had previously commanded the 3rd Panzer Brigade (1938–39) and the 3rd Panzer Division (1939–40). He was promoted to general of panzer troops on November 9, 1944.

4. Gustav-Georg Knabe (1897–1972) was the former commander of the 15th Motorcycle Battalion (1941).

5. Correlli Barnett, *The Desert Generals*, 2nd ed. (Bloomington, IN: 1982), p. 156.

6. Baron Kurt von Liebenstein (1899–1975) was the commander of the 164th Light Afrika Division. He was captured when Army Group Afrika was destroyed in Tunisia in May 1943. Later he was a major general in the Bundeswehr.

CHAPTER XI: FRIEDRICH FUERST

1. Bradley et al., vol. 4, pp. 143–45.

2. Hermann Hoth was born in 1885 and attended a number of cadet schools. He entered the army as a Faehnrich in 1904 and was commissioned in the infantry in 1905. Although an infantryman by trade, he proved to be an excellent

commander of motorized and armored forces. During World War II, he commanded the XV Motorized Corps (1938–40), 3rd Panzer Group (later Army) (1940–41), 17th Army (1941–42), and 4th Panzer Army (1942–43). He was promoted to general of infantry in 1938 and to colonel general on July 19, 1940. Hitler did not appreciate his opinions on the deteriorating situation on the Eastern Front and forced him into retirement on November 30, 1943. He was never reemployed. He was captured by the Americans, tried as a war criminal, and was sentenced to 15 years in Landsberg prison in late 1948. He was released in April 1954 and retired to Goslar am Harz, where he died on January 25, 1971.

3. The 34th Infantry Division was created at Koblenz (Wehrkreis XII) in August 1939 and remained in the Saar or Eifel until the invasion of France. Later it was on occupation duty in Belgium, before crossing into Russia on June 22, 1941. It fought at Minsk, White Russia, and Smolensk, and was advancing on Moscow when Fuerst assumed command. Later it fought at Orel, Poltava, and Cherkassy, and was crushed at Uman in April 1944. It was later rebuilt and served in northern Italy (Ligurien) until the end of the war. Georg Tessin, *Verbaende und Truppen der deutschen Wehrmacht und Waffen-SS im Zweiten Weltkrieg*, 16 vols. (Osnabrueck: 1973–81), vol. 4, pp. 34–35.

4. *Division z.b.V. 442* was formed in Wehrkreis VI with Landschutzen battalions. It was initially assigned to the 5th Army on the Lower Rhine. It was sent to central Russia in January 1943. Tessin, vol. 10, p. 182.

5. The 442nd Division was not officially dissolved until August 24, 1944, but it had already ceased to exist.

CHAPTER XII: FRIEDRICH-CARL VON STEINKELLER

1. Keilig, p. 331.

2. The 60th Panzer Grenadier Division "Feldherrnhalle" was formed in southern France in June 1943 to replace the 60th Motorized Infantry Division, which had been destroyed at Stalingrad. After the second 60th was destroyed during Operation Bagration, a third FHH unit, the 13th Panzer Division "Feldherrnhalle," was formed. It also served on the Eastern Front and most of it was destroyed at Budapest in February 1945. The remnants of the FHH surrendered to the Russians at Deutsch-Brod in May 1945.

CHAPTER XIII: HANS JOACHIM VON KRONHELM

1. The author wishes to thank the colonel's son, Eberhard von Kronhelm, for kindly providing information about his father.

2. The II/45th Motorized Artillery was formed at Wetzlar in late 1939 as a GHQ (General Headquarters) unit under Wehrkreis IX. It was attached to the field component of the military district (IX Corps) in November 1939.

3. Oberkommando der Wehrmacht., *Kriegstagebuch des Oberkommando der Wehrmacht (Wehrmachtfuehungsstab)*, 8 vols. (Frankfurt/Main: 1961), vol. II,

pp. 1387, 1394; Kurt Mehner, ed., *Die Geheimen Tagesberichte der deutschen Wehrmachtfuehrung im Zweiten Weltkrieg, 1939–1945,* 12 vols. (Osnabrueck: 1984–95), vol. 5, p. 330; vol. 6, p. 546; Samuel W. Mitcham, Jr., *Panzer Legions:* pp. 190–92; Horst Scheibert, *Die Traeger des deutschen Kreuzes in Gold* (Friedberg: n.d.), p. 209; Rolf O. G. Stoves, *Die 22. Panzer-Division, 25. Panzer-Division, 27. Panzer-Division und 233. Reserve-Panzer-Division* (Friedberg: 1985), pp. 195–262, 301; Tessin, vol. 4, p. 253; vol. 6, p. 319; vol. 10, p. 93; Martin Windrow, *The Panzer Divisions* (London: 1985), p. 12.

4. Helmut Michalik entered the service as a Fahnenjunker in the 1st Dragoons when World War I broke out. He served in the Reichsheer and commanded the 30th Antitank Battalion (1937–40) and the 140th Rifle (later Panzer Grenadier) Regiment (1940–late 1942). After commanding the 27th Panzer, he was a member of the staff of the 18th Army, then besieging Leningrad (1942–44). He was assigned to Army Group South Ukraine in 1944 as a panzer division commander. The records, however, do not indicate that he actually assumed command of a tank division. In any case, he was mortally wounded in July 1944. He was posthumously promoted to major general.

Hans Troeger was born in Plauen in 1896 and entered the Imperial Army as a Fahnenjunker in the 9th Engineer Battalion in 1915. After fighting in World War I, he entered the Reichswehr and was the adjutant of the Higher Cavalry Officer with the Mobile Troops Office in OKH. When World War II broke out, he led the 3rd Motorcycle Battalion in Poland and France (1939–40) and the 64th Motorcycle Battalion in Russia (1940–41). Later he commanded the 103rd Rifle Regiment (late 1941–1942) and was commandant of the School for Battalion Commanders (1942). After leading the 27th Panzer Division (1942–43), he commanded the School for Panzer Troops (1943), the 25th Panzer Division (1943–44), and the 13th Panzer Division (May–September 1944). Along with the bulk of his division, he was captured by the Red Army in Rumania and spent 11 years in Soviet prisons. He was released in 1955 and died in 1982.

5. Naturally, the 127th Panzer Battalion did not take its equipment with it. It was left in Russia. The men were sent to Versailles, France.

CHAPTER XIV: EDUARD CRASEMANN

1. U.S. War Department, "Histories of 251 Divisions of the German Army Which Participated in the War (1914–1918)," Document no. 905 (Washington, DC: 1920), pp. 308–11; Bradley et al., vol. 2, pp. 474–75.

2. The High Command of the Army was headquartered at Zossen, which was about 20 miles south of Berlin.

3. See U.S. War Department, "Handbook on German Military Forces," Technical Manual TM-E 30-451 (Washington, DC: 1945), pp. I-21–I-22.

4. Baron Hans-Karl von Esebeck was wounded near Tobruk on May 13, 1941. He recovered and later commanded the LVII Panzer Corps (1943–44) on the Eastern Front.

5. F. W. von Mellenthin, *Panzer Battles: A Study in the Employment of Armor in the Second World War* (Norman, OK: 1956), p. 93.

6. J. A. I. Agar-Hamilton and L. C. F. Turner, *Crisis in the Desert, May–July 1942* (Cape Town: 1957), p. 66.

7. Barnett, p. 156.

8. Heinz Randow later commanded the 21st Panzer Division, following the death of General von Bismarck. He was killed in action in Tripolitania on December 21, 1942.

9. Tessin, vol. 4, p. 208.

10. Hans Boelsen (1894–1960) was an incredibly well-educated man who started his military career as an eighteen-year-old war volunteer (*Kriegsfreiwilliger*) when World War I broke out. He became a Fahnenjunker in the 180th Infantry Regiment in late 1914 and was commissioned the following year. He served as a platoon leader in infantry and machine gun companies (1915–17) and as a battalion adjutant and a deputy regimental adjutant. Late in the war he was assigned to the staff of the 242nd Infantry Division. Discharged from the service with an honorary promotion to first lieutenant in 1919, he obtained two doctorates. He rejoined the service as a captain in 1934 and spent three years as a company commander (1934–37) before serving as a staff officer with the 33rd Infantry Division (1937–38) and as a tactics instructor at the Infantry Schools at Potsdam and Doeberitz (1938–39). He then served as adjutant (IIb) of Panzer Group von Kleist (later 1st Panzer Army) and fought in France and the Balkans. He assumed command of the II Battalion of the 111th Rifle Regiment in May 1941 but was severely wounded on the fifth day of Operation Barbarossa. When he returned to duty in July 1941, he commanded the 160th Motorcycle Battalion. He fell ill in December 1941 and did not return to duty for four months. After spending more than a year as an instructional group leader on the staff of the Infantry School at Doeberitz, he returned to the front as commander of the 111th Panzer Grenadier Regiment. He returned to Germany to attend the brief Division Commanders' Course at Doeberitz in late 1943 and then served as acting commander of the 29th Panzer Grenadier Division (March 1944), the 26th Panzer Division (April–May 1944), the 114th Jaeger Division (May–July 1944), and the 26th Panzer Division again (July–August 1944). He was given permanent command of the 18th Panzer Grenadier Division (September 1944–February 1945) and led the 172nd Special Purposes Division in March 1945. Captured by the Western Allies on March 29, he was a prisoner of war until 1947. He was promoted to major (1938), lieutenant colonel (1941), colonel (1942), major general (June 1, 1944), and lieutenant general (March 1, 1945). Bradley et al., vol. 2, pp. 85–87. He was not tried for any war crimes.

11. See http://www.camp198.fsnet.co.uk//General%20der%20Artillerie%20Eduard%20Crasemann.

CHAPTER XV: FRIDO VON SENGER UND ETTERLIN

1. Ferdinand von Senger und Etterlin and Stefan von Senger und Etterlin, "Senger," in *Hitler's Generals*, ed. Correlli Barnett, p. 388 (New York: 1989).

Notes

2. Senger's son, Ferdinand, served in cavalry and panzer grenadier units during World War II. He became an officer, was wounded eight times, and lost his right arm on September 4, 1944, while fighting on the Eastern Front. He was a lieutenant at the time, commanding the 3rd Company of the 24th Panzer Reconnaissance Battalion, 24th Panzer (formerly 1st Cavalry) Division. After studying law at Goettingen University, where he received his doctorate, he joined the West German Army when it was formed in 1955. He rose to the rank of general and was commander-in-chief of the Central Region of NATO when he retired in 1984. In the process, he became an internationally respected authority on armored fighting vehicles and wrote several books on the subject. He died in January 1987.

3. Lieutenant Johann-Gustav von Senger und Etterlin was born on December 12, 1894. He joined the army when World War I broke out and served with the 5th Baden Artillery—his brother's regiment. Johann, however, transferred to the Air Service in 1916 and was assigned to the 12th Fighter Squadron (*Jagdstaffel 12*) in July 1917. He was killed while engaged in aerial combat with British SE 5 fighters. It is possible that he collided with one of his opponents, but this is not certain.

See http://www.islandfarm.fsnet.co.uk for information on German generals held there, including Senger.

4. Frido von Senger und Etterlin, *Neither Fear Nor Hope*, translated by George Malcolm (New York: 1963; reprint, Novato, CA: 1989) (hereafter cited as "Senger").

5. U.S. War Department, "Histories of 251 Divisions of the German Army Which Participated in the War (1914–1918)," Document no. 905 (Washington, DC: 1920), pp. 382–85.

6. Senger, pp. 22–23. General Feldt (1887–1970) was a West Prussian who entered the service as a Fahnenjunker in 1908 and who spent virtually his entire career in the cavalry. He was promoted to lieutenant general in 1942 and to general of cavalry in early 1944. He commanded the 24th Panzer Division until April 1942 and was named military governor of southwest France in July 1942. During the retreat from France, he led the ad hoc Corps Feldt. In February 1945, he became commander of the ad hoc Corps South Jutland in Denmark. He surrendered on May 8, 1945, and was a prisoner of war until December 1947.

7. Carl-Heinrich von Stuelpnagel was born in Berlin in 1886. He joined the army in 1904 and was commissioned in 1906. By 1938 he was a lieutenant general and was deputy chief of operations at OKH. He was promoted to general of infantry in April 1939 and became chief of operations in October. On May 30, 1940, he was given command of the II Corps, which he led in the last phases of the French campaign. He did a poor job in this post and was transferred to head the French-German Armistice Commission in June. Despite this poor showing as a corps commander, he was named commander of the 17th Army on February 15, 1941. During the invasion of Russia, he again did an inadequate job and, on November 25, 1941, he was relieved of his command

by Field Marshal Walter von Brauchitsch, the commander-in-chief of the army. In February 1942—after Hitler sacked von Brauchitsch—Stuelpnagel was appointed military governor of France. He was never given another field command. Deeply involved in the plot to oust Hitler, he was relieved of his duties by Field Marshal von Kluge, the OB West, during the night of July 20, 1944. He was summoned to Berlin the next day, but, on the trip back, he attempted to commit suicide instead—ironically only a few miles from the place Kluge would kill himself three weeks later. He botched the attempt and blinded himself instead. He was hanged in Berlin on August 30, 1944.

8. Senger, p. 60.

9. Ibid.

10. See Hans Wijers, *Storm over the Steppe: The Action of 6. Panzer-Division during the Attempt by LVII Panzercorps to Relieve the Stalingrad Cauldron, 1942* (Coventry: 2001). Also see Helmut Ritgen, *The 6th Panzer Division, 1937–1945* (London: 1982; reprint, London: 1985).

11. The Allies landed in Sicily on July 10, 1943. Hube and his headquarters arrived on July 17. When Senger left, his chief of operations, Lieutenant Colonel Hans Meier-Welcker, became chief liaison officer with the Italian 6th Army. See Samuel W. Mitcham, Jr., and Friedrich von Stauffenberg, *The Battle of Sicily* (New York: 1991).

12. In October 1943, the SS Assault Brigade was sent to Slovakia and was reorganized as the 16th SS Panzer Grenadier "Reichsfuehrer-SS." It returned to Italy, where it fought at Anzio, in the Gustav Line and the Gothic Line battles, and in the retreat through Tuscany. It was sent to the Eastern Front in December 1944 and fought in Hungary and in the Battle of Vienna.

13. Carl-Hans Lungershausen commanded the 164th Light Afrika Division in Egypt and Libya in 1942.

14. General Basso was later arrested for allowing the 90th Panzer Grenadier to leave Sardinia unmolested but was acquitted in a subsequent trial.

15. General Lungershausen continued to command the 90th Panzer Grenadier until December 12, 1943, when he was apparently wounded again. He was not able to return to duty until July 1, 1944, when he was named inspector of Italian units under OB Southwest (formerly South). He held this post until March 1, 1945, when he was placed in Fuehrer Reserve. He was never reemployed. Lungershausen was living in Hamburg in the late 1950s.

16. Senger, p. 288.

17. Keilig, p. 112; Senger, pp. 182–83.

18. Fries was unjustly relieved of his command by Adolf Hitler on January 20, 1945, for his failure to prevent overwhelming Soviet forces from breaking out of the Baranov Bridgehead on the Vistula, south of Warsaw. He was arrested, tried by court-martial in March, and acquitted. He was never reemployed.

19. General Steinmetz was more highly thought of by Senger than by Kesselring. He was nevertheless promoted to lieutenant general on June 1, 1944,

and led the 94th Infantry from January 2, 1944, until the end of the war. Before assuming command of the 94th, Steinmetz had served in General Staff positions, primarily as chief of operations and then chief of staff of the VIII Corps, although he had briefly commanded the 305th Infantry Division (November 1942–February 1943).

20. Senger, pp. 182–83; Keilig, p. 212.

21. Heinrich von Vietinghoff (1887–1952) was a solid East Prussian general who has not received his fair share of credit for the campaign in Italy. He was the commander of the 5th Panzer Division when the war began. Later he commanded XIII Corps (1939–40), XXXXVI Panzer Corps (late 1940–1942), 9th Army (as acting commander) (1942), 15th Army (late 1942–1943), 10th Army (1943–October 26, 1944), OB Southwest (1944–January 15, 1945), Army Group Courland (1945), and Army Group C and OB Southwest (March 10–April 28, 1945).

22. The permanent commander of the 14th Army, General of Panzer Troops Joachim Lemelsen, was suffering from acute catarrh.

23. Friedrich Schulz (1897–1976) was the commander-in-chief of Army Group South. He simultaneously replaced Vietinghoff as OB South on April 28, 1945. Kesselring (now OB West) sacked Vietinghoff for engaging in unauthorized surrender negotiations. Schulz had previously been Manstein's chief of staff in Russia and had also commanded the 28th Jaeger Division, III Panzer Corps, LIX Corps, XXXXVI Panzer Corps, and 17th Army, all on the Eastern Front. He had been named commander of Army Group South on April 2, 1945.

24. Ferdinand von Senger und Etterlin and Stefan von Senger und Etterlin, "Senger," in *Hitler's Generals*, ed. Correlli Barnett, pp. 388–92 (New York: 1989).

CHAPTER XVI: OTTO HEIDKAEMPER

1. Bradley et al., vol. 5, pp. 232–34.

2. Ludwig Beck was born in Biebrich, the Rhineland, in 1880 and joined the Imperial Army as a Fahnenjunker in 1898. Commissioned in the 15th Artillery Regiment in 1899, he served five years as regimental adjutant before being selected for General Staff training in 1908. He graduated in 1911, served on the Great General Staff (1911–14), and was assigned to the staff of the VI Reserve Corps when World War I broke out. Later he was chief General Staff Officer (Ia) of the 117th Infantry and 13th Reserve Divisions (1915–late 1916), and was on the General Staff of the Crown Prince (1916–18) at the end of the war. He remained in General Staff positions until 1929, when he assumed command of the 5th Artillery Regiment. He served briefly on the General Staff of Group Command I in Berlin (1931–32), and then was Artillery Leader IV and deputy commander of the 4th Infantry Division in Dresden (1932), before assuming command of the 1st Cavalry Division on October 1, 1932. He became chief of the Truppenamt (later the General Staff of the Army) on October 1, 1933. In the fall of 1938, he resigned in protest against Hitler's aggressive policies. A

longtime anti-Hitler conspirator, he was deeply involved in the assassination attempt and coup of July 20, 1944. When it failed, Beck shot himself. He had been promoted to general of artillery on October 1, 1935, and was given an honorary promotion to colonel general on November 1, 1938.

3. Walter Goerlitz, *The History of the German General Staff, 1657–1945* (Westport, CT: 1975). For a history of General Staff training, also see Hans Georg Model, *Der deutsche Generalstabsoffizier. Seine Auswabl und Ausbildung in Reichswehr, Wehrmacht und Bundeswehr* (Frankfurt am Main: 1968).

One way did exist to enter the General Staff corps without attending the War Academy. If an officer scored high enough on his Wehrkreis exam, he could be sent to a university for four years to earn a technical degree—usually in engineering. He was then assigned to the Weapons Office in Berlin. Usually such officers served as technical experts during World War II, but a few did command divisions and corps.

4. Alfred Jodl was born at Wuerzburg in 1890. A Bavarian artillery officer, he was chief of operations of the High Command of the Armed Forces (OKW) from 1938 to 1945, except for a brief period in 1938–39 when he commanded Arko 44. He was convicted as a major war criminal and hanged at Nuremberg on October 16, 1946.

Claus von Stauffenberg was a cavalry officer who later became chief logistical officer of the 1st Light (later 6th Panzer) Division. He was involved in raising anti-Communist forces in Russia in 1941–42 and was Ia of the 10th Panzer Division in Tunisia in 1943. There he was critically wounded, losing an arm, an eye, and two fingers. Upon his recovery, he became chief of staff of the General Army Office (1943–44) and chief of staff of the Replacement Army. He led the plot to assassinate Adolf Hitler and was executed on July 20, 1944.

5. Albert C. Wedemeyer, *Wedemeyer Reports!* (New York: 1958), p. 50. General Omar Bradley agreed with Wedemeyer. British Field Marshal Sir Bernard Law Montgomery also considered the German General Staff course vastly superior to the British Army Staff College course he took at Camberly, which only lasted one year and which consisted largely of "hunting and socializing." See Nigel Hamilton, *Monty: The Making of a General, 1887–1942* (London: 1981), p. 151; and Omar Bradley and Clay Blair, *A General's Life* (New York: 1983), p. 80.

6. Franz Halder was born in Wuerzburg, Bavaria, in 1884. He joined the army as a Fahnenjunker in 1902 and was commissioned in the 3rd Bavarian Artillery Regiment in 1904. He attended the Bavarian War Academy in Munich from 1911 to 1914 and, upon graduation, was granted the right to wear the red stripes of a General Staff officer. He served in various General Staff positions in World War I and in the War Ministry in the early 1920s. He alternated between command and staff positions thereafter and became commander of the 7th Infantry Division at Munich in 1935. He returned to the General Staff of the Army in 1936, became chief of logistics in 1937, and was named chief of the General Staff in 1938. He was an off-and-on anti-Hitler conspirator in the 1930s. Hitler finally fired him on September 24, 1942. He was arrested by the

Notes

Gestapo three days after the July 20, 1944, assassination attempt failed and was held at Dachau until May 8, 1945, when he was rescued by the U.S. Army. Halder was released by the Americans in 1947 and later worked for the U.S. Army in Koenigstein and Karlsruhe. He died in Aschau/Chiemsee on April 2, 1972, and is buried in Munich.

7. Wedemeyer, pp. 52–53.

8. The 2nd Light/7th Panzer Division did not receive its signals battalion until October 1939, after the Polish campaign. Even then it only had two companies.

9. Charles W. Sydnor, Jr., *Soldiers of Destruction* (Princeton, NJ: 1977), pp. 47–48, 53, 105, and 105n.

10. By 1940, SS Colonel Baron Cassius von Montigny was suffering from a hemorrhaging stomach ulcer. After his recovery, he was named commandant of the SS Officers' Training School (*Junkerschule*) at Bad Toelz. During a British air raid on November 8, 1940, he died of a massive heart attack.

11. Theodor Eicke was born in Huedingen, in the then-German province of Alsace, in 1892, the 11th child of a railroad stationmaster. He grew up in relative poverty. In 1909, he dropped out of the German equivalent of high school and joined the Rhineland-Palatinate 23rd Infantry Regiment as an enlisted man. He fought on the Western Front in World War I and returned to Germany as a highly embittered and brutal atheist and right-wing extremist. A member of the Nazi Party, he fled Germany in 1932 because the police were after him for conspiracy to commit political murder. He returned after Hitler assumed power in 1933. Later, after a brief incarceration in a mental institution, he became commandant of the Dachau concentration camp. He did such a good job there—by Himmler's standards—that he was promoted to inspector of concentration camps and commander of SS guard units. He also shot and murdered former Brownshirt chief of staff Ernst Roehm in his cell in 1934. This earned the fanatical Nazi a promotion to *SS-Obergruppenfuehrer* (General of SS).

In 1939, the SS guard formations (the "Death's Head" units) formed the SS *Totenkopfdivision*, which eventually became the 3rd SS Panzer Division "Totenkopf." It fought as a motorized infantry division in France and later in Russia. Eicke proved to be a terrible division commander in France, but he did much better against the Red Army in the Soviet Union (1941–43). He was killed in action on the Eastern Front on February 26, 1943, when the reconnaissance airplane in which he was flying was shot down.

12. David Fraser, *Knight's Cross: A Life of Field Marshal Erwin Rommel* (London: 1993; reprint ed., New York: 1995), pp. 207–8.

13. Baron Willibald von Langermann und Erlenkamp was born in Karlsruhe in 1890. He began his career as a Fahnenjunker in the 5th Dragoons Regiment in 1908. After serving in World War I and the Reichsheer, he rose to the command of the 4th Cavalry Regiment in 1935. He was the leader of the I Higher Cavalry Command (1938) and Inspector of Remounts (1938–39). In late 1939, he assumed command of the 410th Special Purposes Division. Promoted to

major general (1940), lieutenant general (1942), and general of panzer troops (June 1, 1942), he commanded the 29th Motorized Division with considerable distinction in France (1940). Later he commanded the 4th Panzer Division (1940–42) and the XXIV Panzer Corps (from January 8, 1942). He was killed in action on October 3, 1942.

14. Dietrich von Saucken (1892–1980) was an extremely capable East Prussian cavalry officer who joined the army as a Fahnenjunker in 1912. During World War II, he commanded the 2nd Cavalry Regiment (1937–late 1940), the 4th Rifle Brigade (1940–December 1941), and the 4th Panzer Division (assumed command, December 27, 1941). Seriously wounded on January 2, 1942, he did not return to active duty until August 24, 1942, as commandant of the School for Mobile Troops. He reassumed command of the 4th Panzer Division on May 31, 1943, and later became deputy commander of the III Panzer Corps (May 1944), commander of the XXXIX Panzer Corps (June 1944), commander of the elite Grossdeutschland Panzer Corps (December 1944), and commander of the 2nd Army in East Prussia (March 1945). A holder of the Knight's Cross with Oak Leaves, Swords, and Diamonds, he surrendered to the Soviets in May 1945 and spent 10 years in Communist prisons. He retired in Bavaria.

Heinrich Eberbach was born in Stuttgart, Wuerttemberg, in 1895. He joined the Imperial Army as an infantry cadet in 1914, fought in World War I, and was discharged in 1919. He then joined the police and rose to the rank of major by 1935, when he rejoined the army. He was given command of the 35th Panzer Regiment in late 1938. After fighting in Poland and France, he took command of the 5th Panzer Brigade in July 1941 and took over the 4th Panzer Division on January 6, 1942. On August 1, 1943, he became a general of panzer troops and took charge of the XXXXVIII Panzer Corps on October 1. On July 5, 1944, he became commander of Panzer Group West in Normandy (which was soon upgraded to 5th Panzer Army). He was named commander of the 7th Army on August 21 and was captured by the British 10 days later, during the retreat from France. He died in Norzingen in 1992 at the age of 95.

15. Martin Wandel was a Berliner. He was chief of staff to the Inspector of Artillery (1935–40), commander of Arko 105 (1940–41), and commander of the 121st Infantry Division before assuming command of the XXIV Panzer. He was promoted to general of artillery, effective January 1, 1943.

Arno Jahr was the former chief engineer officer of the XXXVI Corps and 17th Army and commander of the 387th Infantry Division (February 1, 1942–January 14, 1943). He was promoted to lieutenant general on December 1, 1942.

Karl Eibl (a lieutenant general since December 19, 1942) was an Austrian. He commanded the III/132nd Infantry Regiment (1938–40), the 132nd Infantry Regiment (1940–42), and the 385th Infantry Division (January 1942) before assuming command of the XXIV Panzer. He was posthumously promoted to general of infantry.

Notes

16. Walter Nehring (1892–1983) served in the infantry during World War I but was an early convert to the panzer branch. He commanded the Afrika Korps from March 1942 until he was seriously wounded by an Allied fighter-bomber during the night of August 31–September 1, 1942. He later commanded the XC Corps in Tunisia (late 1942), and the XXIV Panzer Corps (February 1943–March 1945) and the 1st Panzer Army (March 22–May 9, 1945) on the Eastern Front. He surrendered to the Americans on May 9 and retired to Duesseldorf, where he died on April 20, 1983, at the age of 90. In my opinion, he was the best all-round tank commander in World War II.

17. Georg-Hans Reinhardt was born in 1887 and joined the army as an infantry Fahnenjunker in 1907. Commissioned in 1908, he fought in World War I, served in the Reichsheer, and was promoted to major general in 1937. He was promoted to lieutenant general (1939), general of panzer troops (1940), and colonel general (January 1, 1942). He commanded the 1st Rifle Brigade (1937–38), the 4th Panzer Division (1939–40), the XXXXI Panzer Corps (1940–41), and the 3rd Panzer Group (later Army) (October 5, 1941–August 16, 1944).

18. Guenther von Kluge was born in Posen in 1882. Educated at various cadet schools, he entered the army as a lieutenant in the 46th Field Artillery Regiment in 1901. By 1930 he was a colonel, commanding the 2nd Artillery Regiment. He later was Artillery Commander III (1931–33), inspector of signal troops (1933–34), commander of the 6th Infantry Division (1934–35), commander of Wehrkreis VI (1935–38), commander of Army Group 6 (late 1938–1939), commander of 4th Army (1939–41), commander of Army Group Center (1941–43), and commander of OB West (July 2, 1944–August 16, 1944). He was simultaneously commander of Army Group B in Normandy from July 19 to August 16, 1944. He was an on-again, off-again anti-Hitler conspirator. Hitler relieved him of his commands on August 16 and ordered him to return to Germany. Rather than face arrest by the Gestapo, he committed suicide near Metz on August 19, 1944. He had been promoted to field marshal on July 19, 1940.

19. Walter Model was born in 1891 into a family of extremely modest means. He entered the army as an infantry officer-cadet in 1909 and was promoted to field marshal on March 1, 1944. In the meantime, he fought in World War I, served in the Reichsheer, was selected for the General Staff, and became an expert on the technical matters of armament. He served as chief of the Training Department in the War Ministry and chief of the Technical Department of the army in the 1930s. He later served as chief of staff of Wehrkreis IV and later IV Corps (1938–39), chief of staff of the 16th Army (1939–40), commander of the 3rd Panzer Division (1940–41), commander of the XXXXI Corps (late 1941–early 1942), and commander of the 9th Army (1942–January 1944), Army Group North (January–March 1944), Army Group North Ukraine (April–June 1944), and Army Group Center (June–August 1944). He was commander-in-chief of OB West and Army Group B from August 16, 1944 until early September, when he handed command of OB West over to Field Marshal von

Rundstedt. He commanded Army Group B until it was destroyed in the Ruhr Pocket in April 1945. Rather than surrender to the Americans, he shot himself in a wooded area near Duisburg on April 21, 1945. A brilliant tactician, he was nicknamed "the Fuehrer's fireman" and was only given the most difficult assignments.

20. Hans Krebs was born in 1898 and entered the army as an infantry officer-cadet when World War I broke out. During World War II, he served on the staff of OKH (1937–39) and was chief of staff of VII Corps from late 1939 to January 1942. From that point, he served as Model's chief of staff when he commanded 9th Army, Army Group Center, and Army Group B. He was named acting chief of the General Staff of the Army on February 17, 1945. Promoted to general of infantry on August 1, 1944, he committed suicide in Berlin after the city fell—probably on May 3, 1945.

21. Reinhardt commanded Army Group Center from August 16, 1944, to January 25, 1945. He recovered from his wound and died in Munich on November 24, 1963. He held the Knight's Cross with Oak Leaves and Swords.

22. Ferdinand Schoerner was born in Munich, Bavaria, in 1892 and became a public school teacher and a reserve NCO. During World War I, he won the Pour le Merite and a commission in the mountain troops branch. He remained in the service after the war and rose from regimental to army group commander in five years. In the meantime, he earned a reputation for brutality and is considered by many historians to be Hitler's most brutal field marshal. He commanded the 98th Mountain Regiment (1939–40), the 6th Mountain Division (1940–early 1942), XIX Mountain Corps (1942–43), XXXX Panzer Corps (1943–early 1944), 17th Army (March 1944), Army Group South (March 31–July 20, 1944), Army Group North (July 20, 1944–January 18, 1945), and Army Group Center (January 18, 1945–end). Hitler promoted him to field marshal on April 5, 1945, and named him commander-in-chief of the army on April 28, 1945, effective the day Hitler committed suicide (he shot himself two days later). Schoerner then apparently tried to make his way to the Alpine Redoubt but was arrested by members of the 1st Panzer Division on May 18. He was later sentenced to 25 years' imprisonment as a war criminal by the Soviets, but he was released in 1955. The West Germans then rearrested him and tried him for manslaughter. He was sentenced to four-and-a-half years in prison. Schoerner died in poverty in Munich on July 6, 1973.

23. The 464th Infantry Division was formed in Chemnitz as *Division Nr. 464* (also translated 464th Replacement Division) in the fall of 1942. It initially consisted of the 14th Grenadier Replacement and Training Regiment at Leipzig, the 534th Replacement Regiment at Zwichau, the 24th Artillery Replacement Regiment at Altenburg, and assorted smaller units. On March 26, 1945, it was reorganized as an infantry division and was augmented by the addition of the 561st Grenadier Training Regiment from Magdeburg. It was assigned to the LXXX Corps of the 4th Panzer Army, Army Group Center, and held a zone in eastern Saxony.

Notes

CHAPTER XVII: JOHANN MICKL

1. Heinz Richter and Gerd Kobe, *Bei Den Gewehren: General Johann Mickl, Ein Soldatenschicksal* (Bad Radkersburg: 1983).

2. Baron Erpo von Bodenhausen (1897–1945) was promoted to major general on May 1, 1943, and to lieutenant general on November 1 of the same year. (With very rare exceptions, six months was the minimum time in grade a man had to serve as a major general before being promoted again—and even that was considered exceptional.) He led the division from March 1, 1943, until the end of the war, except for a brief period at the very end of the conflict when he commanded L Corps. He committed suicide in early May 1945, rather than surrender to the Russians. He was a former cavalry officer who proved to be a brilliant panzer commander.

BIBLIOGRAPHY

Agar-Hamilton, J. A. I., and L. C. F. Turner. *Crisis in the Desert, May–July 1942*. Cape Town: 1957.

Barnett, Correlli. *The Desert Generals*. 2nd ed. Bloomington, IN: 1982.

Bradley, Dermot, Karl-Friedrich Hildebrand, and Markus Brockmann. *Die Generale des Heeres, 1921–1945*. 7 vols. Osnabrueck: 1993–2005.

Buchner, Alex. *Ostfront 1944*. Translated by David Johnston. West Chester, PA: 1991.

"Colonel Hans von Luck." Obituary, *London Times*, August 1997.

Corum, James S. *The Roots of Blitzkrieg: Hans von Seeckt and German Military Reform*. Lawrence, KS: 1992.

Dupuy, T. N. *A Genius for War*. Fairfax, VA: 1984.

Engelmann, Bernt. *In Hitler's Germany*. Translated by Krishna Winston. New York: 1986.

Fraser, David. *Knight's Cross: A Life of Field Marshal Erwin Rommel*. London: 1993. Reprint, New York: 1995.

Goebbels, Joseph. *Final Entries, 1945: The Diaries of Joseph Goebbels*. Edited by Hugh Trevor-Roper. New York: 1978. Reprint, New York: 1979.

Gordon, Harold J. *The Reichswehr and the German Republic, 1919–1926*. Princeton, NJ: 1957.

Grunberger, Richard. *The Twelve-Year Reich: A Social History of Nazi Germany, 1933–1945*. New York: 1971.

Hart, W. E. (pseudo.). *Hitler's Generals*. New York: 1944.

Heck, Alfons. *A Child of Hitler*. Frederick, CO: 1985.

Irving, David. *Trail of the Fox*. New York: 1977.

———. *The War Path*. New York: 1979.

Keilig, Wolf. *Die Generale des Heeres*. Friedberg: 1986.

Knappe, Siegfried. "Soldaten." Unpublished manuscript in the possession of the author.

Kochan, Lionel. *Pogrom: 10 November 1938*. London: 1957.

Bibliography

Kramarz, Joachim. *Stauffenberg: The Life and Death of an Officer, 15 November 1907–20 July 1944*. London: 1967.

Kursietis, Andris J. *The Wehrmacht at War*. Soesterberg, The Netherlands: 1999.

Lang, Jochen von. *The Secretary*. Translated by Christa Armstrong and Peter White. Athens, OH: 1979.

Lucas, James. *Hitler's Enforcers*. London: 1966.

Luck, Hans von. *Panzer Commanders*. New York: 1989.

Manteuffel, Hasso von. *Die 7 Panzer-Division, 1935–1945: Die "Gespenster-Division."* Friedberg: 1978.

Maser, Werner. *Hitler: Legend, Myth, and Reality*. Translated by Peter and Betty Ross. New York: 1973.

Mehner, Kurt, ed. *Die Geheimen Tagesberichte der deutschen Wehrmachtfuehrung im Zweiten Weltkrieg, 1939–1945*. 12 vols. Osnabrueck: 1984–99.

Meissner, Hans-Otto. *Magda Goebbels*. Translated by Gwendolen Mary Keeble. New York: 1980.

Mellenthin, F. W. von. *Panzer Battles: A Study in the Employment of Armor in the Second World War*. Norman, OK: 1956.

Mitcham, Samuel W., Jr. *Crumbling Empire: The German Defeat in the East, 1944*. Westport, CT: 2001.

———. *The Panzer Legions: A Guide to the German Army Tank Divisions of World War II and Their Commanders*. Westport, CT: 2001.

Mitcham, Samuel W., Jr., and Friedrich von Stauffenberg. *The Battle of Sicily*. New York: 1991.

Oberkommando der Wehrmacht. *Kriegstagebuch des Oberkommando der Wehrmacht (Wehrmachtfuehungsstab)*. 8 vols. Frankfurt am Main: 1961.

Preradovich, Nikolaus von. *Die Generale der Waffen-SS*. Berg am See: 1985.

Richter, Heinz, and Gerd Kobe. *Bei Den Gewehren: General Johann Mickl, Ein Soldatenschicksal*. Bad Radkersburg: 1983.

Ritgen, Helmut. *The 6th Panzer Division, 1937–1945*. London: 1982. Reprint, London: 1985.

Rommel, Erwin. *Infantry Grieft Au*. Potsdam: 1935.

———. *The Rommel Papers*. Edited by B. H. Liddell Hart. New York: 1953.

Scheibert, Horst. *Die Traeger des deutschen Kreuzes in Gold*. Friedberg: n.d.

Senger und Etterlin, Ferdinand von, and Stefan von Senger und Etterlin. "Senger." In *Hitler's Generals*, edited by Correlli Barnett, pp. 375–92. New York: 1989.

Senger und Etterlin, Frido von. *Neither Fear Nor Hope*. Translated by George Malcolm. New York: 1963. Reprint, Novato, CA: 1989.

Stauffenberg, Theodor-Friedrich von. "Panzer Commanders of the Western Front." Unpublished manuscript in the possession of the author.

Stoves, Rolf O. G. *Die Gepanzerten und Motorisierten deutschen Grossverbaende (Divisionen und selbstaendige Brigaden), 1935–1945*. Friedberg: 1986.

———. *Die 22 Panzer-Division, 25 Panzer Division, 27 Panzer-Division, und 233 Reserve-Panzer-Division*. Friedberg: 1985.

Sydnor, Charles W. *Soldiers of Destruction*. Princeton, NJ: 1977.

Tessin, Georg. *Verbaende und Truppen der deutschen Wehrmacht und Waffen-SS im Zweiten Weltkrieg*. 16 vols. Osnabrueck: 1973–81.

Thalmann, Rita, and Emmanuel Feinermann. *Crystal Night*. Translated by Gilles Cremonesi. London: 1974. Reprint, Washington, DC: 1980.

Toland, John. *Adolf Hitler*. New York: 1976. Reprint, New York: 1977.

U.S. War Department. "Histories of 251 Divisions of the German Army Which Participated in the War (1914–1918)." Document no. 905. Washington, DC: 1920.

———. "Handbook on German Military Forces." Technical Manual TM-E 30-451. Washington, DC: 1945.

Wedemeyer, Albert C. *Wedemeyer Reports!* New York: 1958.

Wijers, Hans. *Storm over the Steppe: The Action of 6 Panzer-Division during the Attempt by LVII Panzercorps to Relieve the Stalingrad Cauldron, 1942*. Coventry: 2001.

Windrow, Martin. *The Panzer Divisions*. London: 1985.

Young, Desmond. *Rommel: The Desert Fox*. New York: 1965.

Zweng, Christian, ed. *Die Dienstlaufbahnen der Offiziere des Generalstabes des deutschen Heeres, 1935–1945*. 2 vols. Osnabrueck: 1995, 1998.

INTERNET SOURCES

http://forum.axishistory.com (accessed August 16, 2006)

http://www.austro-hungarian-army.co.uk/biog/mickl.html (accessed August 16, 2006)

http://www.islandfarm.fsnet.co.uk (accessed August 16, 2006)

INDEX OF MILITARY UNITS

Index of Military Units

GENERAL INDEX

Rank listed is the highest attained by that individual.

General Index

General Index

General Index

About the Author

SAMUEL W. MITCHAM, JR., is an internationally recognized authority on Nazi Germany and the Second World War. He is the author of twenty books, including *Panzers in Winter* (Praeger Security International, 2006), *Crumbling Empire* (Praeger, 2001), and *Retreat from the Reich* (Praeger, 2000). A former Army helicopter pilot and company commander, he is a graduate of the U.S. Army's Command and General Staff College.